Arab Spring and Peripheries

The emerging literature on the so-called 'Arab Spring' has largely focused on the evolution of the uprisings in cities and power centres. In order to reach a more diversified and inner understanding of the 'Arab Spring', this book examines how peripheries have reacted and contributed to the historical dynamics at work in the Middle East and North Africa. It rejects the idea that the 'Arab Spring' is a unitary process and shows that it consists of diverse Springs that differed in terms of opportunity structure, the strategies of a variety of actors and outcomes. This book looks at geographical, religious, gender and ethnic peripheries, conceptualizing periphery as a dynamic structure that can expand and contract. It shows that the seeds for changing the face of politics and polities are within peripheries themselves. Focusing on the voices of peripheries can therefore be a powerful tool to 'de-simplify' the reading of the Arab Spring and to reshape the paradigmatic schemes through which to look at this part of the world. This book was published as a special issue of *Mediterranean Politics*.

Daniela Huber is a senior fellow at the Instituto Affari Internazionali (IAI) in the Mediterranean and Middle East programme and a Gerda Henkel Guest Researcher at LUISS University. She holds a PhD from the Hebrew University of Jerusalem and an MA degree in International Relations from the Free University of Berlin. Her research interests include EU and US foreign policies in the Middle East, the regional and international dimension of the Israel/Palestine conflict, and contemporary politics in the Middle East. She has worked for the Friedrich Ebert Foundation in Tel Aviv and Berlin and as a Carlo Schmid Fellow at the United Nations in Copenhagen.

Lorenzo Kamel is a Marie Curie fellow at the Freiburg Institute for Advanced Studies (FRIAS) and a senior fellow at the Istituto Affari Internazionali (IAI). He holds a two-years MA in Israeli Society and Politics from the Hebrew University of Jerusalem, a PhD in History from Bologna University, and was a postdoctoral fellow at Harvard University's CMES. His publications include about thirty academic articles on journals such as the *British Journal of Middle Eastern Studies*, *Mediterranean Politics*, *Eurasian Studies*, and 4 authored books, including *Imperial Perceptions of Palestine: British Influence and Power in Late Ottoman Times* (I.B. Tauris 2015).

Routledge Studies in Mediterranean Politics

Series Editor: Frédéric Volpi, *University of St Andrews, Scotland*

The Mediterranean Politics series takes an inter-disciplinary approach which, while generally focused on the disciplines of politics and international relations, also encompasses economics, human geography, sociology and religious studies, in order to shed light on the interconnectedness of polities and societies in the Mediterranean region. The series takes the study of Mediterranean politics as a focal point to examine the global and transnational linkages between the Mediterranean area and the wider world. Showcasing cutting edge new research on regional, transnational and comparative politics, it provides a forum for the discussion of Mediterranean politics with special reference to the interaction between European and Middle Eastern and North African countries.

The Struggle for Influence in the Middle East
The Arab Uprisings and Foreign Assistance
Federica Bicchi

Twenty Years of Euro-Mediterranean Relations
Richard Youngs

Civil Society and Political Reform in Lebanon and Libya
Transition and constraint
Carmen Geha

Arab Spring and Peripheries
A decentring research agenda
Daniela Huber

Dynamics of Transformation, Elite Change and New Social Mobilization
Egypt, Libya, Tunisia and Yemen
Heiko Wimmen and Muriel Asseburg

EU Neighbourhood Policy in the Maghreb
Implementing the ENP in Tunisia and Morocco before and after the Arab Uprisings
Iole Fontana

Arab Spring and Peripheries

A decentring research agenda

Edited by
Daniela Huber and Lorenzo Kamel

Routledge
Taylor & Francis Group

LONDON AND NEW YORK

First published 2016
by Routledge

2 Park Square, Milton Park, Abingdon, Oxfordshire OX14 4RN
711 Third Avenue, New York, NY 10017

Routledge is an imprint of the Taylor & Francis Group, an informa business

First issued in paperback 2018

Chapters 1–4 and 6–9 © 2016 Taylor & Francis
Chapter 5 © Sylvia I. Bergh & Daniele Rossi-Doria

British Library Cataloguing in Publication Data
A catalogue record for this book is available from the British Library

ISBN 13: 978-1-138-99966-4 (hbk)
ISBN 13: 978-1-138-39322-6 (pbk)

Typeset in Times
by diacriTech, Chennai

Publisher's Note
The publisher accepts responsibility for any inconsistencies that may have arisen
during the conversion of this book from journal articles to book chapters, namely
the possible inclusion of journal terminology.

Disclaimer
Every effort has been made to contact copyright holders for their permission to
reprint material in this book. The publishers would be grateful to hear from any
copyright holder who is not here acknowledged and will undertake to rectify any
errors or omissions in future editions of this book.

Contents

CONTENTS

Citation Information

The chapters in this book were originally published in *Mediterranean Politics*, volume 20, issue 2 (July 2015). When citing this material, please use the original page numbering for each article, as follows:

CITATION INFORMATION

For any permission-related enquiries please visit:
http://www.tandfonline.com/page/help/permissions

Notes on Contributors

Sylvia I. Bergh is a Senior Lecturer at the International Institute of Social Studies, Erasmus University Rotterdam, the Netherlands. Her research interests include decentralization and local governance, natural resources management and migration, with a geographical focus on Morocco, the Middle East and North Africa. Her most recent works can be found in the *Journal of North African Studies, Mediterranean Politics* and the *International Journal of Public Administration.*

Khaled Elghamry is an Associate Professor at Ain Shams University, Egypt. His research focuses on discourse analysis, syntax and computational linguistics.

Mark Farha is an Assistant Professor of Politics and International Relations at the Doha Institute for Graduate Studies. He served as an Assistant Professor of Government at the School of Foreign Service, Georgetown University, Qatar from 2008 to 2015. He received his PhD from Harvard University in 2007 and focuses on the history and politics of secularism and sectarianism in the modern Middle East.

Irene Fernández-Molina is a Lecturer in Middle East Politics and International Relations at the University of Exeter. She has worked as a research fellow at the College of Europe in Warsaw, a Schuman Fellow at the European Parliament in Brussels and a PhD research fellow at the Universidad Complutense de Madrid, where she received her PhD. Her research interests include foreign policy analysis and conflict analysis with a particular focus on the Maghreb, as well as EU foreign policy and Euro-Mediterranean relations. She is the author of *Moroccan Foreign Policy under Mohammed VI, 1999–2014* (Routledge, 2015).

Edwige A. Fortier is a Research Associate at the University College London Department of Infection and Population Health in the Centre for Sexual Health and HIV Research. Her research interests include transitions from authoritarian rule, democratisation and in particular, civil society actors and groups working with marginalized communities, such as sexual minorities affected by HIV. She also works as an Adviser to the Community, Rights and Gender Department at the Global Fund to Fight AIDS, Tuberculosis and Malaria.

Daniela Huber is a senior fellow at the Instituto Affari Internazionali (IAI) in the Mediterranean and Middle East programme and a Gerda Henkel Guest Researcher at LUISS University. She holds a PhD from the Hebrew University of Jerusalem and an MA degree in International Relations from the Free University of Berlin. Her research interests include EU and US foreign policies in the Middle East, the regional and international dimension of the Israel/Palestine conflict, and contemporary politics in the Middle East. She has worked for the Friedrich Ebert Foundation in Tel Aviv and Berlin and as a Carlo Schmid Fellow at the United Nations in Copenhagen.

Lorenzo Kamel is a Marie Curie fellow at the Freiburg Institute for Advanced Studies (FRIAS) and a senior fellow at the Istituto Affari Internazionali (IAI). He holds a two-years MA in Israeli Society and Politics from the Hebrew University of Jerusalem, a PhD in History from Bologna University, and was a postdoctoral fellow at Harvard University's CMES. His publications include about thirty academic articles on journals such as the *British Journal of Middle Eastern Studies*, *Mediterranean Politics*, *Eurasian Studies*, and 4 authored books, including *Imperial Perceptions of Palestine: British Influence and Power in Late Ottoman Times* (I.B. Tauris 2015).

Maryam Khalid is a Lecturer in Politics and Law at Macquarie University, Australia. Her research focuses on gender, race and international relations.

Salma Mousa is a PhD candidate at the Department of Political Science at Stanford University, where she focuses on questions of tolerance, secular governance and democracy in the Middle East.

Daniele Rossi-Doria is a PhD candidate at the International Institute of Social Sciences, Erasmus University of Rotterdam, the Netherlands. His research focuses on rural development in Morocco and explores community-based resource management, water governance and forms of collective action.

Ángela Suárez Collado is a Postdoctoral Fellow at the Political Science Department and the Research Group in Comparative Politics at the University of Salamanca, Spain. Her research focuses on social movements and local politics in North Africa and Moroccan migration in Europe.

Arab Spring: The Role of the Peripheries

DANIELA HUBER[*] & LORENZO KAMEL[**,†]

*Istituto Affari Internazionali (IAI), Rome, Italy, **Department of History, Cultures and Civilizations, Bologna University, Bologna, Italy, †Center for Middle Eastern Studies, Harvard University, Cambridge, MA, USA

ABSTRACT   *The emerging literature on the so-called 'Arab Spring' has largely focused on the evolution of the uprisings in cities and power centres. In order to reach a more diversified and in-depth understanding of the 'Arab Spring', this article examines how peripheries have reacted and contributed to the historical dynamics at work in the Middle East and North Africa. It rejects the idea that the 'Arab Spring' is a unitary process and shows that it consists of diverse 'springs' which differed in terms of opportunity structure, the strategies of a variety of actors and the outcomes. Looking at geographical, religious, gender and ethnic peripheries, it shows that the seeds for changing the face of politics and polities are within the peripheries themselves.*

Since the self-immolation of Tunisian street vendor Mohamed Bouazizi in December 2010 triggered the so-called 'Arab Spring', the academic literature has sought to come to terms with an unexpected phenomenon. Much of the literature had previously focused on explaining authoritarian resilience (Schedler, 2006; Schlumberger, 2007; Heydemann, 2007) in the Middle East and North Africa (MENA) and only few academic works had observed the dynamics at work in the region that eventually led to the Arab Spring (Bayat, 2010; Beinin & Vairel, 2011). What distinguished these works was their focus on the changes in the lives of ordinary people or of groups which were outside of the usually observed power orbit. These works have been in line with similar trends in other disciplines that have started to highlight the importance of the everyday and local lifeworlds, for example in conflict resolution (Heitmeyer, 2009; Mitchell, 2011; Williams, 2013) or history 'from below' (Hobsbawm, 1997; Cronin, 2012).

Nonetheless, most of the literature which has evolved on the Arab Spring, has once more focused on a top-down approach that has either explored – on the structural side – the socio-economic and political context within which the Arab

Spring emerged (Springborg, 2011; Bellin, 2012) or – on the actors' side – the (re) action of regimes (Heydemann & Leenders, 2011), established actors such as Islamist parties (Al-Anani, 2012; Guazzone, 2013; Pioppi, 2013), foreign powers (Teti, 2012; Huber, 2013; Börzel et al., 2015) or of the protest actors themselves (Ottaway & Hamzawy, 2011; Pace & Cavatorta, 2012). This obviously makes sense since these actors have been the drivers of the defining moments of the uprisings. However, if we want to reach a more diversified and in-depth understanding of the Arab Spring and of its broader context and implications, it is necessary to look beyond established power centres and examine these epochal developments also in their 'margins'. The first research venues have opened in this respect (Abu-Lughod, 2012), but such studies are limited and not always easy to pursue since they require field research in geographically remote or socially singled-out areas that are usually difficult to access for outsiders.

The contributors to this volume have either been part of these communities or have established contacts with them through previous field work. Thus, a key contribution of this special issue is empirical stock-taking of the reaction and contribution of peripheries to the historical processes currently unfolding in the Middle East and North Africa. Each contribution gives a voice to a specific periphery and this volume can therefore convey the complexities and nuances of the Arab Spring by looking at peripheries and their interactions with actors in the centre.[1] It rejects the idea of the existence of a static and largely homogeneous Arab world, as well as the idea of the Arab Spring as a unitary process.

'Arab Spring' is not a fully appropriate term to describe the recent past and the present of most of the Arab countries. The name itself is not used, if not disliked, in the MENA region, where an increasing number of persons prefer to opt for expressions such as 'al-marar al-Arabi', or 'the Arab bitterness' (Kamel & Elkholy, 2015). Furthermore, the concept of the Arab Spring was born out of a misguided association with the 'European Spring' of 1848 with the aim, so common in the last few centuries, to read the Middle East through ideas and symbols created by and functional to the West. Finally, 'Arab Spring' gives the impression that millions of people in the Arab world can be lumped together into one largely undifferentiated phenomenon. So why do we use this expression? First, for recognition purposes. Arab Spring has been the most frequent term used to reflect the dynamics triggered by the uprisings in diverse MENA countries; indeed, and as this volume shows, many peripheries framed their protests as 'Arab Spring' for recognition purposes. Secondly, in contrast to terms such as 'Arab Awakening' (Pollack, 2012), which has an orientalist connotation implying that millions of people in the Arab world were 'sleeping', or 'Islamist Winter' (Totten, 2012; Israeli, 2013), which has been used to shift the focus to perceived security threats, Arab Spring resonates with the democratic transition paradigm. This sits well with the aim of this volume, namely to tease out theoretical implications on the role which peripheries can play in the political, social and cultural transformation[2] of autocratic countries in MENA and, vice versa, the impact this transformation can have on peripheries. Furthermore, other terms like Arab revolutions carry a theoretical baggage whose application to the phenomenon we describe is debatable. Arab uprisings refers to large demonstrations in the capitals, while we prefer to include also smaller protests in remote areas in the phenomenon. 'Arab Spring' is less concise or loaded in theoretical and practical terms and so allows us to see the phenomenon as a broader chain of protests of diverse scales, time periods, geographical locations and issue areas across the whole spectrum of MENA societies which has triggered processes of political, socio-economic and cultural transformation at the local, national, regional and international levels.

Peripheries and the Arab Spring

As history from below, a term first used in the 1930s by French historian Georges Lefebvre, is commonly considered as an attempt to understand 'real' people, the perspectives offered by peripheries represent a way to get a deeper understanding of one of the most debated issues of our times. In *The Making of the English Working Class*, Edward P. Thompson (1964) came to the conclusion that England's transition from a predominantly agrarian to an industrial society could not be understood without an appreciation of the daily experiences of the people who lived that transition. Equally true, *mutatis mutandis*, is that a more reliable picture of the events that are currently taking place in most of the Arab countries needs to shed light also on peripheries. By studying the role of peripheries in the events currently unfolding in the MENA, we can better assess the extent of the Arab Spring – its depth and breadth – and learn about its effects across the whole spectrum of the involved societies, possibly also about its durability and sustainability. We can therefore better examine ongoing processes which might challenge or back the dogma of 'authoritarian resilience' which has already re-emerged in the academic literature. The three contributions on the Arab Spring in peripheries in Morocco are particularly instructive in this respect: they show that what came to be known as the 'Arab Spring' started earlier than December 2010 – the Sahrawi tent protests began in October 2010 – and continues to smoulder in remote regions such as the Rif.

Furthermore, through the study of peripheries, virtually all detached from established power, much may be revealed not only about the daily lives and the narratives of the 'powerless' but also about the nature of the 'powerful' (Cronin, 2012). For this purpose, the concepts of centre and periphery should not be dichotomously understood in terms of power versus powerlessness. 'Periphery' is a concept that has been most extensively developed in (post)colonial studies and critical theory, but Martina Ghosh-Schellhorn (2006) has warned against the recurring dangers of the binarism of the colonially based centre–periphery paradigm. For a long time the rhetoric of postcolonialism has in different ways been placed still within colonialism, perpetuating the idea that established power is the sole, and sometimes even the main, dispenser of values and knowledge, while the periphery is assumed as submissive. John and Jean Comaroff (1992: 181–213) have pointed out that in the heyday of British colonialism, Africa was far from being a periphery; rather, it was the centre of colonialism, the context where the values and practices associated with colonialism were shaped and formed.

Friedman (1994) has highlighted how centre–periphery can also be seen as a dynamic structure which can expand, contract, fragment and be re-established throughout cycles of shifting hegemony – a useful concept when looking at countries in transition which undergo rapid contractions and expansions in the public space as the contribution of Edwige Fortier (2015) highlights. Through perceiving centre–periphery as a dynamic structure, peripherality acquires a permeable function that shifts peripheries at the centre as 'peripheral centres' or 'central peripheries' (Ghosh-Schellhorn, 2006). Also Stein Rokkan has conceptualized the periphery dynamically as an opportunity structure. He has pointed out that peripherality can be defined horizontally as well as vertically, with the first referring geographically to 'an outlying area within the territory controlled by a centre' (Rokkan, 1999: 114) and the second to an interaction system between groups. Thus, a periphery can be a space, as well as a group characterized by distance, difference and dependence in three distinctive domains of social life: politics, culture and economics (Rokkan, 1999: 115). Largely based on this definition, the concept of 'periphery' in this volume applies to both *spaces* and *groups* which are characterized by (1) *their difference*, be this a geographical, religious, gender or ethnical difference or even political apathy, and (2) *their distance* from and dependence on a powerful centre constraining but not necessarily blocking their ability to influence political decision making, cultural standardization, or their socio-economic life.

By studying peripheries so defined, this volume also seeks to push the reader to unthink dominant conceptualizations and to overcome what is generally perceived as an active centre and a submissive periphery. Marginality, almost always imposed by oppressive structures, does not prevent peripheries from opposing and, at times, undermining the centre. While peripheries might often be unsuccessful in the short term, they are able to provide counter-hegemonic alternatives and largely pro-active and non-hierarchic views that challenge a centre in the long term. Maryam Khalid (2015), for instance, points out in this volume that even though the political activism of gender peripheries has occurred at the margins of the mainstream, it has nonetheless challenged the boundaries of dominant MENA and western categories of gender and sexuality and, in particular, what peoples in these categories can be and do. Peripheries should therefore not be victimized. While very much interested in bringing peripheries back into the present history, the editors and contributors of this volume have also been careful to avoid any romanticization of the human beings that compose them. In other words, we avoided any easy temptation of transforming these people into simple victims of history or of focusing just on 'heroic' or revolutionary phases in their lives. Rather, we are interested in the agency of peripheries and in challenging dominant understandings of the Arab Spring through this approach.

Concretely, this volume looks at a whole spectrum of diverse types of peripheries: the first two contributions explore gender peripheries: Edwige Fortier (2015) sheds light on the potentialities and boundaries members of the homosexual community in Tunisia encountered during and after the Arab Spring, while Maryam Khalid (2015) explores how gender peripheries resisted their mainstream representations in both western and Arab media during the Arab Spring. The next contribution by Mark

Farha and Salma Mousa (2015) focuses on religious peripheries, Christians in Egypt and Syria. This is followed by three contributions on Morocco, which include ethnic and geographic minorities: Sylvia Bergh and Daniele Rossi-Doria (2015) look at population in rural areas in the Atlas mountains, Ángela Suárez Collado (2015) analyses the evolution of protests in the Rif region and Irene Fernández Molina (2015) examines the impact of the Arab Spring on civil protest in the Western Sahara territory. Finally, the last article by Khaled Elghamry (2015) focuses on the empowering role social media can play for peripheries – an issue that has been largely neglected in the evolving literature on the role of social media in the Arab Spring (see Elghamry, 2015). Thus, this volume displays high variance in terms of types of peripheries and the political opportunity structures they are placed in.

The country cases include Egypt, Morocco, Syria and Tunisia and thus diverse political systems. While Tunisia has gone through regime change and is on a road to transition (El-Khawas, 2012), Egypt has experienced a period of regime changes, but its transition might have failed (Brown, 2013) or 'has only just begun' (Gelvin, 2012). Morocco has mainly reacted with reforms to the protest movements in the country (Barany, 2013; Yom & Gause, 2012), while the Arab Spring in Syria has been met by a violent reaction from the regime (Heydemann & Leenders, 2012). Regarding variance in peripheries, there are gender, geographical, political, religious and ethnic peripheries and many of them also display a combination of two of these criteria, e.g. Berbers living in geographically remote areas. Furthermore, these peripheries also vary in terms of their distance from and dependence on a powerful centre: Christians in Syria, for example, might have better ties with political elites in their country than Sahrawis in Western Sahara with Moroccan political elites. Sahrawis, in turn, might have a locally deeper rooted mobilization structure than Christians in Syria.

Thus, the variances in political context, as well as periphery, provide us with diverse configurations of opportunity structures of peripheries and the strategies they choose in their interactions with the centre that should lead to varying outcomes across cases. This allows us to track diverse patterns of responses and contributions of peripheries to the Arab Spring on one hand and the conditions under which peripheral agency can be successful in a given structure on the other, and so enables a comparative discussion of the overarching research question of this volume: how have peripheries reacted and contributed to the Arab Spring and which impact did this have on peripheries in turn?

Analytical Frame

All contributions analyse this question in terms of the opportunity structure of a periphery, the strategies which agents chose in their interaction with the centre, and the outcome they achieved in terms of transforming their opportunity structure. As has been pointed out above, both periphery and centre are seen as related opportunity structures which can expand and contract. Periphery and centre therefore provide certain constraints and opportunities to interactions between actors from periphery and centre. These interactions are determined by power, whereby power, however, is not seen as one-sided and static, but as relational and dynamic. It is seen as 'the production, in and through social relations, of effects that shape the capacities of actors to determine their circumstances and fate' (Barnett & Duvall, 2005). Strategies adopted by actors in the periphery can transform their very constitution as a periphery (their opportunity structure). Thus, we assume that the three categories of opportunity structure, strategies and outcomes are related, dynamic and circular.

As this special issue focuses on periphery, the operationalization of opportunity structure is pursued from the viewpoint of peripheries. Regarding the political context, opportunity structure includes the institutionalized political system of a country, the state's capacity and propensity for repression towards peripheries[3] and the accessibility of a periphery to central political actors: the government, parliament, bureaucracy or the judiciary. This accessibility can, however, be a double-edged sword, since a state can also seek to co-opt a periphery in order to take the wind out of its sails. The political opportunity structure also involves the mobilizing structure within which agents adopt their strategies.[4] This structure is located at the meso level, with political parties, trade unions, civil society, social movements and the media. It has diverse dimensions: the mobilization structure in the centre; the mobilization structure in the periphery itself; and a transnational mobilization structure – that is, existing networks with foreign organizations. Also the socio-economic context provides opportunities or constraints for peripheries. Factors like poverty, (un)employment/employment in the shadow economy, social security, health, education or an adequate standard of living all determine the capacity of a periphery to interact with actors in the centre. The manipulation of socio-economic factors can be actively used by the latter to demobilize the former. Finally, there are also leading cultural norms which can constrain a periphery. A dominant discourse of 'othering' a periphery in a society, for instance, decisively constrains the possibilities of a periphery. Opportunity structure is not a static concept, but this volume is looking at its expansions and contractions, also (but not exclusively) as a result of the strategies adopted by actors in the periphery.

The second category – *strategies* – observes the interaction between actors in the periphery and centre in the political, socio-economic and cultural domains. In the political domain, strategies can include alignments with the political elite or with parties, trade unions, civil society organizations or social movements in the centre. Peripheries can also mobilize international actors, networks or media to apply pressure on their own governments from abroad (Risse et al., 1999). Strategies can also include violent resistance or unco-ordinated resistance at the level of everyday life. In the socio-economic domain, strategies involve boycotts or strikes, the acquisition of foreign aid or the setting up of social welfare groups within a periphery itself. In the cultural domain, a periphery can challenge a dominant normative discourse through diverse means such as literature, the use of social media or the everyday demonstration of a certain lifestyle. Finally, a periphery can also be apathetic and not adopt any strategy to improve its situation.

Lastly, this volume also observes the *outcome* of such strategies. 'Objective' outcomes focus on the transformation of a periphery – that is, of its expanding or contracting opportunity structure in the political, socio-economic and cultural domains: the transformation of the periphery. Subjective outcomes involve the perception of empowerment of a marginalized actor. This category is therefore based on the assessment of peripheries themselves in terms of their own role in transforming their peripherality.

While each contribution of this volume sets its own focus within these three central categories, all give a voice to the periphery itself, its opportunities and constraints, activism and self-perception and so focus on the agency of marginalized individuals and communities. While they do not represent in any way a homogeneous group – they populate different areas and face different socio-economic conditions – they are in different ways and forms taking part in a process that, far from being a simple awareness about oppression, aims at finding alternative ways of resistance.

Overview of the Articles

In the first contribution to this special issue, *Edwige Fortier* (2015) argues that while the landscape for civil society in Tunisia has widened with the establishment of several thousand associations between 2011 and 2013, vulnerable groups, including sexual minorities, perceived and experienced increased degrees of marginalization. Some members of the *Tunisian LGBT community* chose to engage in a range of strategies to advocate recognition and freedom from discrimination combining strategies of 'publicity' and 'visibility' such as participating in public demonstrations with symbols such as the rainbow flag, appropriating social media such as Facebook, establishing a formal association to combat stigma and discrimination against minorities, including LGBT, publicly countering homophobic statements through mass petitions, and working through a range of national and regional networks. Nevertheless, these actors also believed they encountered increased marginalization at the individual/personal level as an outcome of this growing visibility at the political and socio-cultural level. Actors who were hoping to maximize expanding opportunities to widen the discursive arena, such as LGBT activists, ultimately had to weigh the benefits of visibility to advocate for greater overall inclusion against freedom from discrimination, over the risks of further violence and insecurity. Fortier concludes that some peripheries effectively stand to become more marginalized during the transition to democracy than previously under authoritarian rule.

Complementing Fortier's article, *Maryam Khalid* (2015) looks at *gender peripheries* (women and non-heterosexual people) from a discursive angle. She argues that discourses that influence and shape dominant western understandings of the role of women and non-heterosexual peoples in the 'Arab Spring' have (re) produced orientalist logics that marginalize those who do not conform to particular gendered understandings of the roles of various peoples in the MENA; discourses in the Arab world, too, have deployed specific (binary) understandings of gender and sexuality to exercise control over groups of peoples. Nonetheless, Khalid shows how gender peripheries have pursued their own strategies in these discursive opportunity structures. On a broad level, the calls for freedom and justice that marked the protests of the 'Arab Spring' intersect with the aims of those seeking to change dominant understandings of gender and sexual identities and roles. However, these peripheries have had varying success in changing dominant discourses of gender and sexuality. While political engagement in traditional forums has not always been fruitful, peripheral groups concerned with gender and LGBT rights have been able to find other avenues to challenge discourses. The importance of online forums in contemporary political movements has also been significant and can be seen as an opportunity-structure shift that has been utilized by groups who have (and continue to have) limited access to the institutions of the state to voice and act on their own understandings of rights related to gender and sexuality.

The special issue then turns from gender to religious peripheries. In their comparative analysis of *Christians in Syria and Egypt*, *Mark Farha* and *Salma Mousa* (2015) argue that the status quo ante under al-Assad and Mubarak, though democratically deficient, put a (temporary) lid on civil hostilities and afforded Christian minorities a modicum of secular protection and even prosperity. They show that while Syrian Christians were not considered a peripheral group in Syria insofar as many of them were represented in the political and socio-economic centre, Egyptian Christians suffered from a 'double-periphery' status as excluded religious minorities and as socio-economically marginalized. While Syrian Christians were largely absent in the protests, the strong Coptic presence in the Egyptian uprising is undeniable. Syrian Christians fear the religion-based, peripheral designation that may come with an Islamist-driven revolution, negating a long history of social prominence through state-espoused structures of business and political opportunities. Meanwhile, many Egyptian Christians had little to lose by overturning a regime that compounded their status as a religious, political and socio-economic peripheral group (sharing the last two designations with most Sunni compatriots). Revitalized political participation among Egyptian Copts has allowed the community to make tentative political gains. Coptic political activity directly before, during and since the revolution unmistakably refutes previous assumptions of depoliticization and self-imposed isolation.

The next set of contributions focuses on diverse areas in Morocco. *Sylvia Bergh* and *Daniele Rossi-Doria* (2015) look at the *mountainous areas south of Marrakech*. In contrast to the Rif and Western Sahara (analysed in the two following contribution), this region's opportunity structure did not include already existing well-organized mobilization structures. Analysing the differences between the urban-based activism and the rural protest, Bergh and Rossi-Doria find that while the F20M tried to mobilize rural populations for its purposes, the rural populations did not try to mobilize F20M for theirs. This divergence has its origin in the different understanding of what the demand for social justice represented in the two areas: while the urban-based activists focused on the constitutional arrangements and demanded mainly political change, the population in the rural areas prioritized access to basic infrastructures and services and economic development issues. Hence, peripheral populations did not discursively connect their mainly socio-economic demands to the civic democratic struggle of the central movement. Rural protests started before the formation of the F20M and continued afterwards, but the rural peripheries continue to be marginalized and rural people do not have a very positive view, if any, of the constitutional achievements brought by the F20M.

Ángela Suárez Collado (2015) then analyses the evolution of popular *protest in the Rif* within the Moroccan context of contention. In the case of the Rif, reactions and demands appeared in response not only to the evolution of popular mobilizations in Morocco but also to changes in Moroccan political life prior to the beginning of street protests in the country. Furthermore, they also displayed the persistence of old and new postcolonial problems related to issues such as transitional justice, territorial imbalances and the impacts generated by the neo-patrimonial system. Collado argues that peripheral actors showed agency in conducting their own strategies, using the opportunity structure opened at state level to advance their own agenda, and that they were empowered by the idea that peripheral opposition was necessary for pressuring the centre to pursue political and social change. In the case of the Rif, the previous existence of rooted mobilizing structures around regional demands at the meso level, especially local associations and groups and regional forums of civil society, permitted regional protesters to develop an active and independent role. The most noteworthy outcome of protests in the Rif is the end of the perception of threat among the Rifian public regarding its commitment to regionalist activism, above all among local youth which has been politicized and activated by the Arab Spring. A regional sense of belonging among Rifian youth has been further promoted by the way in which protests developed in the region. Moreover, the regionalist mobilization structures have also become denser and more diverse, including the diaspora.

Similar findings are identified in the following article, by *Irene Fernández Molina* (2015). She points out that *Sahrawi civil protests* in the Western Sahara territory under Moroccan control intensified just before the Arab Spring broke out and can indeed be seen as the first chapter of the Arab uprisings. The emergence and empowerment of Sahrawi civil protests and pro-independence activism inside the Western Sahara territory under Moroccan occupation have to be seen in the context of varying sets of opportunity structures which this peripheral movement has actively seized in the past two decades by symbiotically combining domestic non-violent resistance and international 'diplomatic' activities. The Arab Spring has been a particularly fruitful window of opportunity in this regard. Building on comparatively rich mobilization structures at the local, inter-Sahrawi, Moroccan and international levels, Sahrawis have successfully been able to frame the local Gdeim Izik protest in a favourable universalistic paradigm which has enhanced their international standing, while opportunities have broadened relatively also at Moroccan state level. Molina argues that while objective outcomes seem meagre as the protests in occupied Western Sahara did not lead to better socio-economic conditions or greater political autonomy, subjective outcomes are important, most notably the recognition gained – or seized – from three significant others: the Moroccan state, the Polisario Front and the international community, which has helped Sahrawis to strengthen and crystallize their own identity.

The final contribution by *Khaled Elghamry* (2015) looks at the peripheral theme of this special issue through a media perspective. It examines the expansion and contraction of *an emerging alternative media structure* before, during and after the protests of 25 January 2011, and shows that alternative media have empowered peripheries for which it provided a platform to make their voice heard. Peripheries have employed their strategies within this new, emerging alternative media structure, not only through documenting events in geographically remote areas, but also by constituting a platform for bringing the role of ethnic and gender peripheries in the protests to the centre, and by engaging previously apolitical sectors of society. At the same time, this alternative media machine has also been empowered by peripheries since they provided it with critical mass, contributing to the overflow from the virtual space to the real world. The existing opportunity structure has been deeply challenged, not only in the media sphere which has started to change, but also in the political realm. Initially, the core held onto its power as a state-run media machine through which it attempted to 'peripheralize', but it failed to do so in the January/February 2011 period. Following this, in the interim period, social media continued to serve as an alternative to mainstream media and to contribute to an opening of the general media landscape. In the long term, however, the alternative media structure may again contract. A marked comeback of the traditional media machine is likely, as can be seen in the current decline in the social media impact on public opinion and the path of events in the political sphere where the alternative (both in media and politics) is returning to the periphery.

The *conclusions* by the editors summarize the main findings of the contributions. This special issue shows that the 'Arab Spring' consists of diverse 'springs of different kinds' – an expression initially coined by Michelle Pace (2013) for the Palestinian Spring. Different Arab Springs, however, have not only taken place across diverse countries but also across distinct sections of societies within countries. Several contributions to this volume show that the Arab Spring has been used as a framing claim by peripheries to lend political weight to their own protests which is one of the reasons why the uprisings accumulated a critical mass to become a powerful political phenomenon. This volume therefore serves as a reminder to look beyond the centres when seeking to understand attempted or accomplished processes of transformation. The Arab Spring is not a unitary process but a whole variance of processes which differed in terms of space (diverse countries, diverse areas in countries), time (the Ghedim Izik protests in Western Sahara started already in October 2010, while protests in the Rif are still ongoing), substance (demands for civil and political rights, equality rights, material claims, autonomy), strategies (from violence to apathy), involved actors (social movements, civil society organizations or individual actors) and outcomes (from regime repression to empowerment of peripheries).

Conclusions

More than three decades ago African-American poet Pat Parker wrote that 'revolutions' are neither neat nor pretty and certainly not quick (Parker, 1983). This

10

is even more the case considering the marginalized contexts in which peripheries are struggling and resisting in order to sustain their views and projects.[5] They are increasingly determined to change their system of 'co-cultural oppression' from within (Orbe, 1998). The American author and activist bell hooks used these words to frame her (and maybe indirectly also their) efforts:

> I am located in the margin. I make a definite distinction between that marginality which is imposed by oppressive structures and that marginality one chooses as a site of resistance – as location of radical openness and possibility ... we are transformed, individually, collectively, as we make radical creative space which affirms and sustains our subjectivity, which gives us a new location from which to articulate our sense of the world. (Hooks, 1990: 145 and 153)

Such a subjective transformation has also been found for the peripheries studied in this volume which are increasingly struggling to empower themselves and pursue their own expectations. Their efforts are not taking place in a vacuum but in a historical phase that, in a growing number of areas in the MENA, is witnessing a shift from states to societies. For decades, the major issues concerning the region have been addressed by states or state-like actors. Today, states are taking a step back and non-state actors are moving in. While this has become maybe most evident in the breakdown of statehood in the MENA and the rise of actors like the self-proclaimed 'Islamic State' (IS) on which the western media is focusing, this volume has explored the role of peripheries in this process. New spaces are now available to these peripheries and an unprecedented sense of empowerment is in the air. Thus, instead of a top-down reform process as suggested by Marwan Muasher (2014), which seems particularly unrealistic now that the old authoritarian establishments are making their way back to power, the region might more realistically witness a transition toward inclusiveness through a bottom-up process of self-empowerment triggered by peripheries.

These processes might not be immediately discernible as they happen outside of the media's focus, but might be of higher long-term importance. For instance, women's growing contribution to their households and their increased involvement in activism in rural Upper and Lower Egypt did not yet lead to greater power: the harmful aspects of patriarchy have in some contexts worsened and a new patriarchal structure has emerged (Kamel & Elkholy, 2015b). Nonetheless, as local women are turning the 'political revolution' into a cultural and moral one in their own households, this patriarchal structure is challenged far more deeply than it would be through a change of law at the state level. This is perhaps the major lesson that we can learn about peripheries and their role in the Arab Spring: the seeds for changing the face of politics and polities are within the peripheries themselves. Each of them has handled its marginality in different ways, but all of them are part of a broad process that will change political, social and cultural structures in the long term.

Conversely, what does this mean for the 'powerful'? As Khaled Elghamry (2015) highlights, the powerful had for long underestimated peripheries, when they disregarded them in the initial moments of the uprisings, then sought to represent them as outcasts, before finally being forced to acknowledge the critical mass they had accumulated. The powerful had to shatter their own prevailing stereotypes when reacting to peripheries in the Arab Spring. This also applies to the western machinery of politicians, media, think tanks or academics that are engaged in or with the region. In *The Myth of Marginality* Janice Perlman (1979) pointed out that the prevailing stereotypes about the residents of the favelas of Rio de Janeiro were empirically and analytically misleading. *Mutatis mutandis*, it can be argued that the imaginary western construct of the Arab world has now been deeply challenged, even though it has not been shattered, as the contribution of Maryam Khalid (2015) shows. Also the recent concept of the 'Arab youth' has emerged as a new tool to read the Arab Spring born out of the necessity to rely on an interpretative framework that, however, does not necessarily respond to the needs of the local populations. As Bourdieu has argued, youth is 'nothing but a word', implying that referring to youth as a social category is itself a manipulation of the young (Bourdieu, 1993: 94–102). Rabab El-Mahdi noted soon after the Egyptian uprising of January 2011 that 'the underlying message is that these "middle-class" educated youth (read: modern) are not "terrorists", they hold the same values as "us" (the democratic West), and finally use the same tools (facebook and twitter) that "we" invented and use in our daily-lives. They are just like "us" and hence they deserve celebration' (El-Mahdi, 2011). Focusing on the voices of peripheries can therefore be a powerful tool to 'de-simplify' the reading of the Arab Spring, to reshape the paradigmatic schemes through which to look at this part of the world and to realize Eric Hobsbawm's wish to rescue not only 'the stockinger and the peasant, but also the nobleman and the king' (Hobsbawm, 1997: 184–185).

Notes

1. Periphery and centre are not seen in dichotomous terms in this article. Instead of explaining the centre–periphery relations in the logic of the solar system, it would be more appropriate to consider the universe as a model which consists of several solar systems, with many star-suns and their own planets, as Iván T. Berend (1995: 131) argued (see conceptual section of this article).
2. Transformation is conceptualized in this article from the viewpoint of peripheries, not in terms of the democratic transition paradigm (see analytical section).
3. These concepts are adapted from Douglas McAdam (1996: 27).
4. We owe this point to one of the contributors to this volume, Irene Fernández Molina.
5. Soo-Chul Kim noted that 'what is rarely focused on and theorized in the modernist approach … is the lived spaces as the "location of radical openness and possibility", whereby new radical subjectivity can be contextualized, activated and practiced' (Kim, 2007: 8).

Disclosure statement

No potential conflict of interest was reported by the authors.

References

Abu-Lughod, L. (2012) Living the 'revolution' in an Egyptian village: moral action in a national space, *American Ethnologist*, 39(1), pp. 21–25. doi:10.1111/j.1548-1425.2011.01341.x.

ARAB SPRING AND PERIPHERIES

Al-Anani, K. (2012) Islamist parties post-Arab spring, *Mediterranean Politics*, 17(3), pp. 466–472. doi:10.1080/13629395.2012.725309.

Barany, Z. (2013) Unrest and state response in Arab monarchies, *Mediterranean Quarterly*, 24(2), pp. 5–38.

Barnett, M. & R.Duvall (2005) Power in international politics, *International Organization*, 59(1), pp. 39–75.

Bayat, A. (2010) *Life as Politics: How Ordinary People Change the Middle East* (Stanford, Calif. Stanford University Press).

Beinin, J. & F.Vairel (2011) *Social Movements, Mobilization, and Contestation in the Middle East and North Africa* (Stanford: Stanford University Press).

Bellin, E. (2012) Reconsidering the robustness of authoritarianism in the Middle East: lessons from the Arab spring, *Comparative Politics*, 44(2), pp. 127–149. doi:10.5129/001041512798838021.

Berend, I.T. (1995) German economic penetration in East Central Europe in historical perspective, in: S. E.Hanson & W.Spohn (Eds) *Germany and the Reconstruction of Postcommunist Societies* (Washington, DC: Washington University Press).

Bergh, S.I. & D.Rossi-Doria (2015) Plus ça change? Observing the dynamics of Morocco's 'Arab spring' in the high Atlas, *Mediterranean Politics*, 20(2). doi:10.1080/13629395.2015.1033900.

Börzel, T., A.Dandashly & T.Risse (2015) Responses to the Arab spring: the EU in comparative perspective, *Journal of European Integration*, 37(1), pp. 1–18. doi:10.1080/07036337.2014.975993.

Bourdieu, P. (1993) *Sociology in Question* (London: Sage Publications).

Brown, N.J. (2013) Egypt's failed transition, *Journal of Democracy*, 24(4), pp. 45–58. doi:10.1353/jod. 2013.0064.

Collado, Á. S. (2015) Territorial stress in Morocco: from democratic to autonomist demands in popular protests in the rif, *Mediterranean Politics*, 20(2). doi:10.1080/13629395.2015.1033908.

Comaroff, J.L. & J.Comaroff (1992) *Ethnography and the Historical Imagination* (Boulder: Westview Press).

Cronin, S. (2012) *Subalterns and Social Protest: History from Below in the Middle East and North Africa* (New York: Routledge).

Elghamry, K. (2015) Periphery discourse: an alternative media eye on the geographical, social and media peripheries in Egypt's spring, *Mediterranean Politics*, 20(2). doi:10.1080/13629395.2015.1033902.

El-Khawas, M.A. (2012) Tunisia's jasmine revolution: causes and impact, *Mediterranean Quarterly*, 23(4), pp. 1–23.

El-Mahdi, R. (2011) Orientalising the Egyptian uprising, *Jadaliyya*, Available at http://www.jadaliyya. com/pages/index/1214/orientalising-the-egyptian-uprising

Farha, M. & S.Mousa (2015) Secular autocracy vs. sectarian democracy? Weighing reasons for christian support for regime transition in Syria and Egypt, *Mediterranean Politics*, 20(2). doi:10.1080/ 13629395.2015.1033903.

Fortier, H. (2015) Transition and marginalisation: locating spaces for discursive contestation in post-revolution Tunisia, *Mediterranean Politics*, 20(2). doi:10.1080/13629395.2015.1033904.

Friedman, J. (1994) *Cultural Identity and Global Process* (London: Sage Publications).

Gelvin, J. (2012) Conclusion: the Arab world at the intersection of the national and transnational, in: M.L. Haas (Ed.) *The Arab Spring: Change and Resistance in the Middle East* (Boulder: Westview Press), pp. 238–255.

Ghosh-Schellhorn, M. (2006) *Peripheral Centres, Central Peripheries: India and Its Diaspora(s)* (Münster: LIT Verlag Münster).

Guazzone, L. (2013) Ennahda Islamists and the test of government in Tunisia, *The International Spectator*, 48(4), pp. 30–50. doi:10.1080/03932729.2013.847677.

Heitmeyer, C. (2009) 'There is peace here' managing communal relations in a town in central Gujarat, *Journal of South Asian Development*, 4(1), pp. 103–120. doi:10.1177/097317410900400107.

Heydemann, S. (2007) Upgrading authoritarianism in the Arab world, Brookings Saban Centre Analysis Paper Series. Available at http://www.brookings.edu/research/papers/2007/10/arabworld

Heydemann, S. & R.Leenders (2011) Authoritarian learning and authoritarian resilience: regime responses to the 'Arab awakening.', *Globalizations*, 8(5), pp. 647–653. doi:10.1080/14747731.2011. 621274.

Heydemann, S. & Leenders, R. (Eds) (2012) *Middle East Authoritarianisms: Governance, Contestation, and Regime Resilience in Syria and Iran* (Stanford: Stanford University Press).

Hobsbawm, E.J. (1997) *On History* (New York: The New Press).

Hooks, B. (1990) *Yearning: Race, Gender, and Cultural Politics* (Boston, MA: South End Press).

Huber, D. (2013) US and EU human rights and democracy promotion since the Arab spring. Rethinking its content, targets and instruments, *The International Spectator*, 48(3), pp. 98–112. doi:10.1080/03932729.2013.787827.

Israeli, R. (2013) *From Arab Spring to Islamic Winter* (New Brunswick and London: Transaction Publishers).

Kamel, L. & M.E.Elkholy (2015) Youth exclusion and cultural activism in Egypt's Sohag governorate, in: O.Bortolazzi (Ed.) *The Shifts in Philanthropic Practices in Post-Revolutionary Arab World: Civic Engagement, Social Entrepreneurship and Youth Networks* (Bologna: Bononia University Press).

ibid. (Forthcoming 2015b) Waiting and struggling for the revolution. Perceptions from lower and upper rural Egypt, in: M.M.Charrad & R.Stephan (Eds) *Women Rising: Resistance, Revolution, and Reform in the Arab Spring and Beyond* (New York: New York University Press).

Khalid, M. (2015) The peripheries of gender and sexuality in the "Arab spring.", *Mediterranean Politics*, 20(2). doi:10.1080/13629395.2015.1033906.

Kim, S.-C. (2007) *Space, History and Mobility: A Historical Inquiry of Seoul as a Mobile City from 1970 to 2000* (Ann Arbor: ProQuest).

McAdam, D. (1996) Conceptual origins, current problems, future directions, in: D.McAdam, J.D. McCarthy & M.N.Zald (Eds) *Comparative Perspectives on Social Movements: Political Opportunities, Mobilizing Structures, and Cultural Framings* (Cambridge: Cambridge University Press), pp. 23–40.

Mitchell, A. (2011) Quality/control: international peace interventions and 'the everyday.', *Review of International Studies*, 37(4), pp. 1623–1645. doi:10.1017/S0260210511000180.

Molina, I.F. (2015) Protests under occupation: the spring inside Western Sahara, *Mediterranean Politics*, 20(2). doi:10.1080/13629395.2015.1033907.

Muasher, M. (2014) *The Second Arab Awakening. And the Battle for Pluralism* (New Haven: Yale University Press).

Orbe, M.P. (1998) *Constructing Co-Cultural Theory: An Explication of Culture, Power, and Communication* (Thousand Oaks: Sage Publications).

Ottaway, M. & A.Hamzawy (2011) Protest movements and political change in the Arab world, Carnegie Endowment for International Peace. Available at http://carnegieendowment.org/2011/01/28/protest-movements-and-political-change-in-arab-world/1xu

Pace, M. & F.Cavatorta (2012) The Arab uprisings in theoretical perspective – an introduction, *Mediterranean Politics*, 17(2), pp. 125–138. doi:10.1080/13629395.2012.694040.

Pace, Michelle (2013) An Arab 'Spring' of a different kind? Resilience and freedom in the case of an occupied nation, *Mediterranean Politics*, 18(1), pp. 42–59. doi:10.1080/13629395.2012.745705.

Parker, P. (1983) Revolution: it's not neat or pretty or quick, in: C.Moraga & G.Anzaldúa (Eds) *This Bridge Called My Back: Writings by Radical Women of Color* (New York: Kitchen Table, Women of Color Press), pp. 238–242.

Perlman, J.E. (1979) *The Myth of Marginality: Urban Poverty and Politics in Rio de Janeiro* (Berkeley: University of California Press).

Pioppi, D. (2013) Playing with fire. The Muslim brotherhood and the Egyptian leviathan, *The International Spectator*, 48(4), pp. 51–68. doi:10.1080/03932729.2013.847680.

Pollack, K.M. (2012) *The Arab Awakening* (Washington, DC: Brookings Institution).

Risse, T., Ropp, S.C. & Sikkink, K. (Eds) (1999) *The Power of Human Rights: International Norms and Domestic Change*, Cambridge Studies in International Relations 66 (New York: Cambridge University Press).

Rokkan, S. (1999) *State Formation, Nation-Building, and Mass Politics in Europe: The Theory of Stein Rokkan: Based on His Collected Works* (Oxford: Oxford University Press).

Schedler, A.P. (Ed.) (2006) *Electoral Authoritarianism* (Boulder: L. Rienner).

14

Schlumberger, O. (2007) *Debating Arab Authoritarianism: Dynamics and Durability in Nondemocratic Regimes* (Stanford: Stanford University Press).

Springborg, R. (2011) The political economy of the Arab spring, *Mediterranean Politics*, 16(3), pp. 427–433. doi:10.1080/13629395.2011.613678.

Teti, A. (2012) The EU's first response to the 'Arab spring': a critical discourse analysis of the partnership for democracy and shared prosperity, *Mediterranean Politics*, 17(3), pp. 266–284. doi:10.1080/13629395.2012.725297.

Thompson, E.P. (1964) *The Making of the English Working Class* (New York: Pantheon Books).

Totten, M. (2012) Arab spring or Islamist winter? *World Affairs Journal*, February. Available at http://www.worldaffairsjournal.org/article/arab-spring-or-islamist-winter

Williams, P. (2013) Reproducing everyday peace in North India: process, politics, and power, *Annals of the Association of American Geographers*, 103(1), pp. 230–250.

Yom, S.L. & G.Gause (2012) Resilient royals: how Arab monarchies hang on, *Journal of Democracy*, 23(4), pp. 74–88. doi:10.1353/jod.2012.0062.

Transition and Marginalization: Locating Spaces for Discursive Contestation in Post-Revolution Tunisia

EDWIGE A. FORTIER

School of Oriental and African Studies, University of London, London, UK

ABSTRACT *Transitions to democracy nourish expectations for an expansion of space for political liberalization, redistribution and recognition. From 2011 to 2013, the landscape for civil society in Tunisia widened with the establishment of several thousand associations. However, during this period vulnerable groups, including sexual minorities, perceived and experienced increased degrees of marginalization. This article analyses the* potentialities *and* boundaries *for members of homosexual communities in Tunisia as they manoeuvre through a post-revolution transition characterized by rapid expansions and contractions of the public sphere. It highlights the competing priorities within the public sphere, in particular those voices left on the periphery as a multiplicity of issues are presented for discursive contestation and argues that some groups effectively stand to become more marginalized during the transition to democracy than previously under authoritarian rule.*

> *I was, I am and I will remain an activist. I will stay in this county,*
> *it is mine and I will not let it go.*
>
> *—(LGBT activist, Tunisia)*[1]

In October 2011, Tunisia was the first post-'Arab Spring' country in the Middle East and North Africa to hold democratic elections. Transitions to democracy nourish expectations among a range of stakeholders, from individuals to the international community, for an expansion of space for political liberalization, redistribution and recognition. From 2011 to 2013, the landscape for civil society in Tunisia quickly widened with the establishment of several thousand new associations. As a consequence of the deregulation of the former and more rigid associational laws, organizations in the public sphere were able to engage more openly in a broad range of activities including civic activism, human rights, social welfare initiatives and direct outreach work with deprived communities across the country.[2] From January to October 2011 it is estimated that 1,700 new associations were created, with a further 600 civil society organizations registering between October 2011 to March 2012 (European Union, 2012: 5).

Individuals acting inside Tunisia's public sphere also re-appropriated the concept of *muwatana* (مواطنة) 'fellow citizens/compatriot' or the French *citoyenneté* or 'citizenship', where citizens felt engaged and mobilized as equal partners in the future of the country, with or without the state to accompany them along the way. This took the form of local collections for deprived communities, Tunisian students living overseas raising money to purchase emergency transportation for their local town, and even neighbourhood members meeting in a family's garage to plan support to marginalized women (Interview II, 2012). However, it is often easy to overlook the groups and actors that find spaces contracting around them as the priorities for democratization are outlined and the hierarchy of concerns push certain groups to the periphery. This tightening of certain spaces for individuals (and their rights) also underscores the complexity and unstable nature of democratization itself. Issues perceived as 'contentious' are sidelined in favour of those seen as 'acceptable' in the public sphere featuring the imaginings of a country's new national identity.

The concerns of sexual minorities in many countries in the Middle East and North Africa are often overshadowed and groups acting for/on behalf of homosexual communities are routinely persecuted when the line between discretion and visibility is crossed. Vulnerable groups, including sexual minorities, have perceived and experienced increased degrees of marginalization since the Tunisia uprising in 2010–11. As a specific case study, I follow the experiences of members of one of the homosexual communities in Tunisia that established the organization *Damj* ('reintegration') to further defend human rights and the rights of minorities, including lesbian, gays, bisexuals and transgender populations (LGBT).

This article observes how the *boundaries* and *potentialities* for sexual minorities in the public sphere in Tunisia evolved during the transition to democracy. It also describes the strategies homosexual communities employed to make advances in a highly contested and unstable post-revolution opportunity structure as described in the Introduction to this special issue by Huber and Kamel, as well as the key sites of conflict and contestation they encountered. I argue that these groups, which already represented a social periphery before the revolution, risk becoming more marginalized – even threatened – by the turbulence of shifting and dominant revolutionary priorities. Moreover, there is the dilemma that some vulnerable groups may experience greater freedom and security within liberal-authoritarian regimes than during transitions to democracy. This article begins by situating research with sexual minorities within the context of the disparate objectives of LGBT communities. It then articulates the concepts this study applies within the overall analytical framework of this volume, namely the diverse strategies vulnerable groups can adopt in a public sphere characterized by routine expansions and contractions; these openings and closures are partially caused by the conflation between sex and 'moral panics' during transitions to democracy. Finally, the article describes empirically the multiple advances and challenges sexual minorities encountered in Tunisia in the two years following the uprising.

Researching Sexual Minorities in the Arab World

Similar to conceptualizations of 'civil society' within liberal frameworks, issues of homosexual identity and liberation have become linked to modernization trajectories. As will be further explored by Khalid in the subsequent article in this special issue on gender and sexuality in the 'Arab Spring', a country is increasingly deemed 'modern' depending upon the policies and laws it has in place to combat inequality and discrimination against LGBT communities.[3] Furthermore, homosexual groups/organizations themselves are bestowed the recognition of modernity depending upon their chosen degree of visibility in the public sphere as activists calling for universal human rights, freedom from discrimination and violence, or 'liberation'. Jason Ritchie (2010) allows space to conceptualize 'different kinds of visibilities' in relation to how LGBT activists and groups express and seek out defining (or not) their own homosexuality(ies) in relation to the western gay international. However, some scholars rely upon more homogenous understandings of how sexual identity is understood in regions outside the West, perhaps a tacit form of *Orientalism in reverse*. Joseph Massad (2002: 363), for example, argues that the discourse of the gay international 'Both produces homosexuals ... where they do not exist, and represses same-sex desires and practices that refuse to be assimilated into its sexual epistemology'. Massad (2002: 373) contends that there is no evidence of LGBT movements anywhere in the Arab world or 'Even of gay group identity outside of the small groups of men in metropolitan areas such as Cairo and Beirut'. However, Massad and other proponents of the 'homosexual behaviour' supposition negate the agency of homosexual actors in these countries whilst simultaneously side-lining the more fundamental issues of homophobia and violence. Both Ritchie and Rahul Rao underscore the inherent inconsistencies in Massad's arguments whilst acknowledging the 'Hierarchies and supremacism that lurk within the cosmopolitan politics of LGBT solidarity' (Rao, 2010: 176).

When considering what these diverse agents were trying to achieve following the uprisings across the Middle East and North Africa (and the strategies they adopted to achieve these aims), it is more constructive to avoid approaches which rely primarily upon 'essentialist diffusionism' (Chabot & Duyvendak, 2002: 697–740). Chabot and Duyvendak (2002: 700–704) argue that analyses which take for granted that ideas and social movements originate in a western core and enter 'receptive communities' in the non-western periphery, trickling down to 'traditional followers' at the bottom, negate '*How* such cross border dissemination evolves or *why* it occurs in some times and places and not others'. They contend rather that transnational diffusion involves considerable 'reinvention and pragmatist agency' on the part of the actors themselves (2002: 707). This requires the acknowledgement of the tensions between 'globalizing' and 'localizing' when considering the overall objectives of these heterogeneous movements (Warner, 1993: xii). In determining the exact boundaries and potentialities for these actors, a more profound analysis is required to ascertain whether or not, and to what degree, these groups are seeking political recognition and participation in the broader public sphere.

Following the uprisings in the Middle East and North Africa, limited research has so far looked to the impact on minority groups, sexual minorities in particular. This study focuses on the agency and voices of the activists as they depict their own perceptions and experiences during Tunisia's national endeavour toward a greater standard of democracy. This article was developed based on field research supported through the University of London School of Oriental and African Studies over the course of several months in Tunisia in 2012 and a follow-up visit in 2013 as part of my doctoral thesis into how the public sphere functions during transitions to democracy. The research relies primarily on in-depth interviews among a range of actors, namely with associations working in the domains of HIV/AIDS and human rights, alongside interviews with multilateral institutions and journalists.[4] As with other research conducted following the Arab uprisings, the timing of the interviews often shaped the response of the interviewee (Gunning & Baron, 2013). Whilst I encountered an incredible openness among the different associative actors working with marginalized communities in 2012, unfortunately upon my return in 2013 I found that for many the residue of authoritarian rule had resurfaced.

Conceptualizing Strategies of Sexual Minorities in Periods of Transition

Sexual minorities in the Middle East and North Africa often find themselves on the periphery of their political and socio-cultural environment both spatially and in terms of difference or 'Otherness'. The recognition these groups achieve is contingent, on the one hand, on the (combination) of strategies they adopt and, on the other, on the spaces in which these strategies are chosen and pursued. Given the often precarious situation of minorities in transitions, I introduce additional concepts to the analytical framework of this collective volume, namely the diverse strategies of visibility sexual minorities can choose in the context of rapidly expanding and contracting 'public spheres' – a phenomenon often caused by 'moral panics' in periods of transition. The 'public sphere' effectively represents both a spatial arena to allow for multiple publics to engage in discursive contestation as well as a Habermasian ideal for rational critical discourse in which equal individuals participate as part of a larger public (Habermas, 1989). In this particular context, the 'public sphere' is to be understood neither as a singularity of publics nor as a multiplicity of publics (Fraser, 1990) but rather as a continuum between singular and plural as this domain expands and contracts perpetually throughout the different transformations of the state. As the 'public sphere' can also be characterized through Seteney Shami's (2009: 15–16) articulation of the notion of the 'integrative promise', this concept is able to provide disparate perspectives on civil society, private and public domains, urban social movements and sexual identity. In principle it serves as an analytical frame to observe the boundaries and potentialities different actors face in seeking recognition following the 2010–11 Tunisia uprising.

Such recognition could be related to identity, rights or simply the freedom from discrimination and violence. Nancy Fraser identifies a shift in the post-socialist terrain in which groups of actors are no longer simply 'economically defined classes' seeking an end to exploitation and means to greater distribution. Rather, these actors are also 'culturally defined' groups and 'communities of value' seeking to preserve their identities and to attain recognition (Fraser, 1997: 2). However, Fraser's contribution in this field is not simply that 'communities of value' are not required to choose between strategies which advocate either for distribution or recognition. Her primary impact lies in underscoring the difficult choices subaltern and marginalized groups must routinely make between strategies of publicity and visibility, and the protection that invisibility and discretion can offer. She argues:

> It is not correct to view publicity as always and unambiguously an instrument of empowerment and emancipation. For members of subordinate groups it will always be a matter of balancing the potential uses of publicity against the dangers of the loss of privacy. (Fraser, 1997: 116)

In supporting public spheres that can allow for a multiplicity of views and counter-publics to emerge through discursive contestation, 'communities of value', such as homosexual communities, will encounter greater space to manoeuvre for recognition. She contends that 'Democratic publicity requires positive guarantees of opportunities for minorities to convince others that what in the past was not public ... should now become so' (Fraser, 1990: 71).

However, during transitions to democracy, it is not only possible to observe a public sphere with multiple conflicts and contentions among its disparate actors, but also the rapid expansions and contractions this domain experiences within a brief amount of time. These expansions and contractions are in part a result of emerging socio-political and socio-cultural dynamics that have a remarkable impact on the various groups that emerge during transitions as 'publics' and on those which will be designated as 'peripheral'. Such dynamics also affect the designation of the hierarchy of concerns for the transition to democracy within the public sphere, a catalogue of priorities that is articulated and re-articulated regularly. Therefore homosexuality can also become peripheral as an issue by virtue of its distance to mainstream socio-political issues.

Dennis Altman (2001: 2) aptly characterized sexuality as an area of 'constant surveillance and control' despite its inherent designation as that which is also 'natural and private'.[5] Thus, when analysing new and emerging discourses on sexuality, the question of *who* gains from speaking about them should also be explored. Emerging discourses on sex are examined in this study through the concept of 'moral panics'. Altman (2001: 143) argues that '"Moral panics" can be understood both as specific populist reactions, and as calculated appeals by political and economic elites to these reactions as ways of winning popular support for other policy shifts'. Inciting such moral panics can lead to rapidly evolving political and socio-cultural contestation which inevitably can expand and contract the spaces available for sexual minorities.

How have the spaces for recognition of sexual minorities during the Tunisian transition to democracy expanded and contracted? Which strategies have members of homosexual communities employed to make advances in a highly contested and unstable post-revolution opportunity structure? What were the key sites of conflict and contestation they encountered? Ultimately, has the year 2011 reversed long-held assumptions of possibilities for political pluralism and liberalism in the Middle East and North Africa? Or is there likely to be a continuum of expansions and contractions in these spaces as not only the political but also the socio-cultural environment simultaneously create and destroy alliances, visions, approaches, concepts and ideologies as these 'democratic experiments' evolve?

Expanding and Contracting Spaces

At present it is illegal to engage in same-sex conduct in 78 countries and in five countries – the United Arab Emirates, Mauritania, Saudi Arabia, Yemen and Sudan – the death penalty can be invoked for homosexual activity (see also Whitaker, 2006: 112, 123).[6] Those countries which have retained the death penalty all justify this punishment based on the foundations of Islamic law (Whitaker, 2006: 112). For other countries in the region, the penalty for sodomy in Bahrain is ten years' imprisonment; seven years in Kuwait; five years in Libya and Qatar; three years in Algeria, Oman, Morocco, Somalia and Tunisia; and one year in Lebanon and Syria (Whitaker, 2006: 123). The number of individuals prosecuted or arrested for same-sex offences in the Middle East and North Africa remains impossible to determine.

Alongside formal legal codes which persecute same-sex behaviour throughout the region, there is also discrimination, harassment and violence committed by state security forces as well as by individuals and groups at the community level acting on their own sense of moral authority. There are examples across the Middle East and North Africa of the flagrant abuse of authority against homosexual communities and equally homophobic acts committed by individuals that consequently, through non-response, can indicate sanctioning by state entities. For example, in May 2001, 52 men were sent to trial after a police raid on a Cairo discothèque known as 'Queen Boat'; 23 of the men were convicted and sentenced to prison terms of one to five years for 'immoral behaviour and contempt of religion' (Human Rights Watch, 2004: 2). Since this time, Human Rights Watch (2004: 2) has reported that it was aware of more than 170 men whose cases under the Egyptian law of 'debauchery' were brought before prosecutors. Furthermore, in March 2012, international human rights groups urged Iraqi authorities to investigate targeted killings against approximately 15 teenagers perceived to be gay. Young people with 'emo-like' features such as tight-fitting clothes and 'alternative' hairstyles were brutally stoned, beaten or shot (Associated French Press, 2012). It is even reported that some victims had their heads smashed with concrete blocks. The minister of interior continues to deny any homophobic or 'anti-emo' killings took place. Finally, in July 2012, Human Rights Watch reported that 36 men were arrested in Beirut in an adult cinema. The men were subjected to anal examinations to determine whether or not they were homosexual (Human Rights Watch, 2012). These events, *at a minimum*, reflect the degree of stigmatization and violence against sexual minorities throughout the Middle East and North Africa.

In part, this discrimination stems from discourses which situate homosexuality within the context of an imported phenomenon, or 'western borrowing', as well as firmly within colonial discourses. Moreover, these discourses allow intermittent moral panics to (re)surface at *peculiar* times resulting in targeted discrimination and, in some cases, brutality. Brian Whitaker (2006: 140) attributes these crackdowns against homosexual communities on the part of the government as serving to 'Appease moral outrage and make an example of a few people, but not so many as to cast doubt on the public fiction that there is little or no homosexuality in the country'. Since the 2010–11 uprising, LGBT communities in Tunisia have experienced noteworthy advances and have been able to manoeuvre in the public sphere to advocate for greater rights for sexual minorities and freedom from violence. However, they have simultaneously faced considerable contractions in the space to operate at the political as well as socio-cultural level.

Some Openings, in Some Places

In 1996, post-Apartheid South Africa became the first country in the world to explicitly integrate protections for the rights of gays and lesbians into its constitution (Croucher, 2002: 315). Since 1996, South African courts have decriminalized sodomy, ruled in favour of gay employees seeking benefits for their partners and supported immigration appeals for foreign partners of homosexual South Africans. Sheila Croucher (2002: 324) explains:

> In South Africa, the availability of an anti-Apartheid master frame, rooted in respect for human rights and equality for all, helped galvanize gays and lesbians and to legitimate their demands in the eyes of politicians and society as a whole.

Given the historical precedent for increased opportunities in putting greater rights for minorities high on the agenda in other countries that passed through extreme periods of political transition, it should come as no surprise that soon after the 2011 Arab uprisings, different actors mobilized to take maximum advantage of these new spaces opening up in Tunisia. Some of Tunisia's gay and lesbian activists worked quickly to maximize what could be achieved in what was perceived as a limited window of opportunity. A Tunisian journalist for an online news journal explained during the interview for the research: 'This space was wide open – there was no police, no government, the political groups were not structured, anything was possible' (Interview III, 2012).

In one of the first instances, homosexual communities participated in the *Atakni* ('leave me in peace') rally in October 2011 in protest at the significant conservative backlash against the broadcasting of the film *Persepolis*' (see Chawki, 2011) and to counter threats to the principle of free expression. It is reported that several dozen youths carried the large rainbow flag marked with the word 'PEACE' (Collins, 2012: 105). There was also a Tunisian online magazine *GayDay*, founded by a group of 'like-minded individuals' and maintained by editor-in-chief Fadi Krouj just after January 2011.[7] In addition, 2012 marked the first year in Tunisia where members of LGBT communities publicly celebrated the International Day against Homophobia and Transphobia (IDAHOT), launching a declaration on behalf of these different communities. The statement reaffirmed LGBT rights by advocating, 'Stunned by the wind of revolt blowing over Tunisia, they no longer hid themselves, they fought for the right to employment and for dignity, as well as for sexual liberties' (Krouj, 2012).[8]

Not long after the Tunisian uprising, three male activists, Moazzam, Nasser and Kader, worked to establish the non-profit charity the Tunisian Association for Justice and Equality or *Damj* ('reintegration') in Arabic.[9] The word *Damj* was chosen by the founders because it signified inclusion and alluded to the continued *exclusion* of minorities and vulnerable groups in Tunisia at the time. The men all worked as LGBT activists before the revolution and collaborated together through their work at one of the larger HIV/Aids associations in Tunis. *Damj* acquired its official associational status in October 2011, formally articulating its work to defend human rights and the rights of minorities, including the rights of LGBT. Kader, one of the principal founders of the organization, explained during the interview for the research:

> We labelled the application as 'the fight against stigma and human rights' because we felt it needed to be as general as possible in order for it to be accepted … The LGBT were some of the first groups to come out and speak about human rights before the revolution and we are the Tunisians who have been outwardly demonstrating against these injustices. On our marches and participation in the demonstrations, before and now, we bring the two flags – the LGBT flag and the Tunisian flag! (Interview I, 2012)

He stated that as a new association, 'We want to continue to mobilize young people to take this fight forward and to be strong advocates'. On the association's Facebook page (added in summer 2013) the organization outlines its goal to participate in spreading the culture of universal human rights, while specifically: anchoring the principles of citizenship and equality among Tunisian citizens; highlighting the factors which exacerbate marginalization and vulnerability; combating all forms of stigma and discrimination; developing partnerships and networks of mutual aims and understanding as they pertain to the fight against stigma and discrimination, and promoting human rights. Finally, the association stipulates that it aims to support individuals in precarious situations, those who are victims of injustices, to help them to attain their own physical and moral integrity. In a follow-up research interview with one of the founders in March 2013, Nasser, who was also involved in the high-profile Tunisian graffiti urban art group *Zwela* (see Ben Mhenni, 2013), said that his association was working to advocate the National Constituent Assembly to include issues of equality and justice for minorities in the constitution. He hoped that *Damj* would be able to strengthen the rights of minority groups, including members of LGBT communities, and to document human rights abuses as a stronger advocacy tool for rights reform (Interview IV, 2012 & 2013).

In addition to the establishment of *Damj* after January 2011, different groups such as the Human Rights Observatory and the Tunisian Association for Minorities also came forward to engage more in the protection of individual human rights, including the rigorous documentation of human rights abuses against homosexual communities which some would argue increased since the uprising (see Mersch, 2012). Moazzam, one of the other founders of *Damj*, explained that there was significant violence and aggression against homosexual men, including homicide (Interview V, 2012). He added:

> And of course we never see this information in the media, our friends tell us. There is no protection, there is not as much security, and this creates many problems. The law does not favour MSM (men who have sex with men). (Interview V, 2012)

In response to this perception of increasing violence, a group of human rights lawyers came together to form the Human Rights Observatory. The organization aimed to observe and collect information related to HIV and human rights violations including problems of abuse. The information would be used to advocate greater attention to universal human rights. In an interview with Walid, one of the principal proponents of the Observatory, he explained that regionally the issue of human rights was a very serious challenge indeed. He stated:

> We will have to act now or we will lose this space. We have to adopt our discourse now so that this is not eventually turned against us. The rise in conservative discourse is worrying, and so we can no longer work as we did before. (Interview VI, 2012)

In addition to the establishment of the different forms of associations that aimed to work with minority groups since the 2010–11 uprising, there were also a host of regional initiatives that arose specifically to address how the revolutions across the Middle East and North Africa would impact upon LGBT communities. In *Sex and the Citadel*, Shereen El Feki cites the example of the establishment in 2010 of *Mantiqitna Kamb* ('our region's camp'). The regional network provides the opportunity for individuals working in LGBT communities to participate in clandestine workshops on issues such as sexuality, gender and activism, as well as training in life skills. The network stipulates that its key aim is to connect less through gay identity and more through Arab identity (El Feki, 2013: 270). Through the regional network, Kader and Nasser were able to attend a meeting organized in Turkey shortly after January 2011 of over 70 members of LGBT communities throughout the region. Nasser explained:

We wanted to make sure that everyone at this meeting was from this region as we felt this was *our* problem and we need to come up with our *own* solutions. So we tried to exchange experiences of this [the Arab Spring] and learn from each other. (Interview IV, 2012 & 2013)

In a follow-up interview regarding the regional meeting, he remarked 'We felt we needed to be prepared because we were afraid of the worst … There were many ideas but there were also so many different priorities among these (LGBT) groups' (Interview IV, 2012 & 2013).

Finally, activists and academics working in HIV/Aids, in particular with homosexual communities, used the finalization of the 2012–16 National Strategic Plan (NSP) to Fight AIDS in Tunisia as a primary example of the advances that could be made in the post-revolution window of opportunity. Bio-behavioural surveys conducted in 2009 and again in 2011 indicated HIV prevalence of 4.9 and 13 per cent in men having sex with men (UNAIDS UNGASS, 2012: 8). Given these higher levels of prevalence, the NSP not only highlighted strategic objectives to intensify targeted prevention and education work with sexual minorities, but it also underscored the need to conduct advocacy regarding the current legal and juridical frameworks in Tunisia – namely the legal code 230[10] – which persecutes and criminalizes same-sex behaviour with up to three years in prison (Minister of Public Health, 2012: 45). Radi, an academic and activist who worked on many of the HIV bio-behavioural studies conducted among youth and key populations at higher risk in Tunisia, argued that he and his colleagues would not have had the courage to produce a similar NSP before January 2011. He stated during the interview:

The NSP went through without exceptions … Each time different actors are saying 'now is not the time to be doing work on MSM' but we now have very real and worrying data so now IS in fact the time to push these boundaries and now is the time to act … But this can go against our objectives if we are not careful. (Interview VII, 2012)

Contracting Individual Liberties

Before the Tunisian uprising the former regime supported interventions to engage in outreach work with homosexual communities and permitted the United Nations Development Programme (UNDP) and the Joint United Nations Programme on HIV/AIDS (UNAIDS), for example, to conduct in-depth research on multiple categories of homosexual practice across Tunisia. Since the revolution, however, a sequence of highly public incidents have re-animated national discussions and subsequent moral panics on the 'moral–ethical' dimensions of homosexuality (Collins, 2012: 104).

After January 2011, there was a rise in public conservative or Islamic discourse(s) at the political and socio-cultural levels (Borsali, 2012; Meziou-Dourai, 2012). Perhaps for the first time Tunisians were experiencing just how conservative their society really was as all issues were open for contestation, even debates which many thought would not be revisited, such as temporary marriage, polygamy, the 'problem' of single mothers, abortion and even more recently female excision (Khalsi, 2012). Sex was back on the agenda, causing the public sphere to become increasingly destabilized in part due to a 'moral panic'. In post-revolution Tunisia, one was able to distinguish two facets of a 'moral panic' – the moral panic concerning the secular response to the growing emergence of Salafist ideology and their physical presence in the public sphere; and, specific to this case, the increasing conservative backlash against 'liberal' behaviour and identity attributed to the immorality and corruption of the former regime. This sense of 'identity recovery' manifested in various forms at the level of the 'street' when the post-revolutionary judiciary and security systems were at their weakest.

For example, in February 2011, during what was considered as a 'wave of violence', it is estimated that 2,000 'Islamists' attacked a *maison close* (legally sanctioned brothel) in the old town of Tunis, followed by similar attacks on the *maisons closes* in Medenine, Sfax, Kairouan and Sousse, while sex workers were chased out and some of the establishments boarded and bricked over (Bensaied, 2011). 'Salafists' also gathered in Sidi Bouzid in May 2012 to burn down bars and physically threaten the owners in protest against the sale of alcohol in the town (Ltifi, 2012). Moreover, it was reported that between 2012 and 2013 more than 100 cases of fire and looting were targeted at *zawiyas* (Sufi lodges) by Salafist forces (Blibech et al., 2014). Not only was the subject of women through the symbols of the headscarf and the *niqab* 'strategic terrain' in post-revolution Tunisia for national identity recovery, but minority groups and 'behaviours' such as among sex workers and sexual minorities also became targets for purifying the nation of the 'impiety' associated with the former regime (Haugbolle & Cavatorta, 2012). In effect, sex was used in conjunction with 'moral panics' by the 'Islamists' to demonstrate the immorality associated with the Ben Ali regime (or secular regimes in general), as well as by secular groups to highlight the extreme 'Islamist' tendencies of *Ennahda*. From each side, despite the peripheral nature of the issue, debates concerning sexual minorities were being articulated within a heavily charged terrain. It is this conservative backlash against 'liberal' behaviour that largely dictated the strategies LGBT communities would employ to advance their objectives.

Moreover, shortly after I arrived in Tunisia in January 2012, a lengthy YouTube video depicted the newly appointed minister of interior (and eventually prime minister in 2013), Ali Laarayedh, engaging in a sexual act with a male fellow inmate in a prison cell (Baeder, 2012a). The video was allegedly filmed while he was imprisoned for nearly 15 years as an opposition figure under Ben Ali. The broadcasting of the video sparked outrage and condemnation within the government, the media and the public sphere, and allowed many to further underscore the cruel tactics of the former Constitutional Democratic Rally (RCD) party and the security apparatus of the shadow state. However, the video also served to highlight the more general phenomenon of homophobia in the Arab world and globally. During the research interview Kader stated: 'Homosexuality is used to humiliate someone in the worst way possible, it is the first thing someone raises now to humiliate and embarrass ... to delegitimize political figures for example (referring to the video)' (Interview I, 2012).

During the two years following the 2011 Arab uprisings, spaces for political expression and for democratic liberalization in the political realm expanded; however, socio-cultural spaces in the public sphere regarding what was acceptable in the post-revolution era simultaneously contracted. Often individuals would remark that 'now is the right time to talk about everything in Tunisia', yet it seems in reality 'everything' had its limits. For example, homosexuality in Tunisia is virtually forbidden at three principal levels. At the political level Article 230 of the Tunisian penal code criminalizes same-sex relations. At the religious level, homosexuality, whilst not being officially *haram* in the Qur'an, is forbidden in *shariah* with punishments varying according to the school of *fiqh* (Islamic jurisprudence). Finally, at the socio-cultural level, homosexuality is highly stigmatized in the media and at the community level, in families and in the workplace. Kader explained in the interview, 'Our society is schizophrenic, people say one thing and do the complete opposite' (Interview I, 2012). He used the example of alcohol consumption and men in bars drinking, yet saying in the same breath homosexuality is *haram*. He stated:

> The act of homosexuality is one thing, speaking about it is another. It is not the act that is forbidden here it seems. It is saying you are 'homosexual'. When you want to express yourself, it is here where the problems begin. (Interview I, 2012)

In the interview with Nasser, he remarked that shortly after the 2010–11 uprising the different LGBT communities of Tunisia became afraid; eventually it was reported that hundreds of sexual minorities left the country. Nasser and Kader had both been subject to physical violence after 14 January 2011 through attacks in known 'safe spaces' for homosexual men. Nasser explained:

> Before the 14th, the gay community in Tunisia did not necessarily live freely, but at least we lived in security ... Since the 14th, homophobic acts are clear and direct. Now everyone gives himself the right to criticize our way of dressing, to stare or to physically assault us. (Interview IV, 2012 & 2013)

His friend and colleague Kader was physically beaten trying to protect one of the known safe spaces from entry by intruders. When I remarked to Kader that this must have been very traumatic, he shrugged his shoulders and said *'je reste et je résiste encore'* – I am staying and I am still resisting (Interview I, 2012).

Some would argue that during the Ben Ali regime, LGBT communities were not singled out as repression was targeted at political dissent in the form of opposition. However, after the uprising, as one member of an LGBT community in Tunisia remarked, 'Don't forget the Islamist parties who are trying to play the role of judge right now, and who view homosexuality and the gay community as a product of the former regime. They call it "rot" that must be cleaned away' (quoted in Crary, 2011). Some also explained that whilst there is a specific penal code in Tunisian law which penalizes same-sex acts, it was not applied in practice (Mersch, 2012).

Nevertheless, members of homosexual communities reported having direct experience of the law being applied in theory as well as in practice even following the revolution. During the interview, Nasser described a friend who was reportedly robbed and beaten. The two perpetrators were caught by the police but they argued to the police that the victim was homosexual. Soon the victim himself was threatened with 11 months' incarceration under penal code in Article 230. Eventually he received a jail sentence of two months, and was forced to sign a confession that he was homosexual and had broken the law; often similar arrests are made under the offence of *'atteinte a la pudeur'* – or being at risk of offending the moral sensibilities of the population (Interview IV, 2012 & 2013).

There was (and continues to be at the time of writing) a blurred conflation between the legal, the religious and the moral in the transition government, media and society in post-revolution Tunisia. For example, the newly appointed minister for human rights, Samir Dilou, demonstrating the emerging heteronormative discourse on the part of the government as described by Khalid (2015), was quoted in a television interview in February 2012 speaking of homosexuality as 'a perversion to be medically treated' and that 'freedom of expression has its limits' (quoted in Baeder, 2012b). Of concern for human rights activists in Tunisia was this notion of *'pas les droits de l'homme, mais les droits de certains hommes'* – not of human rights but of rights only for some (Interview VI, 2012). Furthermore, in response to the demonstration organized on 28 January 2012 for liberty (and against violence), during which the LGBT rainbow flag was again featured, a Tunisian talk show host (who also interviewed the minister for human rights during which the aforementioned comments were made) condemned the protestors on his Facebook page, writing: 'Do we need further strife because a very small minority expresses its perversion ... not caring about the feelings and the sacred beliefs of a majority' (quoted in Baeder, 2012b)?

In an interview with Ouroub, a country representative for one of the United Nations Tunis-based offices, she explained:

> In a way they [homosexuals] were a bit protected by the former system, but now this is perhaps the population which is the most stigmatized by the government, by the police and the larger society. They have suffered a lot of violence and unfortunately with this population they also have the highest HIV prevalence. (Interview VIII, 2012 & 2013)

Moreover, she remarked, 'So in a sense you have this enormous new opening but also very high and somewhat new stigma that was not there before' (Interview VIII, 2012 & 2013). One of the founders of *Damj*, Moazzam reluctantly admitted during the interview:

> They [*Ennahda*] played on their words, on God and on religion, this is what I see at this time. Nothing is sure for the rights of homosexuals, personally I do not feel safe, I even have friends who have left the country out of fear ... Now, I do not want to live here. (Interview V, 2012)

Reports of discrimination and violence against LGBT communities in Tunisia both before and after the 2010–11 uprising spurred members to advocate for the addition of freedom from stigma and hostility/aggression to the democratic reform agenda. However, advocacy for the expansion of the post-revolution socio-political agenda was met with voices encouraging caution at home and abroad as members of the public sphere warned 'now is not the time'. For example, I interviewed a group of journalists from a newly established Tunisian English-language news website who had published an article on homosexuality in Tunisia, just less than one year after the uprising (Samti & Belkhiria, 2012). The piece drew a range of responses from both within and outside the homosexual population. Muammar, one of the founders of the website, explained during the interview that when the article was being developed they asked a number of members of LGBT communities if the transition government should prioritize issues for homosexual populations. They reported that most, if not all, said no, 'this was not the time'; furthermore, several of those consulted felt it would never be a good time (Interview III, 2012). The article cites Fedi: 'Despite his strong conviction about the need for legally guaranteed rights for the homosexual community, [he] thinks that it is still too soon to officially demand them from the government'. Fedi explained: 'Such a move would only destabilize the situation in which we are living, and cause more violence and more insecurity' (quoted in Samti & Belkhiria, 2012).

These voices of caution also come from the 'liberal' associations themselves, which filtered and prioritized the reform agenda within the public sphere. For example, following the comments made by the minister of human rights against homosexuality (Baeder, 2012b), a number of members of LGBT communities signed a petition advocating for the homophobic comments made by the minister to be addressed by the Tunisian League of Human Rights as an illustration of the need to tackle homophobia in the new constitution. Despite the petition and open confrontation during one of the meetings of the organization, the human rights association concurred 'now is not the time to address these issues in Tunisia'. Even when one looks outside the country across the Middle East and North Africa in the post-Arab Spring era, other members of LGBT associations advised against engaging in overt advocacy for greater rights for homosexual communities, such as establishing new LGBT associations. For example, El Feki describes a member of a well-known LGBT organization in Lebanon counselling caution to homosexual communities in Egypt, stating:

Now is not the time to say in Egypt 'I want to establish an LGBT organisation'. There are foundational things that need to be laid first. You're talking about a society in a huge sway of transition, and the building blocks of a more open and democratic society need to be laid down first. (El Feki, 2013: 269)

During transitions to democracy the space available for the 'Other', in particular minority groups, shrinks as actors manoeuvring in the public sphere attempt to make as many 'wins' as possible without thwarting or reversing gains made. Voices are regularly marginalized in the name of democracy (and consensus) as some members of civil society are side-lined in favour of a singular, 'acceptable' public sphere featuring or modelled upon what Tunisia's new national identity should resemble, rather than a multiplicity of publics operating in this domain. Consequently, one then begins to witness a minority that could move with relative freedom under the former system, finding itself being excluded from the imaginings of the newly emerging Tunisian 'modern state'. During my return visit to Tunisia in March 2013, I learned that all three of the men who established *Damj* to defend human rights at the national level left Tunis for reasons of security – feeling unsafe as homosexual men in post-revolution Tunisia (Interview IV, 2012 & 2013). Activists Moazzam and Kader were given asylum in Europe and the United States, and Nasser moved outside of Tunis to an environment where he could find more like-minded peers. Nasser remarked that he thought Kader never recovered from the violence he experienced soon after January 2011. He explained that many of his own friends had left Tunisia following the uprising and that this has been a difficult time for him and his peers (Interview IV, 2012 & 2013). He ended by saying that there are regular homosexual attacks and that individuals are even killed (Ben Ammar, 2012). The reason given, he explained, is that it never relates to homosexuality (but rather to random untargeted criminal violence) so these instances of homosexual attacks continue to be impossible to prove.

Conclusion

Sexual minorities and the touchstone issue of homosexuality encompass three conceptual understandings of the 'periphery' in Tunisia following the uprising in 2010–11 – that of space, difference and distance. Throughout the transition in Tunisia, a variety of shifting priorities were fiercely contested within the discursive arena whereby dominant publics, both liberal and conservative, sought to marginalize the 'Other' to the periphery in order to constrain their possibilities (see Kamel & Huber, 2015). This marginalization was further facilitated through 'moral panics' produced at the political and socio-cultural levels seeking manifold forms of transitional justice associated with the impiety and corruption of the former regime. These 'moral panics' also heavily featured sex as a topic for national debate. Multiple discourses on sex consequently permitted both the liberal and conservative factions to emphasize the other's unsuitability to govern post-revolution Tunisia. Each side could gain as these discourses scapegoated minorities and marginalized new voices attempting to emerge in the burgeoning public sphere. This marginalization was equally exacerbated by 'liberal' actors manoeuvring nervously in the public domain who were fearful of losing gains made over 'peripheral' issues during the transition. Actors who were hoping to maximize expanding opportunities to widen the discursive arena, such as LGBT activists, ultimately had to weigh the benefits of visibility to advocate for greater overall inclusion against freedom from discrimination over the risks of further violence and insecurity.

Some members of LGBT communities were able to make remarkable advances within the post-revolution opportunity structure in Tunisia. These actors explicitly chose to engage in a range of strategies to advocate recognition and freedom from discrimination alongside the manifold priorities thrown into the public sphere for discursive contestation. Actors working within these communities combined strategies of 'publicity' and 'visibility', such as participating in public demonstrations articulating the need for recognition through symbols such as the rainbow flag; appropriating social media such as Facebook to demonstrate solidarity with IDAHOT; establishing a formal association to combat stigma and discrimination against minorities, including LGBT; publicly countering homo-phobic statements through mass petitions; and working through a range of national and regional networks such as human rights groups, to articulate solutions to challenges for sexual minorities in Tunisia.

Nevertheless, these actors also believed they encountered increased margin-alization at the individual/personal level as an outcome of this growing visibility at the political and socio-cultural level – even from among 'liberal' actors within the public sphere itself urging 'now is not the time'. This highlights in particular the tensions between liberalism and pluralism, whereby in effect pluralism can entail the negation of discursive contestation during transitions to democracy. So whilst on one level they would adopt strategies of publicity and visibility at the socio-political level to advocate for greater rights and recognition, they would utilize tactics of discretion and invisibility at the socio-cultural level to fight for freedom from violence. Therefore, there is an inherent trade-off or significant boundary for LGBT activists who seek greater recognition and participation in the public sphere – the loss of individual liberties for political liberties; a trade-off which can hardly be sustained in an environment where discursive contestation and the 'Other' are met with intimidation and violence.

The example of the issue of homosexuality in Tunisia – and in some contexts what can often represent a benchmark for democracy – demonstrates that during post-revolutionary transitions, whilst associative spaces for enhanced political expression may expand, concurrently spaces for supporting minority populations may contract – even, in some cases, arousing nostalgia for a dictator. These expansions and contractions could be understood as perpetual features of the 'modern' state itself, where in the drive towards democratization and consensus new spheres of discursive contestation will be created in the public domain while concurrently old spaces will be destroyed. Actors manoeuvring in the public sphere encounter in effect a 'permanent revolution' (Arendt, 1963: 41) in which disparate views will be open to contestation and manifold priorities will often emerge as dominant over 'peripheral' views. Hence, democratization may spell the necessary inclusion of conservative agendas alongside liberal ones in which minorities, such as sexual minorities, can be further pushed to the periphery by political as well as socio-cultural forces. Perhaps these tensions can best be captured by one of the interviewees' own words: 'There are some openings in some places, but these are not openings for everyone – it depends on what exactly these openings are' (Interview VII, 2012).

Disclosure statement

No potential conflict of interest was reported by the author.

Notes

1. Interview I, 2012.
2. During the first phase of Tunisia's transition the 'High Authority for the Realization of the Objectives of the Revolution, Political Reform and Democratic Transition' was established to oversee the transition from revolution to elections. Among its many remits it was also tasked with modifying the text on associational laws. For additional information see Zemni (2014) and Guellali (2011); and decree laws no. 14 of 23 March 2011 and no. 27 of 18 April 2011.
3. Countries that have recently adopted laws to criminalize same-sex behaviour, such as Uganda in 2014, are internationally condemned (see Saner, 2013).
4. All interviews referred to and referenced in this article were conducted by the author for this research unless specified otherwise; the names of the interviewees have also been changed to protect their identity.
5. Foucault has situated the inter-manipulation of sex and power – and in particular the multiplication of discourses on sex – in the beginning of the eighteenth century when there 'emerged a political, economic and technical incitement to talk about sex ... in the form of analysis, stocktaking, classification and specification' (Foucault, 1978 [Hurley ed., 1998: 24]).
6. Speech by the RT. Hon. John Bercow, MP, Speaker of the British House of Commons to the Kaleidoscope Trust IDAHOT event, 16 May 2012, http://www.kaleidoscopetrust.com/features-bercow-speech-5-12.php. It is important to note that some activists and academics (such as the International Gay and Lesbian Association) cite 81 countries as outlawing same-sex acts and Iran is also reported to invoke the death penalty for sodomy; this also does not include the passing of the Uganda Anti-Homosexuality Act in February 2014 that criminalizes same-sex acts.
7. http://gaydaymagazine.com/
8. Déclaration du 17 mai de la communauté LGBT Tunisienne, 17 May 2012 as featured in Krouj (2012).
9. Homosexual women also eventually became involved in the development of the organization *Damj* soon after its official establishment in Tunisia.
10. See: http://www.jurisitetunisie.com/tunisie/codes/cp/cp1200.htm

References

Altman, D. (2001) *Global Sex* (Chicago: University of Chicago).

Associated French Press (2012) Rights groups urge Iraq to investigate 'emo' killings, Al Arabiya.net, 16 March, Available at http://english.alarabiya.net/articles/2012/03/16/201079.html.

Arendt, H. (1963) *On Revolution* (London: Penguin Books).

Baeder, C. (2012a) Release of unauthenticated prison-Sex video denounced in defence of Tunisian interior minister, Tunisia-Live.net, 19 January, Available at http://www.tunisia-live.net/2012/01/19/release-of-unauthenticated-prison-sex-video-denounced-in-defense-of-tunisian-interior-minister/.

Baeder, C. (2012b) Tunisian human rights minister's remarks spark debate on homophobia, Tunisia-Live. net, 09 February, Available at http://www.tunisia-live.net/2012/02/09/tunisian-human-rights-ministers-remarks-spark-debate-on-homophobia/.

Ben Ammar, S. (2012) Les Islamistes Tuent des Gays de Peur de se Regarder dans leur Propre Miroir, Tunisie News.Com, 5 August, Available at http://www.tunisie-news.com/chroniques/dossier_636_islamistes+tuent+gays+peur+se+regarder+dans+leur+propre+miroir.html.

Ben Mhenni, L. (2013) Le Graffiti n'a pas Bonne Presse dans La Révolution Tunisienne ... , Opinion-Internationale.com, 12 September, Available at http://www.opinion-internationale.com/2013/09/12/le-graffiti-na-pas-bonne-presse-dans-la-revolution-tunisienne_14738.html.

Bensaied, I. (2011) Les Islamistes s'attaquent aux maisons closes, France24.com, 18 March, Available at http://www.france24.com/fr/20110318-prostituees-tunis-tunisie-prostitution-bordel-avenue-bourguiba-mosquee-islamistes.

Blibech, F., A. Driss & P. Longo (2014) Citizenship in post-Awakening Tunisia: power shifts and conflicting perceptions, *Euspring,* Feb.

Borsali, N. (2012) Tunisie: 8 mars 2012 ou le défi égalitaire, La Presse de Tunisie, 12 March, Available at http://www.lapresse.tn/16102014/46691/tunisie-8-mars-2012-ou-le-defi-egalitaire.html.

Chabot, S. & J.W. Duyvendak (2002) Globalisation and transnational diffusion between social movements: reconceptualising the dissemination of the Gandhian repertoire and the 'coming out' routine, *Theory and Society,* 31(6), pp. 697–740. doi:10.1023/A:1021315215642.

Chawki (2011) Video-Manifestation Contre La Violence et Pour La Liberté d'Expression sous le Signe 'A3ta9ni.', Tunisienumerique.com, 16 October, Available at http://www.tunisienumerique.com/urgent-manifestation-contre-la-violence-et-pour-la-libete-dexpression-sous-le-signe-de-a3ta9ni/81060.

Collins, R. (2012) Efféminés, gigolos, and MSMs in the cyber-networks, coffeehouses, and "secret gardens" of contemporary Tunis, *Journal of Middle East Women's Studies,* 8(3), pp. 89–112. doi:10.2979/jmiddeastwomstud.8.3.89.

Crary, D. (2011) Gays in Egypt, Tunisia worry about post-revolt era, Associated Press, 22 May, Available at http://www.guardian.co.uk/world/feedarticle/9657249.

Croucher, S. (2002) South Africa's democratisation and the politics of gay liberation, *Journal of Southern African Studies,* 28(2), pp. 315–330. doi:10.1080/03057070220140720.

El Feki, S. (2013) *Sex and the Citadel: Intimate Life in a Changing Arab World* (London: Random House).

European Union (2012) Rapport de Diagnostic sur la Société Civile Tunisienne, Mission de Formulation Programme d'Appui a la Société Civile en Tunisie, Mars.

Foucault, M. (1978) *The History of Sexuality 1: The Will to Knowledge,* trans. Robert Hurley (London: Penguin Books).

Fraser, N. (1997) *Justice Interruptus: Critical Reflections on the 'Postsocialist' Condition* (New York: Routledge).

Fraser, N. (1990) Rethinking the public sphere: a contribution to the critique of actually existing democracy, *Social Text,* (25/26), pp. 56–80. doi:10.2307/466240.

Guellali, A. (2011) Pathways and pitfalls for Tunisia's new constituent assembly, *Think Africa Press,* 14 October, Available at http://thinkafricapress.com/tunisia/elections-2011-pathways-pitfalls-new-constituent-assembly.

Gunning, J. & I. Baron (2013) *Why Occupy a Square: People, Protests and Movements in the Egyptian Revolution* (London: Hurst).

Habermas, J. (1989) *The Structural Transformation of the Public Sphere: An Inquiry into a Category of Bourgeois Society,* Translated by Thomas Burger and Frederick Lawrence (Cambridge: Polity Press).

Haugbolle, R.H. & F. Cavatorta (2012) Beyond Ghannouchi: Islamism and social change in Tunisia, *Middle East Research and Information Project (MERIP),* 42(262), pp. 20–25.

Huber, D. & L. Kamel (2015) Arab Spring: The Role of the Peripheries, *Mediterranean Politics,* 20(2). doi:10.1080/13629395.2015.1033905.

Human Rights Watch (2004) *In a Time of Torture: The Assault on Justice in Egypt's Crackdown on Homosexual Conduct* (New York), Available at http://www.hrw.org/sites/default/files/reports/egypt0304_0.pdf.

Human Rights Watch (2012) Lebanon: stop "tests of shame," 10 August, Available at http://www.hrw.org/news/2012/08/10/lebanon-stop-tests-shame.

Khalid, M. (2015) The peripheries of gender and sexuality in the 'Arab Spring', *Mediterranean Politics,* 20(2). doi:10.1080/13629395.2015.1033906.

Khalsi, R. (2012) Excision ... ou les prédictions d'un psychopathe, *Le Temps* (Tunis), 14 Feb.

Krouj, F. (2012) Editor-In-Chief of Gayday magazine Fadi Krouj comments on international day against Homophobia, 18 May, Available at http://www.tunisia-live.net/2012/05/18/editor-in-chief-of-gayday-magazine-fadi-krouj-comments-on-international-day-against-homophobia/.

Ltifi, A. (2012) Salafists burn down bars, liquor stores while police are passive in Sidi Bouzid, Tunisia-Live.net, 20 May, Available at http://www.tunisia-live.net/2012/05/20/salafists-burn-down-bars-liquor-stores-while-police-are-passive-in-sidi-bouzid/.

Massad, J. (2002) Re-Orienting desire: the gay international and the Arab world, *Public Culture*, 14(2), pp. 361–386. doi:10.1215/08992363-14-2-361.

Mersch, S. (2012) No gay rights revolution in Tunisia, Deutsche Welle, 7 November, Available at http://www.dw.de/no-gay-rights-revolution-in-tunisia/a-16364172.

Meziou-Dourai, K. (2012) A propos du mariage coutumier: attaque frontale contre le code du statut personnel, *Le Temps* (Tunis), 4 Feb.

Minister of Public Health and the National Program to Fight HIV and STIs (2012) *National Strategic Plan to Respond to HIV and STIs in Tunisia 2012-2016*.

République Tunisienne Ministère de la Sante Publique (2012) Rapport d'Activité sur La Riposte au SIDA—Tunisie, *UNAIDS UNGASS Report*, March.

Rao, R. (2010) *Third World Protest: Between Home and the World* (Oxford: Oxford University Press).

Ritchie, J. (2010) How do you say "come out of the closet" in Arabic?: Queer activism and the politics of visibility in Israel-Palestine, *GLQ: A Journal of Lesbian and Gay Studies*, 16(4), pp. 557–575. doi:10.1215/10642684-2010-004.

Samti, F. & J. Belkhiria (2012) Gay Tunisia: 'a don't ask, don't tell' situation, Tunisia-Live.net, 27 January, Available at http://www.globalgayz.com/gay-tunisia-a-%E2%80%9Cdon%E2%80%99t-ask-don%E2%80%99t-tell%E2%80%9D-situation/.

Saner, E. (2013) Gay rights around the world: the best and the worst countries for equality, The Guardian.com, 30 July, Available at http://www.theguardian.com/world/2013/jul/30/gay-rights-world-best-worst-countries.

Shami, S. (2009) *Publics, Politics and Participation: Locating the Public Sphere in the Middle East and North Africa* (New York: Social Science Research Council).

Warner, M. (1993) Introduction, in: Michael Warner (Ed.) *Fear of a Queer Planet: Queer Politics and Social Theory* (Minneapolis: University of Minnesota Press).

Whitaker, B. (2006) *Unspeakable Love: Gay and Lesbian Life in the Middle East* (London: Saqi).

Zemni, S. (2014) The extraordinary politics of the Tunisian revolution: the process of constitution making, *Mediterranean Politics*, pp. 1–17. doi:10.1080/13629395.2013.874108.

Interviews

Interview I, Kader, Activist and Supervisor of Key Populations and Outreach Worker, HIV/AIDS association, Tunis, 30 Jan. 2012.

Interview II, Soraya, Programme Co-ordinator, *Femmes et Citoyenneté*, Tunis, 22 Mar. 2012.

Interview III, Muammar, Jason and Maha, Journalists, Tunisian online journal, Tunis, 30 Jan. 2012.

Interview IV, Nasser, Activist and Supervisor of Peer Education and Outreach Work, HIV/AIDS association, Tunis, 27 Jan. 2012 and 14 Mar. 2013.

Interview V, Moazzam, Activist and Outreach worker with Sex Workers, HIV/AIDS organization, Tunis, 24 Jan. 2012.

Interview VI, Walid, Human Rights Lawyer, Activist and Founder of Human Rights Observatory, Tunis, 16 Feb. 2012.

Interview VII, Radi, academic, Université de Sfax, Tunis, 7 Feb. 2012.

Interview VIII, Ouroub, country representative, United Nations organization, Tunis, 16 Jan. 2012 and 13 Mar. 2013.

The Peripheries of Gender and Sexuality in the 'Arab Spring'

MARYAM KHALID

Faculty of Arts, Macquarie University, Sydney, Australia

ABSTRACT   *In much of the world, those who do not perform 'mainstream' understandings of gender and sexuality find themselves on the 'peripheries': these individuals and groups are often located outside of institutionalized power, beyond state power structures and often lack the power of representation vis-à-vis those who wield discursive authority (actors such as the state and mainstream media). The power relations that underscore the production of knowledge and identities in this way are discursive, functioning to normalize and naturalize them. This article examines how some representations of gender and sexuality are privileged over others in both western and MENA mainstream discourses relating to the 'Arab Spring'; how those whose voices have been underrepresented in the mainstream attempt to represent themselves; and how this impacts on the political activities of women and LGBT groups in the MENA.*

Introduction

Gender and sexuality are central to understanding the concept of 'periphery'. The construction of these identity categories, and the placement of particular peoples within them, have been deployed to delineate those who are 'outside' of the 'mainstream'. These identity categories mark out a range of activities, behaviours, identities and peoples as 'acceptable' or 'deviant' by reference to dominant understandings of sexuality and gender (and in doing so reproduce these understandings). In much of the world (not only in Arab or Muslim contexts), those who do not conform to mainstream constructions of 'acceptable' performances of gender and sexuality often have limited access to both institutionalized power *and* discursive power. For example, those identifying as women and LGBT are often located outside of political power structures, but can also lack the discursive power of representation in mainstream discourses. Discursive and political power is intertwined as the ability to effectively shape representations can afford or limit the power to participate in elite politics. Interrogating the function of dominant understandings of gender and sexuality in mainstream discourses allows us to unpack

35

the power relations that underscore the production of knowledge and identities in these discourses, and how these representations (and the knowledges they create) impact on and make possible particular courses of action.

In terms of the so-called 'Arab Spring',[1] understanding *how* representational practices function is central to understanding the peripheries of the MENA region, in terms of both their local activities and, their role in broader (transnational and global) discourses. In this article, I argue that gender and sexuality are central to dominant MENA and western discourses of the 'Arab Spring' and particularly to those who, in these discourses, are characterized by their 'differences' vis-à-vis 'acceptable' or normalized identities, actions, behaviours and so on. These discourses reproduce dominant understandings of gender and sexuality that are narrow, restrictive and deployed in ways that both construct and represent these groups as 'peripheries' and limit their access to (discursive and material) power. Gender and sexuality function to order both MENA and western mainstream discourses in ways that marginalize those who do not perform the gender and sexual identities central to these discourses. However, this is not to say that peripheries (such as women, LGBT people and the various activist feminist and LGBT groups in the MENA region) are completely restricted by these discourses or that they have not played a key role in the 'Arab Spring' (and beyond). They have taken an active role in politics in the MENA (see, inter alia, Fortier, 2015; Khalil, 2014a; Rama, 2013; Kreps, 2012; Radsch, 2012); although their political participation generally (although not always) occurs at the margins of the mainstream, it serves to challenge the assumptions that shape mainstream discourses. Through their activities, writings and speech acts, they have challenged the boundaries of dominant MENA and western categories of gender and sexuality and, in particular, what people in these categories can be and do. For example, women's and LGBT movements have challenged dominant discursive structures (western and local) through a range of activities in the 'Arab Spring' (these will be explored further in this article).

In particular, these peripheral people, groups and ideas challenge dominant western understandings of politics in the MENA. This is not to deny the discursive and material restrictions that constrain gender and LGBT activism. What is problematic, particularly in western discourse, is the focus on victimization of these groups, and thus the denial of their agency. I pay special attention to this issue as it is under-critiqued in mainstream western discourses on MENA politics, and on the 'Arab Spring' in particular. The 'Arab Spring' must be read in the context of long-standing western discourses on the MENA, which are shaped by orientalist logics that are themselves gendered. This is important because it is these discourses that influence and shape dominant western understandings of the role of women and non-heterosexual peoples in the 'Arab Spring', which (re)produce orientalist logics that marginalize those who do not conform to particular gendered understandings of the roles of various peoples in MENA. To this end, this article revisits Edward Said's theory of orientalism and frames it as a discourse that is inherently gendered in that it prescribes certain roles to sexed bodies (for example, women and LGBT people as passive victims, men as aggressive, backward). I deploy this theoretical framework to examine how some representations of gender and sexuality are privileged over others in both western and MENA mainstream texts (popular, political and media) in the context of the 'Arab Spring'. Examining how those whose voices have been underrepresented in the mainstream attempt to represent themselves, and how this impacts on the political activities of women and LGBT groups in the Arab world, allows these discourses to be challenged. In particular, I focus on how these groups have destabilized or challenged mainstream orientalist representations of gender and sexuality in the context of their activities in the 'Arab Spring'.

Representation and Power: Discourse as Analytic Method

Gendered and sexualized discourses have historically been central to regulating and controlling knowledges and peoples. The construction of these discourses has been predicated on binary understandings of gender and sexuality. Binary understandings of gender, sex and sexuality (reflected in the construction of dominant gendered and sexualized identity categories such as male–female, straight–gay), and the attachment of particular behaviours to them (for example, feminine, masculine) is *naturalized* in dominant discourses. Such categorizations of identity (including, but not limited to, gender and sexuality) are discursive because what they tell us about the world and the people in it is '(re)constructed through … an ordering of terms, meanings, practices that forms the background presuppositions and taken-for-granted understandings that enable people's actions and interpretations' (Milliken, 1999: 92). Discourses, then, are 'structured, relational totalities' that 'delineate the terms of intelligibility whereby a particular "reality" can be known and acted upon' (Doty, 1996: 6). That is, language, meaning and 'reality' are not imbued with 'natural' or 'pre-given' 'meaning' but are incomprehensible to us without discourse as an interpretive tool. 'Reality', 'knowledge' and the discursive practices that 'create' them must be analysed 'not to reveal essential truths that have been obscured' (as mastery of knowledge is impossible given no one has perfect information), but rather to uncover *how* certain representations influence the production of knowledge and identities, and how these representations and the knowledge they create make possible particular courses of action (Doty, 1996: 5).

Discursive regimes work to create meanings and attach them to certain subjects and objects, which in turn creates and justifies certain possibilities and actions, and excludes or limits others. Instrumental to this is the construction and representation of 'the world', prescriptions of 'proper' or 'acceptable' behaviour for the 'types' of people in it, and of the actions and events that take place in it. As Jutta Weldes explains, '[d]ifferent representations of the world entail different identities, which in turn carry with them different ways of functioning in the world, are located within different power relations and make possible different interests' (Weldes, 1996: 287). Interrogating the representations of various peoples, ideas, places, things and so on in discourses is important because the power to construct a dominant discourse enables the privileging of some knowledges and 'truths' over others.

The apparent obviousness of what is meant by identity markers like 'men' and 'women' is precisely why gender, as a critical tool that seeks to lay bare the power relations that shape our understandings of the world, is useful. For example, constructs of the 'Middle Eastern woman', 'Muslim woman' and 'Arab woman' have been used, often interchangeably, for a range of political, cultural and ideological projects (Zine, 2006). Although often deployed by colonial and imperial powers, these categories are constructed and regulated by a range of actors, including those within the MENA (Zine, 2006: 35). The function of gender in imperial projects specifically is intertwined with orientalism.

This discourse has a history (and longevity) which is central to interrogating the gendering of the 'Arab Spring' in western discourses, and for understanding how these representations interplay with those produced in the MENA. Orientalism as a critical tool was most comprehensively developed by Edward Said (1978). In this understanding, orientalism is a discourse that is predicated on an artificial division of the world into 'East' and 'West', and requires the (re)production of stereotyped images of peoples along these lines. Understanding orientalism as a *gendered* discourse in which representations become 'fact' uncovers a system of representations that produces and renders intelligible specific categories such as 'East', 'Arab', 'Muslim', 'West', 'civilized', 'barbaric', and organizes them according to binary logics and in hierarchical ways that reflect the function of mainstream understandings of gender and sexuality. Recently, for example, the deployment of gendered and sexualized ideas about various 'types' of people discursively enabled the 'War on Terror' and its military interventions by drawing on traditional understandings of gender, sexuality and race to situate 'the West' as superior to 'the East' (Khalid, 2011). As I will demonstrate, the basic assumptions of orientalism (as a gendered discourse) are reflected in dominant western representations of the 'Arab Spring', most significantly in the deployment of gender and sexuality to construct 'the West' as enlightened in contrast to a backward and barbaric 'East'.

Critical engagement with such discourses and the representations that are (re) produced in them, undertaken largely through alternative readings of these discourses and representations, serves to show them as contingent. In this article, I do this by looking at dominant sources of information on women and LGBT people in the 'Arab Spring' as 'texts'. By 'texts' I am referring not only to written words and speech acts, but also physical actions, legal frameworks (legislation and so on) – anything that conveys information that shapes the ways in which we understand the world. The producers of such information, for my research, include both 'official' (government or state) entities and mainstream media sources. I interrogate these using a discourse analysis (DA) approach: this means interrogating representations by looking for instances of presupposition and predication (the presentation of background knowledge as 'true'), and pre/proscription (whereby certain qualities are linked to subjects and objects). My research is underscored by the understanding that peripheral groups, while characterized by distance, difference and dependence in political, cultural and economic life, are not entirely powerless; rather, they pursue possibilities of resistance. To this end, I also employ techniques of deconstruction and juxtaposition to demonstrate the ways in which peripheral groups have operated in the MENA since the early events of the 'Arab Spring' in 2010.

The 'Arab Spring': Between Orientalism and Authoritarianism

The political developments in the MENA since 2010, often referred to as the 'Arab Spring', have seen varying levels of change through the MENA. The most effective uprisings took place against the governments of the non-Gulf states of the MENA; generally poorer and with less revenue from natural resources, these states had largely failed to respond to some of the most basic needs and aspirations of their citizens. As W.J. Karim (2011: 604) explains, many MENA governments have been 'alienated from their own people, who seek 'employment, better living standards, and democratic freedom'. 'Long-dismissed as prisoners of the "Oriental soul"', Agathangelou and Soguk write, the many who participated in the uprisings and complex transitional processes taking place in the MENA 'have shattered the familiar presumption that only a Western European or a North American is the authentic agent of direct (i.e. unmediated) democracy and political change' (2011: 551, 552).

However, in much mainstream western discourse, this period in Arab politics has been characterized as something unusual. That is, these events are taken to signal a new-found political awareness of Arab citizens across the MENA; this was particularly well-captured in the *Financial Times'* characterization of the 'Arab Spring' as an 'awakening' (Financial Times, 2012). The implication is that, until the events following Mohamed Bouazizi's self-immolation in Tunisia, political engagement among the masses in the MENA had been dormant. This reading of political engagement in the MENA is hardly new – it continues a long tradition of denying Middle Easterners agency by defining them almost entirely in terms of dominant western assumptions around political engagement. The decades of political activity amongst ordinary Middle Easterners is marginalized in this narrative, rendered invisible, shaped by the orientalist narrative of the 'eastern other' as inherently backward and unable to progress. It also points to the dominant orientalist narrative of the contemporary MENA as too weak to progress politically (citing the lack of democracy in the region) and yet strong enough to pose a threat to 'us' (Tuastad, 2003).

The events of the 'Arab Spring' were too visible and widespread to be ignored in western discourses. However, in mainstream western discourses, they have generally been taken as indicative that the Middle Eastern 'other' has finally realized the superiority, if not the inevitability, of the (neo)liberal political logic (Agathangelou & Soguk, 2011: 552). That is, the dominant narrative is that the 'other' has now come to accept that to be 'like us' in 'the West' is to 'progress'. This ignores the role that 'the West' (and the US in particular) has played in shaping political economy in the MENA; the policies of economic liberalism that have empowered some in the region have largely marginalized the desires and needs of most in the MENA (Ali, 2011; Karim, 2011). The situation in which the uprisings and protests of the 'Arab Spring' took place is then 'partly a consequence of their [MENA states'] dependence on US support' that is itself geared toward institutionalizing a particular type of development geared toward specific economic and political ideals that are thought to best reflect what the peoples of the MENA 'need' (Karim, 2011: 604).

Gender Peripheries in MENA and the Local and Western Discursive Opportunity Structures

It is in the above context that mainstream western discourses around gender and sexuality in the political events in the MENA in the 'Arab Spring' must be understood. That is, the orientalist logics that shape dominant western discourses of the East' have not only painted 'the eastern other' as backward/underdeveloped/ uncivilized/undemocratic and so on, but have also deployed specific understandings of gender and sexuality as central to this. For example, gendered orientalist understandings of 'us' and 'them' in the 'War on Terror' functioned to situate 'the West' as civilizationally superior to 'the East' by locating gender inequality in 'the East'; the construction of 'other' women as passive victims rather than active and agential was central to this (Khalid, 2011). As will be explained further on in the article, this is central to understanding the transnational opportunity structures for peripheries as it sets further discursive limits on the very peripheries it claims to be concerned with. This is not to say that specific (and narrow) understandings of gender and sexuality only shape western discourses and have not played a central role in shaping the discursive and material situations in which feminist, LGBT and women's, groups in the MENA work. Rather, the point here is that, as I will illustrate, western discourses on the 'Arab Spring' have centred on gender (largely understood in these discourses as the treatment of women) and sexuality in 'reading' the events of the 'Arab Spring' in ways that function to reaffirm orientalist tropes of 'eastern' backwardness and barbarism. This both privileges dominant discourses of gender and LGBT issues in the MENA and effectively marginalizes groups already on the peripheries of these discourses, and overlooks the varied functions of logics of gender and sexuality in the MENA.

This narrow understanding of 'gender' is unsurprising given the centrality of broader functions of gender in many societies (including non-western *and* western societies). Feminist scholarship has long identified that gender (in particular the construction of 'ideal' womanhood) is central to the construction and control of social communities and nations in particular. While masculine traits are generally central to the construction of the state as 'protector' of citizenry, women play a feminized role as discursive and biological reproducers of 'the nation' (Nagel, 1998; Yuval-Davis, 1997). Feminist analyses have illustrated that women's citizenship is tempered by the state's construction of 'private' familial relationships (such as marriage and child rearing) in ways that reinforce male-headed family structures and encourage the (re)production of traditional roles for women and men that centre on a binary understanding of gender and women's primary role (Yuval-Davis, 1997: 625–626). The peripheries this article is concerned with are also affected by discourses that construct genders and gender roles along binary lines. Gendered discourses impact on the dynamics between the periphery and core by shaping and constraining the political, socio-economic and cultural context in which those who are 'outside' the 'mainstream' find themselves.

The aims, activities and struggles of MENA feminist, women's and LGBT movements must be understood in terms of their complex relationship with broader nationalist struggles in the region, as well as contemporary authoritarian governments (themselves at least partly the product of engagements with powerful neoliberal states and institutions) and their repression of civil society(ies) in the region. These movements are heterogeneous, responding to, shaped by, functioning within and challenging a range of circumstances from levels of modernization and development to avenues for political participation. Not only do dominant discourses determine what 'legitimate' knowledge about gendered and sexed bodies (e.g. naturalizing binary genders, placing people within binary gender categories and setting clear boundaries of acceptable performances of these gender identities), but in doing so they set the limits of, for example, what kinds of feminist agendas can effectively be pursued. For instance, feminist scholars of the MENA point out that state-sanctioned women's groups had been bound up with the nationalist agendas that co-opted feminist agendas insofar as they could serve the state's purpose (Khalil, 2014a: 131).

Generally, women's agitation for rights relating to political participation, education and work have been legitimized through their inclusion in the discourses of (often male-dominated) elite politics. However, issues such as reproductive rights, violence against women and LGBT rights are underrepresented in 'mainstream' movements and are less prominent in state-sanctioned agendas (Al-Ali, 2003). The effect of this is to limit, both discursively and materially, the boundaries of 'acceptable' feminist activism; in effect, it also discursively prescribes what women can be and do. To challenge this is to be at odds with not only 'proper' womanhood, but also the nation itself; feminist activism which challenges dominant (often state-led) discourses of women's activism has often led to accusations of collusion with imperial interests (Zine, 2006). Indeed, the discourse of authoritarian government itself is gendered, (re)producing masculine/feminine divisions that are heteronormative (shaped by understandings of heterosexuality as 'norm' and 'ideal'), and privileging the former over the latter (Khalil, 2014b).

Discourses on Gender and Sexuality during the 'Arab Spring'

Peripheries have found expanded opportunities to engage in activism and challenging dominant norms around gender and sexuality in the 'Arab Spring', but have also faced obstacles in terms of negotiating the changing political contexts across the region. The discourse of gender, sexuality and political engagement has evolved since 2010, and can be analysed through examining events, actions and written and verbal representations in this context. Both gender and LGBT issues and groups, to varying degrees, remained situated at the margins of (even outside) dominant discourses of the 'Arab Spring'.

Initially, western and Middle Eastern media images of the protests that began in Tunisia and Egypt largely featured men (Al-Ali, 2012: 27). For example, a *Foreign Policy* photo essay contained one image of a woman (not in a protest context) out of 13 (Foreign Policy, 2012). In mainstream Arab media, women's involvement was read in various ways. In Egypt's state-run NileTV, archives on the 'Arab Spring' have few references to gender activism in terms of the protests. Those articles that do mention women tend to do so in the context of 'women and children'. Placing women in a category with children serves to infantilize them, thus denying their agency. This effectively situates women, along with children, outside the revolutionary activities of the 'Arab Spring'. This was also done in a more explicit way. An article in the pan-Arab newspaper *Al-Quds Al-Arabi* characterized women's rights activism as lying outside the 'core' concerns of the 'Arab Spring', despite its protesters' slogans of equality and removal of oppressive government. Rather, an article in the paper explained that, in the Egyptian context:

> with the generals still holding on to power, the secular parties struggling in the ballot boxes against the Muslim Brotherhood, and the youth confronting the police firing at them in the streets of Cairo, the liberation of women should not be added to the current agenda. (Quoted in Mourad, 2014: 69)

However, the involvement of women in the protests could not be ignored completely. A broad range of women participated in the protests, including those who had a strong history of activism, those who had not participated in organized political action before, working women and housewives (Pedersen & Salib, 2013: 257). Rather than simply supporting men, women were on the 'frontlines' of the revolutions across the MENA; in Yemen, the symbolic figurehead of the revolution was a female human rights activist in local media (Yadav, 2011). Women were heavily involved in public forums and spaces, not only in terms of protesting on the streets, but also in their online presence. Leil-Zahra Mortada found a lack of acknowledgement of women's participation in these protests in early media coverage and established an online blog for people to submit photos illustrating women's participation (see http://www.sawtalniswa.com/2011/02/women-of-the-egyptian-revolution/). Young activists like Esraa Abdel Fattah (Egypt) and Lina Ben Mhenni (Tunisia) played a prominent role in the online space, as activists aligning themselves with the broader struggles of the Arab masses, as well as specifically feminist agendas to empower women. Abdel Fattah is active in print and television media, and founded a women's organization; Ben Mhenni's activities and influence saw her nominated for a Nobel Prize (Pedersen & Salib, 2013: 256–266).

Women became a particularly important feature in both MENA and western mainstream discourse in light of the sexual assaults that were perpetrated against women involved in protests in Egypt. These media representations illustrate the narrowness of the mainstream media discourse in which gender activists operated in the 'Arab Spring'. In this discourse, women became currency in debates on 'authenticity', 'tradition', 'national identity' and 'civilization', in which the appropriate ways to 'be' female (and therefore, in these discourses, a woman) were policed. Paul Amar explains that Egyptian and western media outlets shifted between the construction of Tahrir as a 'utopian space that forged a new social contract' and 'the moshpit for a hypermasculine mob' (Amar, 2011: 300). Asmaa Mahfouz created and featured in a video protest that went viral in social media and featured in mainstream media outlets. Urging Egyptians to become involved in the protests, she explicitly channelled 'the 'manhood' of Egypt through political action, in order to make legible the violence of the state and challenge the security state's notions of gendered honour' (Amar, 2011: 300). State discourse responded to women's participation and reconfiguring of gender norms by sexualizing them (through accusations, innuendo and physically through assault) (Amar, 2011: 301) and thus reasserting pre-'Arab Spring' discursive boundaries around the limits of appropriate female (and feminine) political action.

In western media, coverage of women in the Arab Spring varied in terms of degree of focus, but retained the underlying logics of gendered orientalist discourse (s) that have structured much mainstream western knowledge of 'the East'. A *New York Times* article on the roots of the 'Arab Spring' attributed the trigger, Bouazizi's self-immolation, to a 'Slap to a Man's Pride' (Fahim, 2011), reflecting dominant understandings of 'honour' that most (if not all) Arab men are perceived to subscribe to. In this context, women's activism became currency in a broader discursive struggle to retain the stability of orientalist and gendered logics that can divide the world into 'progressive West' and 'backward East' through reference to the treatment (but not the agency) of women. A search of Fox News' coverage of the events in the MENA, for example, is notable for its lack of focus on women's activism in the MENA; when women are featured, this is largely in the context of sexual assaults perpetrated by men during protests, or to illustrate that 'they' had now begun to progress by subscribing to 'our' understandings of equality and justice (Sjoberg & Whooley, 2013). As one western journalist explained, '[p]eople in the West recognized themselves in the faces of the young female protesters, and they were pleased that people in these countries were not as different as many had previously believed' (von Rohr, 2011).

Representations of one particular incident of sexual violence which captured the attention of the western media – the assault against CBS journalist Lara Logan in Tahrir Square in 2011 – drew explicitly on orientalist logics, and reflected dominant western western understandings of gender and sexuality as much as they attempted to shed light on these understandings in the MENA. While western journalism tended to represent Tahrir as undisciplined to the point of lacking any leadership or direction in terms of political activism, there was some reluctance initially to cast all Arabs as possessing an uncontrolled hypermasculine sexuality. Rather, hypermasculine violence was seen as a tactic employed by the authoritarian Egyptian state (Amar, 2011: 301). As the Lara Logan story unfolded, however, the discourse shifted from one directed at the authoritarian state to 'the predatory culture' of Muslim/Arab[2] men. Focusing on Logan's femininity, and her blonde hair as symbolic of 'the West', the attack became evidence of the uncontrolled sexuality of the male 'other' (Amar, 2011: 301). Such representations effectively presuppose certain things about 'their' culture, predicated on broader and historical discourses of orientalism, in which the hypermasculinity of the 'other' is uncontrolled and a threat to 'our' women (Khalid, 2011).

The sexuality of women was also central to mainstream western discourses, in ways that recall orientalist preoccupations with uncovering the female 'other'. A dialogue, of sorts, between western and Arab discourses illustrated what I mentioned earlier regarding the deployment of Arab women as 'currency' in debates around citizenship, authenticity, tradition and national identity. A prominent example of this was Egyptian Aalia Elmahdy's posting of a nude picture of herself on Facebook, and then on her blog. Elmahdy's act undermined 'the normative social order' in Egypt, but it arguably shocked more than it opened debate (Mourad, 2014: 67). Some reactions to Elmahdy's photograph were violent, or threatened violence; the social norm which they challenged was virulently defended by some Egyptians. Even for those who were otherwise staunch supporters of freedom from oppression, this particular act of expression fell outside the parameters of the Arab protests. Mainstream media representations in the Arab world tended to discursively re-position 'Arab Spring' discourse away from the boundary-challenging message Elmahdy claimed. Some did this by 'slam[ming] her from the point of view of aesthetics, depth, timing and cultural sensitivity', while others erased the significance of the act altogether (Naguibe, 2011). Elmahdy's form of protest was also critiqued for its perceived cultural origins – an op-ed piece in *al-Dustour* asserted that Elmahdy's actions 'followed a style that was adopted in the West as a tool for protest or for the demand for gender equality ... but in our Arab world, such public nudity is related to humiliation, weakness, and the violation of human dignity' (cited in Mourad, 2014: 70). As Mourad explains, 'the sexual was mapped on to the foreign, and sexualized forms of dissent were dismissed as the mimicry of Western culture' (Mourad, 2014: 70). In mainstream western discourses, overlooking that Elmahdy's first publication of her photograph was removed from Facebook (a western-based social media platform) precisely because of her naked body,[3] the reaction in Egypt to Elmahdy's act became evidence of the backwardness of Arab culture, and its limited democratic potential despite the events of the 'Arab Spring'.

The status of LGBT peoples in the MENA has also been discussed in ways that reflect long-standing orientalist logics. A 2013 *TIME* report on LGBT issues in the MENA deployed many of these. The author explained that '[t]he sodomy law in Tunisia, the birthplace of the Arab Spring in 2011, stands as a stark reminder of the discrimination the gay and lesbian community continues to face in the Arab world' (Rayman, 2013). Reminding the reader that Tunisia was the location of the initial protests that set off the revolutionary movements in the Arab world serves to discursively link these to anti-LGBT agendas. 'The East' remains 'othered' through the predication of the initial location of its most prominent popular democratic movement as unable to attain equality of sexuality, rendering the entire region as inherently backward.

As LGBT discrimination comes to stand for the backwardness of 'the East', it also functions as a marker of 'the West's civilization. Central to this is the juxtaposition of the treatment of LGBT communities in the MENA and 'the West', which also serves to construct the authority of the latter in speaking about sexuality in the MENA. The experiences of LGBT peoples in the MENA serve to reinforce civilizational hierarchies, as 'their' treatment of LGBT people is contrasted directly to their status in 'the West', which remains unproblematized. For example, in the *TIME* report cited above, the author consults a western scholar on LGBT peoples in the MENA, who states that calls for 'freedom', 'justice' and 'dignity' in the 'Arab

Spring' will 'take a long time' to take hold in terms of LGBT issues in the MENA 'because Arab societies are traditionally authoritarian and conservative' (Rayman, 2013). This is contrasted with the imaged painted by a gay Tunisian man quoted as saying: 'at least gay people in the West can stand up and say we are here and we exist' (Rayman, 2013). Such representations of 'the East' fail to problematize the discrimination faced by LGBT peoples in the 'West', and serves instead to rearticulate orientalist narratives of the 'undeveloped Other' vis-à-vis the 'advanced West' (Sabsay, 2012). Although the *TIME* report makes (brief) mention of online LGBT activism in the MENA, the struggles – oppression as well as activism – of LGBT peoples in the MENA thus become currency in a long-standing discursive struggle in which 'East' and 'West' are delineated in binary ways, and organized along hierarchical lines.

A particularly prominent story emerging from the 'Arab Spring' in terms of LGBT rights was that of 'Amina Araf'/'Gay Girl in Damascus' hoax ('Amina's' blog was later revealed to be written not by a gay Syrian woman, but a man and woman residing in Edinburgh). The 'Gay Girl in Damascus' blog sought to document the life of a gay woman living through the revolutionary events of the 'Arab Spring'. 'Amina' communicated with journalists, who saw her as an 'authentic voice'; her struggles were reported on by the *Guardian*, CNN and CBS (Bennett, 2011: 187). The story gained particularly significant media attention when it was reported by a 'cousin' that Araf had disappeared, arrested by government security agents. Media outlets pursued the story, and the US State Department became involved in the investigation. The terms of this discourse construct LGBT concerns in the MENA as an 'updated' version of liberation/rescue tropes that have long been deployed in gendered orientalist discourses, which have most often centred on the need to 'save brown women from brown men' (Oğuzhan, 2014: 81–83).

In mainstream Arab media discourse, LGBT issues were not considered central to the freedom being pursued through mass uprisings; this discourse was largely same-sex-phobic, reflecting the long-standing marginalization of LGBT peoples in mainstream national discourse. For example, the 2001 Queen Boat/Cairo 52 controversy in Egypt, where 52 Egyptian men were charged with debauchery and offending religion, very publicly highlighted that same-sex behaviour was policed in Egypt even in the absence of a specific law against this (homosexuality is not a crime in Egypt, although laws like those policing 'debauchery' and 'offences against religion' are used to the same effect) (see Fortier, 2015; Mourad, 2014; Hawley, 2001). The discursive delegitimization of homosexual identity continued in the 'Arab Spring'. For example, a TV appearance by the new Egyptian human rights minister reinforced the conceptualization of non-heterosexuality as something requiring 'medical treatment' (Kreps, 2012: 224). This discursively continues to construct 'natural' (and therefore legitimate) sexual identities in binary ways, and privileges heterosexuality as the norm.

In the context of the 'Arab Spring', Mourad notes that, as with feminist issues, mainstream discourse reflected a 'compromising stance' on issues of sexual freedom (Mourad, 2014: 68). Shalakany (2007: 9) points out that in promoting human rights around sexuality in this context, individuals run the risk of 'being painted supporters of "sexual deviance"'. Discursively, options for challenging dominant understandings of sexuality and identity are closed off; the mainstream discourse of the 'Arab Spring' constructed hierarchies of freedom and oppression. In mainstream discourse, rights around sexuality and gender are at best ignored (with the hope that securing political stability and so-called 'core' rights will open the way for other rights to be considered); at worst, they are constructed as something 'outside' a particular understanding of Arab 'cultural values'. The interplay between mainstream Arab and western discourses illustrates that these issues are currency in competing discursive battles around civilization and identity – the individuals and groups in these peripheries themselves are marginalized.

Peripheries' Strategies: Shifting the Discourse of the 'Arab Spring'

Peripheral groups were thus marginalized in dominant discourses; however, they have demonstrated their agency in a variety of ways. The strategies adopted by the peripheral groups discussed here have been touched on above, in terms of the ways in which their activities have functioned in the construction of dominant discourses on the 'Arab Spring'. However, it is also important to acknowledge the various approaches, ideas, actions and forums for expression these peripheries have utilized outside of dominant discourses. The shifts in the broader 'Arab Spring' toward widespread 'non-institutional activism' (in public spaces and in online spaces through social media platforms such as Facebook, Twitter and online blogs) was very much reflected in the activism of peripheral groups such as women and LGBT people. While the peripheries discussed in this article were represented, to some extent, in mainstream media outlets, social media has generally allowed these groups to represent themselves in their own terms – and, in terms of LGBT movements, they have value as a safe(r) space for activism and for the expression of ideas that challenge a range of dominant constructions of gender and sexuality.

As mentioned earlier, addressing gender (in)equality in terms of official policy and institutions has been, to some degree, limited by the scope set by the state. However, both in the context of the 'Arab Spring' and before it, broader gender activism has been 'decentralized' through the increasing utilization of online space to discuss issues of gender and sexuality, as a tool for organization and as a forum through which to place pressure on new governments in terms of shifting the boundaries of what reform related to gender (and sexuality) should and could entail (Khalil, 2014a: 131). In terms of the political changes taking place in the MENA since 2010, a range of women's groups have taken the opportunity to challenge and interrogate understandings of gender in terms of national identity, as well as legal and constitutional instruments. 'State-defined action', Khalil explains, has been seriously challenged by 'atomised forms of cyber-activism' that can challenge 'state-imposed binaries' (Khalil, 2014a: 131).

Activism in this space has been both individual and group-oriented, both 'new' and continuing a longer tradition of using online forums for activism. Social media has been used as a tool for organizing street protests as well as virtual protests.

It also offered a range of Arab women (Manal Hassan, Nawara Negm, Nora Younis and Dalia Ziada, to name but a few) a forum through which to put forward non-mainstream accounts of the 'Arab Spring' – to both Arab and western audiences. Importantly, women from rural areas also blogged about the revolutions, offering audiences a more nuanced picture of the events themselves, motivating factors and the role of women and women's rights here (Rama, 2013: 38, see also Elghamry, 2015). As Kamal and ElKholy explain in the Egyptian context, women outside urban centres have been active in the events of the 'Arab Spring', 'turning the "political revolution" into a cultural and moral one' through 'alternative ways of resisting' – not only in the 'public sphere' but also in less visible spaces, such as within the home (Kamal & ElKholy, 2014). Women thus have an important role as revolutionaries, especially as citizen-journalists, challenging the representations disseminated by state and mainstream media outlets (Radsch, 2012: 14–16). Importantly, their activism did not reflect the disconnect between gender and so-called 'core' issues displayed in mainstream discourse. For example, a range of Facebook sites organized by Arab women situated women's rights as part of more general topics (Zlitni & Touati, 2012). As Courtney Radsch (2012: 6), notes there are varying levels of internet participation across the MENA, but the audience includes those with greater access to the centres of power than enjoyed by peripheral groups.

LGBT groups have also utilized online spaces to voice their concerns and challenge dominant discourses of sexuality (Kreps, 2012). These spaces, in part, make possible aspects of what Needham explains as 'closet activism' that has been deployed in Egypt. In contrast to open LGBT rights activism, this approach harnesses the movement for freedom and human rights amongst Arab masses, without specifically enunciating LGBT identity (Needham, 2013: 317–319). LGBT peripheries have faced more constraints than feminist groups (at least, those which have had a focus on gender equality between 'men' and 'women') in terms of engaging with dominant discourses of gender and sexuality in traditional political spaces. The online space, offering potential for a less regulated and more anonymous forum than traditional activism, has been utilized by LGBT individuals and groups. For example, the Tunisian-based magazine *Gayday* was launched in 2011 and offers a forum for expression that is not available in mainstream outlets; it also aims to challenge the criminalization of same-sex acts and identities in Tunisia (Abrougui, 2012).

Dominant discourses of sexuality continue to reproduce traditional under-standings of 'appropriate' sexual expression. However, as David Kreps notes, this is more complex than 'mainstream' western discourses of sexuality might suggest. Historically, Arab understandings of sexuality have tended to be fluid: same-sex acts have not necessarily been seen as determinative of sexual identity, and there has been tolerance toward non-heterosexual activity in Arab cultures (Kreps, 2012: 224). Edwige Fortier (2015) makes the point that speaking publicly about non-heterosexual acts is more socially sanctioned than the acts themselves. Similarly, Joseph Massad has argued that non-heterosexual sexual acts themselves are less problematic than what he calls 'western' homosexual identity (Massad, 2007). The discourse that constructs this identity 'produces homosexuals ... where they do not exist' (Massad, 2002: 363). However, as Fortier (2015) warns, the view that LGBT identity does not exist 'outside small groups of men in metropolitan areas' (Massad, 2002: 373) serves to 'negate the agency of homosexual actors in these countries whilst simultaneously side-lining' the discursive and material violence done to those who identify as non-heterosexual (Fortier, 2015). There is increasing desire amongst those Arabs who identify as non-heterosexual to be able to secure the freedom to express their sexual identities on their own terms, whether this happens to accord with 'western' or 'eastern' notions of sexuality (Kreps, 2012).

The opportunities for political engagement also point to an increased possibility of deconstructing and reconstructing dominant discourses of gender and sexuality. An Egyptian student, for example, pointed out in respect of his perception of LGBT issues in the protests that 'As a gay Arab, I feel represented in these protests in every way and I'm confident that one day there will be a gay rights movement sweeping the Arab streets' (quoted in Russeau, 2012). Indeed, those who challenge dominant discursive constructions of gender and sexuality can face accusations of importing 'western culture' and aiding western imperialism. However, as Rasha Moumneh explains, the 'social anxiety brought about by homosexuality is not all that different from conservative fears that arise from the promotion of women's rights and freedoms' (in Russeau, 2012).

Conclusion

This article has analysed the periphery theme of this volume from a discursive angle. It has examined the discursive opportunity structures in which gender peripheries find themselves. Discourses that influence and shape dominant western understandings of the role of women and non-heterosexual people in the 'Arab Spring' have (re)produced orientalist logics that marginalize those who do not conform to particular gendered understandings of the roles of various people in the MENA. 'Local' discourses too have deployed specific (binary) understandings of gender and sexuality to exercise control over groups of people.

Nonetheless, gender peripheries have pursued their own strategies in these opportunity structures and their activism has deeply challenged them. Those whose voices have been underrepresented in the mainstream have attempted to represent themselves through a variety of ways, which, in particular, have destabilized or challenged mainstream orientalist representations of gender and sexuality in the context of the 'Arab Spring' and more broadly.

The changes brought forth in the 'Arab Spring', as with any significant political upheaval, have been unpredictable and fast-paced. In this sense, the strategies of dissent and political engagement chosen by groups seeking to challenge dominant discourses of gender and sexuality in the MENA during this period have been impacted on by events very much out of their immediate control, shaped by a multiplicity of factors and interests. On a broad level, the calls for freedom and justice that marked the protests of the 'Arab Spring' intersect with the aims of those seeking to change dominant understandings of gender and sexual identities and roles. However, these peripheries have had varying success in changing dominant discourses of gender and sexuality. While political engagement in traditional forums has not always been fruitful in this sense, peripheral groups concerned with gender and LGBT rights have been able to find other avenues to challenge discourses. The importance of online forums in contemporary political movements has also been significant in recent years in popular political engagement in the MENA; this can be seen as an opportunity structure shift that has been utilized by groups that have (and continue to have) limited access to the institutions of state to voice and act on their own understandings of rights related to gender and sexuality.

Notes

1. I use scare quotes around this term to denote that it is problematic in terms of the implication of political dormancy amongst the Arab masses in the MENA until the events of 2010 sparked wide-scale protests and uprisings. To speak of an 'Arab Spring' ignores the decades of political agitation around the Arab (and non-Arab) states in the MENA and ignores the wider political context of the lack of success of challenges to authoritarian regimes in the region, which include the support of some of these regimes by the same western states that engage in the construction of discourses of political underdevelopment in the MENA (Khoury, 2011; Teti, 2012: 281; Tyner & Rice, 2012).
2. I use 'Muslim/Arab' here to indicate that these identity categories are too often conflated in dominant (orientalist) discourses.
3. Facebook's terms of service, arguably reflective of mainstream (western) social norms, prohibit content that contains (particular types of) nudity.

Disclosure statement

No potential conflict of interest was reported by the author.

References

Abrougui, A. (2012) Gayday magazine: Tunisia's first LGBT magazine, *Uncut: Freedom of Speech on the Frontline*, 27 March, Available at http://uncut.indexoncensorship.org/2012/03/gayday-magazine-tunisias-first-lgbt-magazine/ (accessed 16 June 2014).

Agathangelou, A. & N. Soguk (2011) Rocking the Kasbah: insurrectional politics, the "Arab streets", and global revolution in the 21st century, *Globalizations*, 8(5), pp. 551–558. doi:10.1080/14747731.2011.622101.

Al-Ali, N. (2003) Gender and civil society in the Middle East, *International Feminist Journal of Politics*, 5(2), pp. 216–232. doi:10.1080/1461674032000080576.

Al-Ali, N. (2012) Gendering the Arab spring, *Middle East Journal of Culture and Communication*, 5(1), pp. 26–31. doi:10.1163/187398612X624346.

Ali, T. (2011) Who will reshape the Arab world: its people, or the US? *The Guardian*, 29 April, Available at http://www.guardian.co.uk/commentisfree/2011/apr/29/arab-politics-democracy-intervention

Amar, P. (2011) 'Turning the gendered politics of the security state inside out?', *International Feminist Journal of Politics*, 13(3), pp. 299–328. doi:10.1080/14616742.2011.587364.

Bennett, D. (2011) A 'gay girl in Damascus': the Mirage of the 'authentic voice' – and the future of journalism, in: R. Keeble & J. Mair (Eds) *Mirage in the Desert? Reporting the Arab Spring* (Bury St Edmonds: Abramis).

Doty, R.L. (1996) *Imperial Encounters: The Politics of Representation in North-South Relations* (Minneapolis: University of Minnesota Press).

Elghamry, K. (2015) Periphery discourse: An alternative media eye on the geographical, social and media peripheries in Egypt's spring, Mediterranean Politics, 20(2), pp. 255–272. doi:10.1080/13629395. 2015.1033902.

Fahim, K. (2011) Slap to a man's pride set off Tumult in Tunisia, *New York Times*, January 2011.

Financial Times (2012) Arab awakening is just the beginning, Editorial December 23.

Foreign Policy (2012) Looking back at the Arab spring, Available at http://www.foreignpolicy.com/articles/2011/12/16/photos_of_the_arab_spring (accessed 7 April 2014).

Fortier, E. (2015) Transition and marginalisation: locating spaces for discursive contestation in post-revolution Tunisia, *Mediterranean Politics*, 20(2) doi: 10.1080/13629395.2015.1033904

Hawley, C. (2001) Anger over Egypt gay trial, *BBC*, 15 August, Available at http://news.bbc.co.uk/2/hi/middle_east/1493041.stm (accessed 16 June 2014).

Kamel, L. & M.E. El-Kholy (2014) Women activism and resistance in rural upper and lower Egypt, *The Hill*, 27 March 2014, Available at http://thehill.com/blogs/congress-blog/foreign-policy/201830-women-activism-and-resistance-in-rural-upper-and-lower (accessed 16 June 2014).

Karim, W.J. (2011) Stratagems and spoils in US policy in the Middle East, *Globalizations*, 8(5), pp. 601–607. doi:10.1080/14747731.2011.621312.

Khalid, M. (2011) Gender, orientalism and representations of the 'other' in the war on terror, *Global Change, Peace & Security*, 23(1), pp. 15–29. doi:10.1080/14781158.2011.540092.

Khalil, A. (2014a) Gender paradoxes of the Arab spring, *The Journal of North African Studies*, 19(2), pp. 131–136. doi:10.1080/13629387.2014.885782.

Khalil, A. (2014b) Tunisia's women: partners in revolution, *The Journal of North African Studies*, 19(2), pp. 186–199. doi:10.1080/13629387.2013.870424.

Khoury, R G. (2011) Drop the orientalist term 'Arab spring', *The Daily Star*, August 17, Available at http://www.dailystar.com.lb/Opinion/Columnist/2011/Aug-17/146410-drop-the-orientalist-term-arab-spring.ashx

Kreps, D. (2012) In/visibility of LGBTQ people in the Arab spring, proceedings of CATaC'12', CATaC, Aarhus, Denmark. 18–20 June 2012.

Massad, J. (2002) Re-orienting desire: the gay international and the Arab world, *Public Culture*, 14(2), pp. 361–386. doi:10.1215/08992363-14-2-361.

Massad, J. (2007) *Desiring Arabs* (Chicago, IL: University of Chicago Press).

Milliken, J. (1999) Intervention and identity: reconstructing the west in Korea, in: J. Weldes, M. Laffey, H. Gusterson & R. Duvall (Eds) *Cultures of Insecurity: States, Communities, and the Production of Danger* (Minneapolis: University of Minnesota Press).

Mourad, S. (2014) The naked body of Alia: gender, citizenship, and the Egyptian body politic, *Journal of Communication Inquiry*, 38(1), pp. 62–78. doi:10.1177/0196859913508782.

Nagel, J. (1998) Masculinity and nationalism: gender and sexuality in the making of nations, *Ethnic and Racial Studies*, 21(2), pp. 242–269. doi:10.1080/014198798330007.

Naguibe, R. (2011) Aliaa's nudity: a different form of protest, *Egypt Independent*, December 11, Available at http://www.egyptindependent.com/opinion/aliaasnudity-different-form-protest (accessed 16 June 2014).

Needham, J. (2013) After the Arab spring: a new opportunity for LGBT human rights advocacy? *Duke Journal of Gender Law & Policy*, 20, pp. 287–323.

Oğuzhan, Ö. (2014) Whose Niqab is this? Challenging, creating and communicating female Muslim identity via social media, *Journal of Media Critiques*, 2, pp. 71–90.

Pedersen, J. & M. Salib (2013) Women of the Arab spring, *International Feminist Journal of Politics*, 15(2), pp. 256–266. doi:10.1080/14616742.2013.796218.

Radsch, C. (2012) Unveiling the revolutionaries: cyberactivism and the role of women in the Arab uprisings, James A. Baker III Institute For Public Policy Paper, Rice University.

Rama, S. (2013) Remembering their role: keeping women involved post-Arab awakening, *Journal of Women and Human Rights in the Middle East*, 1, pp. 31–48.

Rayman, N. (2013) After the Arab spring, no bloom for Arab LGBT rights, *TIME*, 1 July 2013, Available at http://world.time.com/2013/07/01/after-the-arab-spring-no-bloom-for-arab-lgbt-rights/ (accessed 12 January 2014).

Russeau, S.S.K. (2012) A touch of spring for LGBT Arabs, *Inter Press Service*, January 11.

Sabsay, L. (2012) The emergence of the other sexual citizen: orientalism and the modernisation of sexuality, *Citizenship Studies*, 16(5–6), pp. 605–623.

Said, E.W. (1978) *Orientalism* (Hammondsworth: Penguin).

Sjoberg, L., & J., Whooley (2013) New discourse, old Orientalism: a critical evaluation of the 'Arab Spring for women'?, in: J. Davis (Ed) The Arab Spring and Arab Thaw (Aldershot: Ashgate).

Shalakany, A. (2007) On a certain queer discomfort with orientalism, Proceedings of the American Society of International Law 101, 7–11, Available at http://www.aucegypt.edu/GAPP/law/faculty/Documents/PROCEEDINGS.pdf (accessed 16 June 2014).

Teti, A. (2012) The EU's first response to the 'Arab spring': a critical discourse analysis of the *partnership for democracy and shared prosperity*, *Mediterranean Politics*, 17(3), pp. 266–284. doi:10.1080/13629395.2012.725297.

Tuastad, C. (2003) Neo-orientalism and the New Barbarism thesis: aspects of symbolic violence in the Middle East conflict(s), *Third World Quarterly*, 24(4), pp. 591–599. doi:10.1080/0143659032000105768.

Tyner, J.A. & S. Rice (2012) Moving beyond the 'Arab spring': the ethnic, temporal, and spatial bounding of a political movement, *Political Geography*, 31(3), pp. 131–132. doi:10.1016/j.polgeo.2012.01.001.

Von Rohr, M. (2011) Freedoms at risk: Arab women fight to defend their rights, *Der Spiegel*, 29 November.

Weldes, J. (1996) Constructing national interests, *European Journal of International Relations*, 2(3), pp. 275–318. doi:10.1177/1354066196002003001.

Yadav, S.P. (2011) Tawakkul Karman as cause and effect, *Middle East Research and Information Project*, October 21.

Yuval-Davis, N. (1997) *Gender and Nation* (London: Sage).

Zine, J. (2006) Between orientalism and fundamentalism: Muslim women and feminist engagement, in: K. Hunt & K. Rygiel (Eds) *(En)Gendering the War on Terror: War Stories and Camouflaged Politics* (Aldershot: Ashgate).

Zlitni, S. & Z. Touati (2012) Social networks and women's mobilization in Tunisia, *Journal of International Women's Studies*, 13(5), pp. 46–58.

Secular Autocracy vs. Sectarian Democracy? Weighing Reasons for Christian Support for Regime Transition in Syria and Egypt

MARK FARHA[*] & SALMA MOUSA[**]

*Georgetown University School of Foreign Service in Qatar, Education City, Doha, Qatar, **Stanford University, Stanford, CA, USA

ABSTRACT   *With the spectre of post-Spring Islamist rule looming, Christians in Syria and Egypt were forced to choose between quasi-secular autocracy and sectarian populism. The status quo ante under al-Assad and Mubarak, though democratically deficient, temporarily contained civil hostilities and afforded Christians with a modicum of secular protection and even prosperity, the degree of which sheds light on the relative absence of Syrian Christian protestors and the salient Coptic presence during the Egyptian revolution. This article explores how socio-economic and religious peripheral designations intersected with state policy to determine political (in) action amongst Christian minorities in two crucial countries of the region.*

The Pre-Revolutionary State in Syria and Egypt: Revisiting the Virtues of Autocracy

These transgressions on the subjects (*ri'aya*) are a source of our displeasure and discontent, for all Muslims and Christians are equally our subjects, and the matter of the *madhhab* (denomination) is to have no bearing on the governing of politics. It is therefore imperative that everyone enjoy a state of safety to go about his Islam and his Christianity, even as nobody ought to lord over the other.

> (Ibrahim Pasha, Governor of Syria and Lebanon, 1832–40, quoted in Rustum, 1966: 99)

The iron-fisted Ottoman Wali Ibrahim Pasha's determination to protect Christian minorities from communal transgressions may well be taken as an emblematic instance of autocrats safeguarding the civil rights of religious minorities.

52

As concerns Christian minorities in the Middle East, is there really a trade-off between militaristic, repressive yet socially liberal regimes on the one hand, and more democratic, yet illiberal and communalist orders, on the other?

A brief review of the historical record suggests that the case for 'enlightened autocrats' acting as guardians of minorities in the Middle East (as in Europe) is not without foundation (Scott, 1990). From the early stages of state formation, authoritarian and military leaders in the region, such as the Emir Fakhr Eddin II in the seventeenth century Lebanese emirate, Muhammad Ali and Ibrahim Pasha in the nineteenth century, General Fu'ad Chihab from 1958 to 1964 in Lebanon or indeed the Baathist dictatorships of Hafez and Bashar al-Assad in Syria and, to a far lesser degree, Mubarak in Egypt, garnered Christian support by suppressing political sectarianism, curtailing problematic injunctions of *sharī'a* law and grouping religious peripheral groups with the Sunni majority under at least nominally non-discriminatory administrations. Yet it would be mistaken to attribute political stances to ascriptive religious identities pure and simple. As we shall see, Christian preferences for secular autocracies or sectarian democracies cannot be viewed exclusively through the reductive sectarian lens of 'minority vs. majority' or 'Muslim vs. Christian' that neglect the decisive role of class affiliation in determining regime support.

As we will demonstrate, those on the socio-economic peripheries were more likely to protest, with Egyptian Christians suffering from a 'double-periphery' status as excluded religious minorities. Conversely, Syrian Christians were not considered a peripheral group in Syria insofar as many of them were represented in the political and socio-economic center.

The methodology relies on a qualitative analysis of the most prominent Christian platforms on new and social media sites, statements from Christian political and religious leaders, profiles of cabinets and parliaments to determine the political integration of Christians, academic theories on activity and passivity of peripheral groups in the Arab world, polling data (including 25 original surveys conducted by the authors using a 'snowball' approach to the researchers' existing networks) and interviews with pro- and anti-democracy activists. The timeframe considered – the 18 days of the Egyptian revolution and the first year of unrest in Syria – reflects the initial reaction illustrating the hesitation or participation of Christians.

Assessing the Disparate Reaction of Christians during the Egyptian and Syrian Revolts

'In the name of Jesus and Mohammed, we unify our ranks', said Father Ihab al-Kharat in his sermon on 6 February 2011. 'We will keep protesting until the fall of tyranny' (Kennedy, 2011). Despite the widespread assumption of Coptic political passivity, the Coptic Orthodox Church's initial opposition to the revolution, the common belief that Mubarak provided at least titular secular protections to the Coptic minority and the fear of Islamist parties coming to power in a democratic setting, Coptic revolutionaries protested en masse at Tahrir Square. The same Christian presence was not evident at the start of the Syrian uprising in January 2011. The reaction of Syrian Christians ranged from explicitly supporting Bashar al-Assad, remaining silent on the protests, or proposing modest reforms towards political liberalization – making sure not to become explicitly affiliated with the opposition movement. Although fervent Christian pro-regime support is steadily waning, after the first year of unrest, the vast majority of Syrian Christians had not joined the Sunni-led movement and defections remain far from being widespread even after three years of steady escalation (Petrou, 2011: 26). Why did a proportionately larger number of Christians participate in the Egyptian, but not Syrian, uprisings?

From a strictly numerical perspective, most Christians (and Muslims) in both countries did not protest at the start of their respective uprisings. This article therefore explores the discrepancy between Christians as a proportion of the revolutionaries. Whether or not Christians protested in Egypt and Syria depended on two main factors: the extent to which Christians benefited from state secularism, on the one hand, and suffered from the same socio-economic grievances as Muslim protestors, on the other. It would be fallacious to peg either country as 'secular' by rigorous standards of non-discrimination – *sharī'a* is the main source of legislation in both cases and Syria's constitution stipulates that the president must be Muslim, measures introduced in order to bestow a Sunni veil of legitimacy on Alawi, or military-dominated, autocratic regimes, respectively. Yet in terms of secular protections, simply put, it was much easier to build a church in al-Assad's Syria than Mubarak's Egypt – meaning that long-marginalized Copts on the peripheries had less to lose by overthrowing their embattled authoritarian leader than their Syrian co-religionists closer to the centre of power.

As concerns the second factor, this article departs from the assumption that the political and demographic profile of the revolts in Egypt and Syria must be analysed against the backdrop of socio-economic grievances. For at least the past decade, we have seen mounting frustration at worsening economic and living conditions, induced by rampant inflation in food and fuel prices, stagnant nominal wages and plummeting youth employment rates. Class in Egypt is not a function of religion, but of locality – a product of centuries of close communal cohabitation. The geographic and thus socio-economic intertwining of Christians and Muslims rendered both communities peripheral, and so equally susceptible to the frustrations that fuelled the uprising. Comparatively, Syria is more distinctly divided into Christian, Sunni, Alawite, Shi'a and Kurdish towns and villages, with Christians predominantly affiliated with the professional classes with a clear stake in the continuation of the al-Assad regime (Library of Congress, 2011).

Christians in State and Society

Christians constitute around 10 per cent of the Syrian population, representing approximately 2 million citizens, almost every branch of Eastern Christianity and three popes. Syrian Christians traditionally hold a dominant and prestigious role in state and society, despite the presence of a glass ceiling that implicitly denies non-Alawites access to the highest societal echelons. Christians faced almost no discrimination in one of the few remaining Arab states where, as one bishop puts it, 'a Christian can really feel the equal of a Muslim' – rendering Syria a safe haven for persecuted religious minorities (Dalrymple, 2007; Amnesty International, 2008). Such a claim is supported by freedom of worship enshrined in the pluralistic legal code, which allows Christians to settle non-civil matters through Christian courts, dispose of their possessions without the Ministry of Waqf's interference and buy state-subsidized land to build upon freely (Moussalli, 1998: 282). Christmas and Easter are official national holidays, liturgical celebrations are broadcast on the radio and television and government delegates always attend the ordination of a bishop (Moussalli, 1998: 289). Priests are exempt from obligatory military and civil service, religious education includes Christian catechism in the national curriculum, and the Syrian government subsidizes Christian civil society organizations (Moussalli, 1998: 289).

Syrian Christians integrated themselves politically through the founding of the countries' two most significant post-independence political ideologies and the subsequent parties they spawned, which both created a secular, nationalist framework to unite the Sunni majority with minorities under an inclusive banner of Arab identity – the Syrian National Social Party (SSNP) and the ruling Ba'ath Party, both founded by Greek Orthodox ideologues. The al-Assads have remained in power partly due to an unofficial ruling coalition with other minorities at the centre, demonstrated by several high-ranking Christian ministers in the current cabinet ('Syrian People's Assembly', 2015) This informal alliance grants the Alawite rulers loyal allies united by a mutual defence pact of sorts, stemming from collective opposition to hegemonic Sunni rule (Mikhail, 2008: 16).

The experience of Egyptian Christians differs starkly from that of their counterparts in Syria. Although no official figures exist, Copts constitute around 10–15 per cent of the Egyptian population (Ezzat, 2009). The socio-economic position of Copts varies from billionaire tycoons like the Sawiris family to encampments of *zabbaleen* who live in villages entrenched in garbage dumps. The most distinctive feature of Egyptian Copts relative to their co-religionists in the Middle East is that they have hardly ever politically expressed themselves as a religious community (El Khawaga, 1998: 172). Their post-independence rejection of Coptic parties meant that Copts were almost always excluded from national discussions (Zaki Stephanous, 2010: 115). To attribute the depoliticization of the largest Christian community in the Arab world to 'cold rejectionism' is a gross oversimplification, as Copts consider themselves to be not a minority, but fully and ethnically Egyptian (Haykal, 1992; Hanna, 1980). The decline of Copts from public life can be attributed in part to the failure of the Wafd-sponsored ideals of egalitarian pluralism, which meant that Coptic aspirations for a secular society in Muslim Egypt never materialized into an attainable political goal (Nisan, 2002: 142).

Conditions for Copts were mixed under Nasser and decidedly worst under Sadat – but the status of Copts improved significantly under Mubarak (Ayalon, 1999: 55). Similar to the basis of the Christian–Alawite alliance in Syria, the Mubarak regime and the Coptic community opposed Islamist militancy and the accelerated implementation of *sharī'a* while sharing a common interest in a secular state (Ibrahim, 2010: 18). Orthodox Christmas (7 January) became a national holiday, Coptic history was integrated into national textbooks, books on inter-communal relations in Egypt were heavily subsidized, state media expanded Christian programming and media provocation of sectarian tensions became illegal (Makari, 2007: 70; US. Dept. of State, 2011). However, Copts remained systematically excluded from governmental posts, the armed forces, diplomatic corps, judiciary and intelligence services, and were banned from presidential administrative and security bodies (Hamzawy, 2010; Scott, 2010: 83). Copts coped with this peripheralization by adopting a strategy of turning inwards towards the Church to provide goods and services traditionally in the mandate of the state to maintain a status quo existence, legitimizing the clergy as interlocutors in national institutions in the eyes of the community (Ibrahim, 2010: 5; El Khawaga, 1998: 186).

Syrian Christians and the Uprising

Is the alternative to the current regime more democratic? I doubt it. More liberal? I doubt it. More secular? I doubt it. So why should Christians join the revolution, when their situation will be far worse than the present situation?

(Comment on Al-Arabiya article ['Al-kinīsa as-Soriyya', 2012] by a Syrian Christian blogger)

Absence of Syrian Christian Protestors

The simplistic analysis of the Syrian divide – religious minorities on al-Assad's side and the Sunni Arab majority on the other – has 'never captured the nuance of a struggle that may define Syria for generations' ('Fearing Change', 2011). Most Christians continued to demonstrate unwavering support for al-Assad after a year of unrest (Kremer, 2012; Lund, 2012; Berbner, 2011; 'Unknown Future', 2011; 'Live in Fear', 2012). The current situation reflects the historical tendency of the regime to court and co-opt Christians, who subsequently echoed the state narrative blaming foreign and domestic terrorists for the unfolding events. As Michel Kilo, noted Christian political dissident, observed; 'the smell of death is spreading to the houses of those who mourn their martyrs ... while I hear that Christians have just opened two nightclubs in Aleppo' (quoted in Mamarbachi-Seurat, 2011). The most popular 'Syrian Christian' Facebook group (with over 1,000 members) also reflects Christian regime support, stating that Christians only support reforms intended to maintain al-Assad's government and boasts a profile picture evoking Christian imagery of a sheep led by a shepherd with the caption, 'Syrian Christians entrust national security to the Army'.

Secular Protections

Christians in the Middle East have been able to live relatively peacefully under Arab dictatorships, such as those of Saddam Hussein, both Hafez and Bashar al-Assad and Hosni Mubarak, partly because of the subscription of these leaders to the now largely discredited quasi-secular Arab Nationalism that characterized twentieth century Arab political discourse. Indeed, Syrian political discourse – that propounded by both the regime and the opposition – until very recently has been marked by an artificial amnesia and suppression of sectarian fault-lines. A similar state of 'sectarian denial' has been recorded by Mariz Tadros in Egypt. In 2012, over a third of the pro-regime Syrians polled in YouGov–Doha Debates survey listed the rise of sectarian violence as their primary reason for supporting the president. Syrian Christians accepted the regime-imposed constraints on their political liberties and exchanged the right to practise their religion for regime loyalty.

Most Christians prefer the devil they know – four decades of a secular autocracy that affords extensive rights and privileges to religious minorities – to an uncertain and potentially dangerous future under Islamists, who will undoubtedly demand a stake in a post-al-Assad Syria ('Sectarian Nerves', 2012). The Greek Orthodox patriarch and Syrian Catholic archbishop justified Christian support for the embattled president because, 'most importantly, we have the freedom to be Christians' (quoted in Berbner, 2011). Such guarantees pushed Syrian Christian liberals to trust the Baath Party and embrace the so-called Damascus Spring when Bashar succeeded his father in 2000. Although the Syrian state nominally privileges Sunni Islam (and, *de facto*, the Alawite elite) in a constitutional sense, discrimination is reserved only for those who jeopardize regime authority.

Fear of Islamists

Christian apprehensiveness over the perceived alternative of a sectarian state is evidenced by pro-regime comments from viewers identifying as Syrian Christians on a YouTube clip of al-Assad and his wife visiting parish-run orphanages and monasteries in Ma'loula: 'Ignatius of Antioch will be martyred once Bashar al-Assad leaves and the Islamist extremists come to power', a view affirmed by survey respondents ('Al-Assad Protects Christians', 2012; '10 Syrian Christians', 2012). A woman in Damascus's ancient Christian quarter, Bab Touma, justified Christian attachment to the ailing regime because 'if the regime falls, [she] will have to wear the veil or leave the country' ('Sectarian Nerves', 2012). Almost a third of pro-regime Syrians polled said that their continued support for al-Assad was based on their belief that his departure would allow Islamic extremists to gain a foothold. These fears are not unfounded – although the initial protests in Dera'a were largely civil in rhetoric, waves of sectarian bloodshed gripped Syria soon after the onset of the revolution (Abu Fadel, 2011).

At the outbreak of protests, reports quickly surfaced of demonstrators chanting 'Christians to Beirut and Alawites to the coffin'. Less than a year later, local and foreign militants such as the Faruq Brigade and the most extreme wing of Syria's opposition, Jabhat al-Nusra, expelled virtually all Christians by force from Homs, hitherto the second largest Greek Orthodox diocese in Syria after Damascus ('Inside Jabhat al-Nusra', 2012). Over 100 anti-Assad groups, including the Free Syrian Army and Syrian National Council, signed a petition in support of Jabhat al-Nusra after the latter had been categorized as a terrorist group by the US administration, calling into question the opposition's secular credentials (Zelin, 2011). The February 2014 takeover of Raqqa by a jihadist group demanding that Christians pay a levy in gold and accept curbs on their faith, or face death, is hardly encouraging ('Syria Crisis', 2014). The flight of 2,000 Christians from the Armenian town of Kessab after it fell to rebel fighters in April 2014 is equally telling of the opposition's alienation of Christians (Armstrong, 2014).

Days before Christmas in 2012, the al-Ansar Brigade, armed with Kalashnikovs, released a video message threatening to attack two Christian towns in Hama if they did not expel pro-regime fighters. Armenian Orthodox Christians picked up arms to defend their neighbourhoods in Aleppo against attacks from the Free Syrian Army as well as the regime's militia (Sherlock & Malouf, 2012). Syrian Christian refugees from the border town of Qusayr fled to Lebanon after rebels equated Christian neutrality with fervent regime support and drove them out of the country (Putz, 2012). Such incidents disconcerted minorities and drove them to rally behind the government, even if they had been sceptical of al-Assad before the uprising. The regime, for its part, fomented anxieties by continually stressing that the greatest fears of the Christian community – Islamists, *sharī'a* law and the prospect of burning churches – would be promptly realized if the regime were to fall (Sheperd, 2011a).

Assurances of Post-Al-Assad Secularism by Revolutionaries

Soon after the uprising was underway, revolutionaries (both Muslim and Christian) tried to allay minority fears by emphasizing a civil rights discourse, dismissing the regime's oft-repeated claim that only the al-Assad-headed Ba'ath Party can protect Christians from radical Islamists as a 'bogus argument meant to frighten the West and divide Syrians from one another' (Kabawat, 2012a). Commitment to a civil state is, however, purported in one American survey (which may admittedly reflect the opinion of Syrian exiles more than current battlefield forces) which found that opposition members ranked the French political system highest (5.45/7), with a theocratic government styled on the Iranian model (predictably) receiving the lowest marks (1.26/7), and a majority of respondents affirming the importance of protecting minorities, including Alawites (4.69/7) (Dorell, 2012).

The Muslim opposition cites the (admittedly small) presence of Christians in the opposition movement, Syria's long history of religious cohabitation and the solidarity among the demonstrators to support its claims of secular aspirations (Blanford, 2011). A Friday protest on Easter weekend was dubbed *'Azimeh* Friday' (Good Friday) in honour of Christians, protest organizers were quick to silence signs of sectarianism amongst demonstrators, and the Facebook groups 'Syrian Revolution 2011' and 'We are All Syria', with over 800,000 members collectively, list a code of ethics against sectarianism (Kodmani, 2011; Patterson, 2011). Ali Sadr Al-Din Al-Bayanouni, former general supervisor of the Muslim Brotherhood in Syria, announced that the party would adopt civil notions of citizenship if it came to power and avowed the importance of separating the crimes of minority elites from the lay members of these sects (Brookings Institute Doha, 2011). Sheikh al-Zouabi, the leader of the Syrian Salafists, stressed the importance of co-operation between protestors, the need for international intervention to protect Syrians of all faiths and the theological kinship of Muslims and Christians (Blanford, 2011). However, the treatment of minorities under Islamist parties remains an open question and claims of good will may mask different realities. Even the most liberal exponents of the Muslim Brotherhood have taken special care never to describe their Syria as 'secular', but only 'civil', with the broader explicit goal of an 'Islamic state' still affirmed. Many Christians, such as Greek Catholic Archbishop Jeanbart, therefore prefer the current situation to a 'mere promise' ('Syrian Archbishop', 2012).

Lack of Socio-economic Grievances

Despite Syria's history of religious pluralism, Muslims and Christians are socio-economically segmented – with the Christian presence in the middle and upper classes contributing to their passivity. The uprising started in the agrarian city of Dera'a, with the disenfranchised, perchance Sunni revolutionaries suffering the most from the strains of population explosion that particularly afflicted the rural poor living in government-neglected peripheries, the urban poor disillusioned with crony capitalism and legions of unemployed youth (Seale, 2011). Inclination to protest is influenced more decisively by class background (and proximity to the political, economic and military centre) than religious affiliation. The two often overlap, however, explaining the potency of sectarianism. The state booty was not so much in the hands of the Alawites as in the possession of a cartel headed by Bashar and Maher al-Assad and members of the related Makhlouf family. A large segment of rural Alawites remain mired in poverty, while, by contrast, the Sunni Nahhas and Jood families of Latakia benefited from regime-espoused 'sweetheart' contracts and are among the most ardent regime loyalists – demonstrating that co-optation is contingent on affiliation with the professional classes rather than sect (Khudra, 2011).

Syrian Christians (especially Greek Orthodox, the most populous Christian sect in Syria) have historically been better educated and more urbanized than Muslims and do not generally belong to the lower classes (Stojanovic, 2013). Proportionately more Christians receive secondary education, join skilled professions and attend western-oriented, private and foreign language schools (Lib. of Cong., 2011). Under Hafez al-Assad, and in particular after the failed 1979–82 uprising, the Sunni underclass with ties to the Muslim Brotherhood was categorically denied state protection, jobs and opportunities, while anti-Islamist, secular Christians established connections (*wāsṭa*) with state officials and rose to socio-economic prominence (Interview III, 2012). Christians are also well represented in Syrian business networks, which have benefited from economic freedoms in a socialist state while preserving the security of the regime (Haddad, 2011; Sheperd, 2011b).

Muslim–Christian relations, and related conceptions of peripheries, are thus closely linked to class and urban–rural divides. According to one Christian woman, a university graduate from Damascus, 'they [protestors] are just rural troublemakers; the government should carry on trying to end this even if it means more deaths' ('Many Syrians', 2011). To be sure, many urban Sunni merchants have exhibited the same disdain for 'rabble' militia wreaking havoc in Aleppo or Damascus. While

Sunnis range from the poorest to the richest strata, as an Armenian Orthodox Syrian comments, 'you can safely say there are no poor Christians' (Interview IV, 2012). One interviewee, a 24-year-old Master's student from Damascus, answered that 'yes, of course being economically well-off has affected the decision not to protest' (Interview I, 2012). Others like Hind Kabawat contend that 'even lower class Christians don't blame the regime for anything. They suffer from Stockholm syndrome and can't imagine an alternative because the state TV says Christians need al-Assad to protect them' (Interview III, 2012).

Hence, even the small proportion of lower class Christians who suffer from the same protest-inducing factors as their Muslim compatriots – high unemployment, a devastating drought in the east, an inefficient public sector, the effects of international sanctions and the post-uprising collapse of the tourism industry – often disassociated socio-economic frustrations from the regime ('Sanctions against Syria', 2011). Indeed, state-sponsored propaganda – like *Donia TV* broadcasts of the funeral processions of Christian soldiers 'assassinated by thugs' alongside hysterical relatives – affirms that the regime has invested much of its energies in intertwining the fate of Christians with its own to scare them into submission, as authoritarian leaders did in Egypt and Iraq in 2011 (Donia TV, 2011).

Although they are better integrated with Muslims in big cities, Christians tend to be geographically segregated to a far more striking extent than their Egyptian counterparts. Since Ottoman times, districts and villages are clearly delineated along sectarian lines, such as the *Wadi al-Nasara*/Valley of Christians consisting of over 30 predominantly Greek Orthodox villages and the majority Assyrian governorate of al-Hasaka, home to the 75 per cent Christian city of Qamishly (Dalrymple, 2007). Members of the Armenian Orthodox Church – the second largest in Syria – are especially prone to self-segregation, rarely mixing with Muslims in less prosperous districts. The reductive Muslim–Christian dichotomy is thus problematic, considering the intrinsic and nuanced relationship between class-based identities and religious affiliations.

Syrian Christians: Alternative Factors Driving Acquiescence

Unwavering regime support emanating from church hierarchies further entrenches Christians in the regime's camp. In a statement dated 15 December 2011, the three Syrian patriarchs declared their absolute rejection of foreign intervention or any other threat to Syrian sovereignty ('Patriarchs' Message', 2012). Throughout 2011, the Armenian Orthodox patriarch instructed churchgoers to obey the government, support the president and keep a low profile (Interview IV, 2012). In September 2011, Lebanese Maronite Patriarch Rai III expressed concern over the future security of the region's religious minorities, urging the international community not to rush into resolutions that could topple al-Assad, a 'poor man who cannot work miracles' ('Rai', 2011). Archbishop Tabé called the demonstrators 'nothing but terrorists', adding that in any political system 'there are always 10 per cent who have to be sacrificed' (quoted in Berbner, 2011). This stance led George Sabra, the Christian president of the oppositional Syrian National Council and acting president of the Syrian National Coalition, to attribute the mass absence of Christian protestors to the lack of church-sponsored mobilization ('Al-kinīsa as-Soriyya', 2012). The Russian Orthodox Church's open support for the al-Assad regime may also be spurring similar attitudes among their Syrian counterparts. It is difficult, however, to determine whether the church response reflects the attitude of its constituents or creates it.

It is similarly problematic to ascertain whether such institutional displays of support on the part of the church are voluntary. The church leadership may well be coerced into obedience, constrained by the watchful eye of a praetorian government brandishing a carte blanche arrest policy born of the 1963 emergency law. Stories of attacks on Christian protestors – including the assassination of Father Basillius of Homs and the beating and detention of 20-year-old student activist Hadeel Kouky and actor Jalal al-Tawil – serve as warnings to their community and demonstrate the systematic silencing of dissident Christian voices, however rare they may be (Massoud, 2012; 'Actor', 2011; 'Al-'ab Basiliūs', 2011). As public statements could differ greatly from private sentiments, Christians may fear not only for their security tomorrow, but also today.

When choosing allegiances, Syrian Christians also consider the tragic experience of neighbouring Iraqi Christians and the on-going post-revolutionary struggle of Egyptian Copts. Syria borders with Lebanon and Iraq, which both deteriorated into sectarian conflicts and widespread Christian emigration in the absence of strong leadership. Much like al-Assad, Saddam Hussein cultivated a close relationship with the fellow minority Christian groups, which were perceived as collaborators and consequently targeted when the regime was toppled in 2003. Bloody sectarian attacks then forced the exodus of at least 330,000 Iraqi Christians to Syria, where refugees settled in Christian areas and brought stories of atrocities at the hands of the Muslim majority (Harrison, 2008; Interview III, 2012). The deeply discouraging effect of the Iraq experience is reflected in a December 2011 YouGov–Doha Debates poll, which found that of the 55 per cent of Syrians polled who supported al-Assad, the most common reason cited (46 per cent) was 'we do not want to see Syria become another Iraq' ('Syria's President', 2011).

The importance of military and political integration with the regime is reflected by Christians serving as generals, pilots and soldiers in the army and officers in the police force. Christians are counted among the late minister of defence Daoud Rajiha and the current Minister of State Joseph Sweid, as well as the head of the Syrian Central bank, Adib Mayaleh (Berbner, 2011). Although the highly influential despotic bureaucracy, presidential guard and intelligence services are controlled in part by an outer governmental layer of religious minorities such as Christians, the informal but dominant inner circle composed of Alawite security elites (and the weak Christian parliamentary presence) suggests that the regime has been cautious about totally co-opting Christians into its centre of decision-makers (Hinnebusch, 2008: 265; Ziadeh, 2011; Mikhail, 2008: 9).

Co-optation is also driven by the Alawites' unofficial incorporation of Christians in a power-sharing minority coalition underpinned by the belief that 'minorities protect minorities'. While constantly pandering to the Sunni majority, the al-Assad regime has historically portrayed itself as the protector of Syria's Christians. This politically expedient act of superficial solidarity led Christians to take comfort in their mutual 'minority-hood'. (Sheperd, 2011a). This strategic alliance stems from the Alawite desire to garner diverse allies to bolster legitimacy and create a pluralistic national identity, the Christian desire to break away from the inferior societal position of minorities and, most importantly, mutual concern of an Islamist takeover spurred by hegemonic Sunni rule.

Egyptian Copts and the Uprising

Coptic problems will not be solved by the revolution. But the struggle of all Egyptians is a separate issue, and the time finally came for the inevitable.

(Ragy Gendi, 52-year-old Copt – Interview VI, 2011)

Presence of Coptic Revolutionaries

Although no exact figures exist, the strong Coptic presence at Tahrir during the 25 January revolution is undeniable (Hennawi, 2011; Alwaṭanī, 2011; Free Copts, 2011; 'Mass in Tahrir Square,' 2012). Maged Adel, a youth co-ordinator and revolutionary from the Kasr el-Dobara Church in Tahrir Square, attests that more Copts were present than their proportion of the population would dictate (Interview V, 2012). Others interviewed maintain that Copts represented about 15 per cent of protestors, commensurate with the Coptic segment of the Egyptian population (Interview VIII, 2012). The Coptic presence in the Egyptian revolution was recognized and acclaimed by both liberals, such as MP Amr Hamzawy, and Islamists, such as Amr Derrag, head of the Brotherhood-founded Freedom and Justice Party in Giza ('New Parliamentarians', 2012; 'Egypt's new Democracy', 2011).

Unprecedented displays of national unity between Christian and Muslim protestors surfaced in the foreground of the global media, attesting to the presence of Coptic revolutionaries. Protest leaders intermittently read verses from the bible and anti-regime slogans, images of cross and crescent side by side were plastered across downtown Cairo and one of the most popular chants was 'Muslim, Christian, one hand!' Copts encircled praying Muslims amid chaos and harassment on Friday, 4 February 2011, with Muslims reciprocating by forming a human shield around Copts holding Mass at Tahrir (Nunns & Idle, 2011: 186; Kennedy, 2011). Despite the withdrawal of the police forces, not one attack on a church was reported during the 18 days of the revolution (Van Doorn-Harder, 2011). The well-publicized stories of Coptic revolutionaries and bloggers Maikel Nabil Sanad and Mina Daniel also attest to Coptic revolutionary activity (Knell, 2012; Knafo, 2011). The emphasis on national identity in Tahrir was key to the success of the revolution, as national unity discourse is the most salient when citizenship is informed by 'Egyptianness' (inclusive of peripheral groups) and weakest when citizenship is informed by religion (exclusive of peripheral groups) (Tadros, 2011).

Trans-sectarian Motivations to Protest

Copts protested for almost identical reasons to their Muslim compatriots. Christians were not immune from the decline of mean living standards, the sharp spike in food and energy prices, rising unemployment and chronic poverty, exacerbated by the government's refusal to up the minimum wage from a meagre $100 to $240 per month (Ismail, 2011). The Arab Opinion Index survey (2011) of 1,200 Egyptians found that corruption (33.1 per cent), a declining economic situation (23.9 per cent) and injustice (21.4 per cent) were the top reasons given by revolutionaries for their participation. As concluded by several Egyptian NGO reports, state-sanctioned corruption, oppression and despotism squandered the rights of Muslims and Christians alike ('PHRA', 2008). These findings are consistent with the recent trend of majorities and minorities in the Arab world being increasingly bound together in the 'threats they face, the rights they claim and the aspirations they voice', and thus equally invested in a shared future (Mitri, 1992: 68).

The agendas and attitudes of Coptic revolutionaries-turned-politicians also attest to the pan-Egyptian motivations to revolt. Mikail Jaber, a member of the Egyptian Union for Human Rights and a candidate for the Shura Council, prioritized agricultural subsidies, youth employment programmes, economic diversification and food security programmes for the poor (Hennawi, 2011). The Free Egyptians Party, founded by tycoon Naguib Sawiris, and Shaheer Ishak's Egypt Freedom Party aim to build a civil democracy that champions social justice, equal rights and the inherent dignity of all Egyptian citizens ('Main Principles', 2011). Official statements released in 2011 by the Holy Synod of the Coptic Orthodox Church following Mubarak's departure saluted Egyptians for 'combating anarchy and ruin, enhancing security, safety, social justice and national unity' in the 'battle against poverty, unemployment and corruption' – a credit to the pan-Egyptian approach of Coptic revolutionaries.

The notion that Copts protested for the same reasons as their Muslim compatriots is reflected in 15 surveys sent to Copts (by the authors) between the ages of 20 and 52 ('15 Egyptian Christians', 2012). Mina Kamal, a 25-year-old pharmacist from Tanta, underlined that 'corruption, minimal wages, inflation and unemployment in every house affecting both Copts and non-Copts needed to stop' (Interview II, 2012). And 41.7 per cent of revolutionaries (compared to 26.3 per cent of non-revolutionaries) said their religious identities were secondary to national or political party affiliations (Arab Opinion Index, 2011). Although Copts undergo additional hardship due to sectarian government policies, Copts distinguish between their struggle as Copts (a product of religious peripheralization) and their struggle as Egyptians (a product of socio-economic and political peripheralization) – with the revolution representing the latter.

Deteriorating Protections: The Myth of Mubarak's 'Secularism'

The decision to protest was made easier for Coptic revolutionaries by the flaws in the Egyptian secular model under Mubarak – with secular protections dismissed as superficial, driven by tactical expediency and declining in quality. Mubarak's administration frequently incited hostility towards minorities to distract attention away from criticisms of the regime, a reality that Coptic revolutionaries were quick to recognize (Elshahed, n.d.). This perspective differs greatly from the image of Mubarak as a protector of all Egyptians, consolidated by amicable public meetings with Pope Shenouda.

Under Mubarak, Copts continued to suffer from discriminatory state policies that disproportionately affected non-Muslims, a relic of the quasi-Islamic state inherited from Sadat. A potent example is the 'Islamization' of the national curriculum, which downplays Coptic history in biased textbooks that promote Islam as the only source of ethics and morality. Coptic protestors also resented the government's refusal to implement a unified legal code for building places of worship, failure to mitigate daily discriminatory practices, statistical underrepresentation of the Coptic population, subordinating legislation to *sharī'a* law and, most significantly, complicity in allowing violent sectarian attacks to be met with impunity (Abdel-Hakim, 2011; 'Egypt's Opposition', 2011). Suffering from 'double peripheralization', Copts thus suffered from government indifference and neglect at best, discrimination and persecution at worst, long before the outbreak of demonstrations – which added insult to socio-economic injury and catalysed Coptic rebellion.

The Copts Who Stayed Home

Despite the strong Coptic presence at Tahrir, pro-democracy Copts were not the majority within their community (Interview VIII, 2012; Interview VII, 2012). Those who chose not to protest preferred a secular autocrat who extended at least titular secular protections to religious minorities to a precarious future under Islamists loudly calling for a *sharī'a* state. Such fears, as in Syria, are not baseless: the Muslim Brotherhood maintained an ambiguous, patronizing stance towards non-Muslim minorities, the Salafist agenda often morphed into anti-Coptic hostility, and well-organized Islamist groups were poised to (and did) capitalize on post-Mubarak instability in order to gain power. Coptic priest Father Boulad reflects the prevalent fear of Islamist rule signalling worsening conditions for Copts: 'right now, [Copts] might be paralysed, but the future could mean death' ('Le père Boulad', 2011). The fear of an Islamist takeover also contributed to the estimated emigration of some 250,000 Copts by the end of 2012 (Khalil, 2011).

The fragmentation at the heart of the Coptic community depended on whether Copts viewed the revolution as an opportunity to reclaim rights and liberties, and perhaps open the door for resolving Coptic issues in the future, or a perilous risk that would grant emboldened Muslim zealots control of Egypt and further alienate Copts – a retreat from public life they can ill afford (Morqos, 2009). Copts were also divided along generational lines; young Copts stood their ground at Tahrir while the older generation remained sensitive to media reports of fast-moving Islamist political gains (Beach, 2011). Coptic revolutionaries were further segmented depending on their perception of Islamists. Some felt that Copts needed to be an integral part of Egypt's political future precisely *because* of the popularity of Islamists. Others still gave little thought to Islamists, hoping that the Islamist threat was an empty fear-mongering tactic employed by Mubarak's regime. After all, the 25 January uprising was not perceived as an Islamic revolution even if it did bring Islamists to power.

Egyptian Copts: Alternative Factors Driving Activity

Though not a primary determinant of political activity, among Copt-specific catalysts to protest was growing frustration with the church leadership, which peaked when, at the height of the protests, Pope Shenouda ordered Copts to stay at home, proclaiming that 'we are with you [Mubarak]', and stating on national television that Copts were not participating in the revolution, omitting any mention of the revolution in the Sunday mass held less than a week after Mubarak's departure (quoted in Sanad, 2011; 'Pope Shenouda's Sermon', 2011). This reflected a continuation of a historical collaboration whereby the church retained autonomy over communal affairs in exchange for mobilizing Christian support for Mubarak's National Democratic Party (NDP). These concessions, however, did not trickle down to the Coptic citizenry, any more than Mufti Ahmed Hassoun or Sheikh Buti's staunchly pro-al-Assad stance in Syria can be taken as barometer for all Syrian Sunnis (Tadros, 2010). Especially following Pope Shenouda's tepid response to the 2010 Christmas eve drive-by shooting in Nag' Hammadi, Copts began to openly question the church's alliance with the regime and resent clerics for overstepping their spiritual mandate and monopolizing Copt–state relations. As many Copts viewed the church's pro-regime stance as unwarranted, unnecessary and illegitimate, some protested not in spite of the church's disapproval, but because of it.

The fresh memory of the Two Saints Church bombing in Alexandria on New Year's Eve 2010/11, mere weeks before the start of the 25 January revolution, had an even stronger effect on the Coptic proclivity to protest. Explosives killed 25 churchgoers and injured more than 200 as over 1,000 worshippers attended the midnight service (Abdel-Fattah, 2011). The incident sparked grassroots anger among Copts and moderate Muslim sympathizers. Although Copts were afflicted by the same inescapable sense of immobility common to all Egyptians, the Alexandria bombing served as a reminder that Copts suffered from additional grievances, leading them to identify the attack as a precursor to the revolution and affirming the link between sectarian violence and revolutionary activity theorized by Coptic scholar Paul Sedra (2011).

Another Copt-specific motivation to revolt was frustration at the disproportionately low political representation of Copts. Although Mubarak fulfilled his constitutional prerogative to appoint Copts to the ten parliamentary seats reserved for underrepresented groups, Copts were disillusioned with out-of-touch candidates chosen by the state, not elected through a popular vote (Khalil & Ramadan, 2010; Tadros, 2011). Copts were similarly excluded in the November 2010 parliamentary elections, where they occupied a paltry 3.5 per cent of seats. From local office to the Shura Council, Copts are likewise absent, largely due to the failure of the NDP to nominate Coptic candidates (Tadros, 2011). Following the 2005 elections, only one of 18 ministerial positions was occupied by a Copt – the relatively insignificant minister of environmental affairs, further fuelling Christian frustration ('Egypt's Cabinet', 2012). Furthermore, (young) Copts may also have identified with the Christian-friendly, liberal-leaning and politically active civil society opposition groups that supported the revolution. However, their efficacy in encouraging Copts, whose associational tradition likewise 'occup[ied] a liberal space that is otherwise limited in Egyptian politics' (Rowe, 2009: 124), to rebel is difficult to determine.

Conclusions

The repressive regimes of al-Assad and Mubarak did provide significant security for minorities, but not unlike the Iraqi case, the 'republic of fear', by curtailing freedom of thought and speech, created a pent-up society of frustration, crony capitalism, perilous socio-economic polarization and dissimulation which is now imploding. With its influx of foreign fighters, Syria today has become a battleground for a Sunni–Shia, Israeli–Iranian, ISIS–al-Qaeda showdown – with Gulf states, Russia, Turkey and the US backing the antagonists financially and militarily, while Syrians themselves serve as ready cannon-fodder (Cole, 2015; Chivers & Schmitt, 2013; Keinon, 2013; Nasir & Macdonald, 2011; Zelin, 2014; Hersh, 2014). We do not, however, discount the domestic drivers of the civil war, even as we do not seek to attribute all the syndromes of state collapse and social disarray to clashing communal identities pure and simple. Rather, sectarianism in each country tended to erupt in its most vicious form to the degree that the peripheralization of class and confession overlapped. The urban Sunni elites (in both Syria and Egypt) occupied even higher echelons of the social pyramid than the Christians, and thus largely remained beholden to the status quo. It is by no means fortuitous that popular uprisings first erupted in the rural and peripheral areas of Tunisia (Sid Abu Zeid), Bahrain and Syria (Idlib, Dera'a, Deir al Zor), while the lucrative sectors of the economy remained in the control of thin elites and nepotistic family networks. Furthermore, Copts protested because of pan-Egyptian grievances, confirming that shared socio-economic conditions can lead national identities to supersede sectarian affiliations. The concept of 'periphery' is thus multifaceted; Syrian Christians fear the religion-based, peripheral designation that may come with an Islamist-driven revolution, negating a long history of social prominence through state-espoused structures of business and political opportunities. Meanwhile, many Egyptian Christians had little to lose by overturning a regime that compounded their status as a religious, political and socio-economic peripheral group (sharing the last two designations with most Sunni compatriots).

In the wake of the 2011 revolts, the Arab world is at an ideological crossroads, unwilling to become a post-revolutionary Iran but unable to become post-revolutionary France, with pluralism – both religious and political – hanging precariously in the balance. As Christians participate politically almost exclusively through secular platforms, elected Islamist governments espousing religiously coloured notions of citizenship could discourage Christian participation in public life by playing up their peripheral status and excluding them from the highest office, thus accelerating the emigration of the region's dwindling Christian population. Although Christians view themselves as an integral part of the national fabric, increasingly strident Islamic fundamentalism heightens minority-centric consciousness among Christians, exacerbating their peripheralization (Mitri, 1992: 67). In this way, Islamists and religious minorities can be seen as peripheral groups, with the former ascending throughout the region to claim the centre hitherto held by relatively pluralistic – if militaristic – Muslim regimes.

However, revitalized political participation among Egyptian Copts has allowed the community to make tentative political gains through the liberal bloc alliance of moderate Christians and Muslims disturbed by sectarian strife, concerned with maintaining national unity and hardships felt by Christians (Carr, 2011; Mitri, 1992: 67). Indeed, Coptic political activity directly before, during and since the revolution (notably at Maspero) unmistakably refutes previous assumptions of depoliticization and self-imposed isolation in solemn acceptance of peripheral relegation. The tenacious Pope Tawadros' co-authoring of the transition roadmap that contributed to Morsi's ousting and the election of Hala Shukralla (a woman and a Copt) as Mohammed El-Baradei's successor at the helm of the Constitution Party are notable examples of political expression emerging within and outside the church. This relatively recent strategy of creating political opportunity structures by engaging with the public sphere should be praised, as Mariz Tadros (2010) argues, as a rare bright spark of 'newfound youth determination to participate in politics and the highest forms of citizen action', and one step closer to Egypt's political centre.

As the polarization of Syrian society intensifies, so too does the eagerness for sectarian revenge – with Christians caught at the centre of this crucible. Betting on al-Assad will provoke the hostility that Christians are desperately struggling to evade, yet siding with the dissidents might incite the wrath of regime troops and accelerate the emergence of a Sunni, sectarian regime. Statements giving lip service to a civil state by elements from the Syrian opposition will do little to redress the underlying demographic, socio-economic, ideological and geopolitical challenges which feed the raging fire of communalism. Whatever trajectory takes shape in Egypt and Syria, the inclusion or exclusion of religious minorities in the ruling bargain will undoubtedly be at the heart of the political predicament of an Arab world in convulsion.

Funding

This work was supported by NPRP [grant number 6-028-5-006 from the Qatar National Research Fund (a member of Qatar Foundation)]. The statements made herein are solely the responsibility of the authors

Disclosure statement

No potential conflict of interest was reported by the authors.

References

10 Syrian Christians between the ages of 23–53, Survey. January 2012. Conducted by authors.
15 Egyptian Christians between the ages of 18–52, Survey. January 2012. Conducted by authors.
Library of Congress, A Country Study: Syria (2011), Available at www.lcweb2.loc.gov/frd/cs/sytoc.html
    (accessed on 10 November 2011).

Abdel-Fattah, M. (2011) Two Saints Church celebrates christmas in black, *Al-Ahram Weekly* (Cairo), 8 January.

Abdel-Hakim, M. (2011) Misr Laysat Kheyr Lel'aqbat, *United Copts*, Available at www.copts-united. com/Arabic2011/Article.php?I=1085&A=43151 (accessed 29 March 2012).

Abu Fadel, Z. (2011) Sectarianism dominates the movement against Syria's government, *The Arab American News* (Dearborn), 24 June.

Actor Jalal al-Tawil Attacked After a Damascus Protest on 19/12/2011 (2011) *Syrian Christians for Democracy*, Available at http://syrian-christian.org/actor-jalal-al-tawil-attacked-in-damascus-protest-on-19122011-arabic/ (accessed 8 August 2013).

Al-'ab Basiliūs Shaheed al-Kinīsa (2011) *Syrian Christians for Democracy*, Available at www.syrian-christian.org/ الأب-باسيليوس-شهيد-الكنيس (accessed 8 August 2013).

Al-kinīsa as-Soriyya 'okherat Mushārakat al-Misiḥiyīn fī al-thawra (2012) *Al-Arabiya*, 4 February 2012, Available at www.alarabiya.net/articles/2012/02/03/192394.html, visited 21 August 2012.

All Egyptians Suffer Discrimination: PHRA (2008) *Egypt News* (Cairo), 26 June.

Amnesty International, Refugees in Syria, Suffering in Silence (2008), Available at www.amnesty.org/en/library/info/MDE14/010/2008/en (accessed 25 September 2011).

Amr Hamzawy Calls on New Parliamentarians to 'Prove Their Loyalty to the Revolution.' (2012) *Al-Ahram Online* (Cairo), 8 January.

Armstrong, M. (2014) Syria's latest battle: the PR fight over sanctuary for Christians, *Christian Science Monitor* (Beirut), 7 April.

Ayalon, R. (1999) Egypt's coptic Pandora's box, in: G. Ben-Dor & O. Bengio (Eds) *Minorities and the State in the Arab World* (New York: Lynne Rienner).

Bashar Al-Assad Protects Christians (2012) *YouTube*, Available at www.youtube.com/watch?v=cQY26A8sbcc (accessed 3 March 2012).

Beach, A. (2011) Fearing Islamists and chaos, some Christians opt to flee, *Egypt Today* (Cairo), 11 April.

Berbner, B. (2011) The tolerant dictator: Christians side with Al-Assad out of fear, *Der Spiegel*, 30 November.

Blanford, N. (2011) Q&A with a Syrian Jihadist: minorities have nothing to fear in post-Al-Assad Syria, *Christian Science Monitor*, 29 September.

Brookings Institute Doha (2011) Lecture by Sheikh Ali Sadr Al-Din Al-Bayanouni, former secretary-general of the Syrian Muslim brotherhood, September 19 (Doha: Diplomatic Club).

Carr, S. (2011) Sectarianism, reconciliation and complexity in Al-Nahda, *Egypt Independent* (Cairo), 16 February.

Chivers, J.C. & E. Schmitt (2013) Arms airlift to Syria rebels expands, with Aid from C.I.A, New York Times, 24 March, Available at http://www.nytimes.com/2013/03/25/world/middleeast/arms-airlift-to-syrian-rebels-expands-with-cia-aid.html?pagewanted=all&_r=1& (accessed 5 February 2015).

Christian Soldier Killed in Syria (2011) *Donia TV*, Available at http://www.youtube.com/watch?v=lVs3z33bodY (accessed 2 November 2011).

Cole, J. (2015) Israel's Syria strike: is it trying to help al-Qaeda vs. Hizbullah & Iran? *Informed Comment*, January 20, Available at http://www.juancole.com/2015/01/israels-strike-hizbullah.html (accessed 5 February 2015).

Dalrymple, W. (2007) Ignore the hype: Syria shouldn't be demonized, *The Spectator*, 27 October.

Dorell, O. (2012) Syrian rebels said to favor democracy, *USA Today*, 23 September.

Egypt's Opposition Demands Unified Law for Building Houses of Worship (2011) *Al-Ahram Online* (Cairo), 14 January.

Egyptian Coptic Christian Mass in Tahrir Square (2012) *YouTube*, Available at www.youtube.com/watch?v=qDGqVUx_3Hc&feature=fvsr (accessed 10 March 2012).

El Khawaga, D. (1998) The political dynamics of the copts: giving the community an active role, in: A. Pacini (Ed.) *Christian Communities in the Arab Middle East: The Challenge of the Future* (Oxford: Oxford University Press).

Elshahed, K. (n.d.) Breaking the fear barrier of Mubarak's regime, *Social Science Research Council*, Available at http://www.ssrc.org/pages/breaking-the-fear-barrier-of-mubarak-s-regime/ (accessed 31 October 2012).

Ezzat, D. (2009) Blessed are the Egyptian people, *Al-Ahram Weekly* (Cairo), 8 January.

Fearing Change, Syria's Christians Back Al-Assad (2011) *New York Times* (Saydnaya), 27 September.

Haddad, B. (2011) *Business Networks in Syria: The Economy of Authoritarian Resilience* (Stanford: Stanford Press).

Hamzawy, A. (2010) Egypt's legitimacy crisis in the aftermath of flawed elections, *Carnegie Endowment for International Peace*, Available at www.egyptelections.carnegieendowment.org/2010/12/02/egypt%E2%80%99s-legitimacy-crisis-in-the-aftermath-of-flawed-elections, 1 December. visited on 10 November 2011.

Hanna, M. (1980) *Na'm Aqbāṭ wa Lākin Miṣriyūn* (Cairo: Madboole' Publishers).

Harrison, F. (2008) Christians besieged in Iraq, *BBC* (London), 13 March.

Haykal, M. (1992) Copts are no minority, *Al-Ahram* (Cairo), 27 April.

Hennawi, H. (2011) Istirdād al-Karāma, *United Copts*, Available at www.copts-united.com/Arabic2011/Article.php?I=1057&A=41630 (accessed 10 October 2012).

Hersh, S. (2014) The red line and the rat line, *London Review of Books*, 36(8), pp. 21–24.

Hinnebusch, A. (2008) Modern Syrian politics, *History Compass*, 6(1), pp. 263–285. doi:10.1111/j.1478-0542.2007.00487.x.

Ibrahim, V. (2010) *The Copts of Egypt: The Challenges of Modernisation and Identity* (London: I.B. Tauris).

In Egypt's New Democracy, Copts feel Sidelined (2011) *The Jerusalem Post* (Cairo), 20 November.

Inside Jabhat Al-Nusra, the Most Extreme Wing of Syria's Struggle (2012) *The Telegraph* (Beirut), 2 December.

International Religious Freedoms Report for 2011 (2011) *US Department of State*, Available at www.state.gov/j/drl/rls/irf/religiousfreedom/index.htm#wrapper (accessed 17 February 2012).

Ismail, S. (2011) A private estate called Egypt, *The Guardian* (London), 6 February.

Jangling Sectarian Nerves (2012) *The Economist*, 7 January.

Kabawat, H. (2012a) The Al-Assad delusion, *The National Post*, January 30.

Keinon, H. (2013) 'Tehran-Damascus-Beirut arc is the greatest danger,' says outgoing Israeli envoy to US Michael Oren, *The Jerusalem Post*, September 17, Available at http://www.jpost.com/Syria-Crisis/Oren-Jerusalem-has-wanted-Assad-ousted-since-the-outbreak-of-the-Syrian-civil-war-326328 (accessed 5 February 2015).

Kennedy, H. (2011) Muslims return favor, join hands with Christian protestors for mass in Cairo's Tahrir square, *New York Daily News*, 7 February.

Khalil, E. & R. Ramadan (2010) Coptic leaders betrayed by parliamentary appointments, *Egypt Independent* (Cairo), 12 December.

Khalil, E. (2011) NGO report: 93,000 copts left Egypt since March, *Egypt Independent* (Cairo), 25 September.

Khudra (2011) What do Sunnis intend for Alawis following regime change? *Syria Comment*, Available at http://www.joshualandis.com/blog/?p=10267&cp=all (accessed 17 October 2012).

Knafo, S. (2011) Maikel Nabil Sanad, on hunger strike in Egypt, is dying: family, *The Huffington Post* (New York), 15 September.

Knell, Y. (2012) Cairo's copts mourn their 'Egyptian Guevara,', *BBC* (Cairo), 15 October.

Kodmani, B. (2011) To topple Al-Assad, it takes a minority, *New York Times*, August 3.

Kremer, S. (2012) Christen in Syrien: Die Angst Vor Dem Sturz Al-Assads, *Tages Schau*, 15 January.

Le père Boulad: Le Printemps Arabe et les Frères Musulmans (2011) *LeBlogCopte*, Available at www.dailymotion.com/video/xonkun_le-pere-boulad-le-printemps-arabe-et-les-freres-musulmans_news (accessed 23 February 2011).

Lund, A. (2012) Syrian Jihadism, *Swedish Institute of International Affairs*, Available at http://www.ui.se/upl/files/76917.pdf (accessed 17 September 2012).

Main Principles (2011) *Free Egyptians Party Website*, Available at www.almasreyeenalahrrar.org/EgyptiansAbroad/OurPrinciples.aspx (accessed 21 December 2011).

Makari, P. (2007) *Conflict and Cooperation: Christian-Muslim Relations in Contemporary Egypt* (Syracuse: Syracuse University Press).

Mamarbachi-Seurat, M. (2011) Honte Aux Chretiens Syriens!, *Le Monde*, 17 September.

Massoud, R. (2012) La menace des chabbiha: 'Ton Beau Visage, Nous le Brûlerons avec l'Acide,', *L'Orient Le Jour* (Beirut), 25 February.

Mikhail, B. (2008) Un Statut Enviable, Ou Une Sérénité Simulée, *Confluences Méditerranée*, 66(3), p. 45.

Mitri, T. (1992) Minorities in the Middle East, in: J. Nielsen (Ed.) *Religion and Citizenship in Europe and the Arab World* (London: Grey Seal).

Morqos, S. (2009) The coptic question, *Al-Ahram Weekly* (Cairo), 31 December.

Moussalli, H. (1998) The Christians of Syria, in: A. Pacini (Ed.) *Christian Communities in the Arab Middle East: The Challenge of the Future* (Oxford: Oxford University Press).

Nisan, M. (Ed.) (2002) *Minorities in the Middle East: A History of Struggle and Self-expression* (Jefferson, NC: McFarland).

Nunns, A. & N. Idle (2011) *Tweets from Tahrir* (New York: OR Books).

Nasir, L. & A. Macdonald (2011) Libyan Islamist commander swaps combat rig for suit, *Reuters*, 11 November, Available at http://www.reuters.com/article/2011/11/11/us-libya-islamist-belhaj-idUSTRE7AA52320111111 (accessed 5 February 2015).

Egyptian Cabinet (2012), Official Egyptian government website, available at www.egyptiancabinet.gov.eg/Cabinet/Cabinet.aspx (accessed 8 October 2012).

Official Statement by the Holy Synod of the Coptic Orthodox Church (2011) *Alwaṭanī*, Available at www.al-Wataninet.com/al-Watani_Article_Details.aspx?A=13245 (accessed 2 November 2011).

Official websites of *United Copts, Alwaṭanī* and *Free Copts* (accessed 23 November 2013).

Patriarchs' Message to their Faithful and to their Fellow Citizens in Syria (2012) *Melkite Greek Catholic Church Official Website*, Available at https://melkite.org/patriarchate/patriarchs%E2%80%99-message-to-their-faithful-and-to-their-fellow-citizens-in-syria (accessed 3 December 2012).

Patterson, M. (2011) Syria in crisis, *America Magazine*, Available at http://americamagazine.org/issue/5124/article/syria-crisis (accessed 31 March 2014).

People's Assembly (2015) Official Syrian government website, Available at http://parliament.sy/index.php?pageLang=en (accessed 8 October 2012).

Petrou, M. (2011) Not just another Arab revolt, *Maclean's*, 124(32), pp. 26–27.

Pope Shenouda's Sermon Omits Revolution (2011) *Egypt Independent* (Cairo), 17 February.

Putz, U. (2012) Christians free from radical rebels in Syria, *Der Spiegel* (Al Qa), July 25.

Rai Urges International Community to Give Al-Assad Time to Implement Reform (2011) *The Daily Star* (Beirut), September 9.

Rowe, P. (2009) Building coptic civil society: Christian groups and the state in Mubarak's Egypt, *Middle Eastern Studies*, 45(1), pp. 111–126. doi:10.1080/00263200802548147.

Rustum, A. (1966) *Bashir Bayna al-Sultan wa al-'Aziz Volume I* (Beirut: Manshurat al-Jami'at al-Lubnaniyah).

Sanad, M. (2011) Bābā Shnūda, wa Tārīkh ṭawīl min Nifāq al-ḥokām, *Maikel Nabil Sanad's Blog*, Available at www.maikelnabil.com/2011/02/blog-post_3584.html (accessed 23 October 2011).

Sanctions Against Syria: As Effective As Bullets, Maybe (2011) *The Economist* (Damascus), December 3.

Scott, H.M. (Ed.) (1990) *Enlightened Absolutism: Reform and Reformers in Later Eighteenth Century Europe* (Ann Arbor, MI: University of Michigan Press).

Scott, R. (2010) *The Challenge of Political Islam* (Stanford: Stanford University Press).

Seale, P. (2011) Averting civil war in Syria, *The Middle East Online*, Available at http://www.middle-east-online.com/english/?id=49164 (accessed 3 March 2012).

Sedra, P. (2011) Copts as Egypt's conscience, *Al-Akhbar* (Cairo), 21 December.

Sheperd, E. (2011a) Al-Assad is not our friend, *Syrian Christians for Democracy*, Available at http://syrian-christian.org/dr-elian-shepherd-blog/ (accessed September 25 2012).

Sheperd, E. (2011b) Syrian Christians and the missed opportunity, *Syrian Christians for Democracy*, Available at http://syrian-christian.org/dr-elian-shepherd-blog/ (accessed 25 September 2012).

Sherlock, R. & C. Malouf (2012) Syria: Christians take up arms for first time, *The Telegraph* (Beirut), September 12.

Stojanovic, D. (2013) Beleaguered Syrian Christians fear future, *Associated Press* (Damascus), 28 October.

Syria Crisis: ISIS Imposes Rules on Christians in Raqqa (2014) *BBC*, February 27.

Syria's Christians Back Al-Assad, Dread Unknown Future (2011) *Sunday Mail* (Damascus), 12 November.

Syria's Christians Live in Fear (2012) *YouTube*, Available at www.youtube.com/watch? v=SieYTLsWaEM (accessed 2 March 2012).

Syria's President Al-Assad- Should he resign? (2011) *Doha Debates and YouGov Poll Report*, Available at www.clients.squareeye.net/uploads/doha/polling/YouGovSirajDoha%20Debates-%20President%20Al-Assad%20report.pdf (accessed 2 March 2012).

Syrian Archbishop Says Give Al-Assad a Chance (2012) *Now Lebanon* (Beirut), January 11.

Tadros, M. (2010) The sectarian incident that won't go away, *Middle East Research and Information Project*, Available at http://www.merip.org/mero/mero030510 (accessed 29 March 2014).

Tadros, M. (2011) A state of Sectarian denial, *Middle East Research and Information Project*, Available at http://www.merip.org/mero/mero011111 (accessed 29 March 2014).

The Arab Opinion Index (2011) *Arab Center for Research and Policy Studies*, Available at english. dohainstitute.org/release/5083cf8e-38f8-4e4a-8bc5-fc91660608b0 (accessed 10 October 2012).

Van Doorn-Harder, N. (2011) Egypt: does the revolution include copts? *Open Democracy*, 10 October.

We Are All Syria (2012) *Facebook*, Available at https://www.facebook.com/We.Are.All.Syria (accessed 19 October 2012).

Why Many Syrians Still Support Al-Assad (2011) *Christian Science Monitor* (Damascus), September 14.

Zaki Stephanous, A. (2010) *Political Islam, Citizenship and Minorities: The Future of Arab Christians in the Islamic Middle East* (Lanham, MD: University Press of America).

Zelin, A. (2011) Rally 'round the Jihadist, *Foreign Policy*, Available at https://www.washingtoninstitute. org/policy-analysis/view/rally-round-the-jihadist (accessed 30 March 2014).

Zelin, A. (2014) The war between ISIS and al-Qaeda for supremacy of the global Jihadist movement, *The Washington Institute*, June, Available at http://www.washingtoninstitute.org/policy-analysis/view/the-war-between-isis-and-al-qaeda-for-supremacy-of-the-global-jihadist (accessed 5 February 2015).

Ziadeh, R. (2011) *Power and Policy in Syria: Intelligence Services, Foreign Relations and Democracy* (Washington, DC: Library of Modern Middle East Studies).

Interviews

Interview I, 24-year-old Masters' student from Damascus. E-mail. 30 January 2012.

Interview II, Mina Kamal, 25-year-old Coptic pharmacist from Tanta. E-mail. 3 January 2012.

Interview III, Hind Kabawat, Senior Research Associate, George Mason University. Skype. 10 April 2012.

Interview IV, 23-year-old Syrian-Armenian from Aleppo. Doha. 8 April 2012.

Interview V, Maged Adel, Youth Coordinator, Kasr el-Dobara church. Cairo. 15 February 2012.

Interview VI, Ragy Gendi, 52-year-old Coptic auditor from Cairo. Abu Dhabi. 19 December 2011.

Interview VII, Wafik, 29-year-old Coptic engineer from Cairo. Cairo. 12 February 2012.

Interview VIII, Wasseem, 35-year-old Coptic telecommunications specialist from Cairo. Cairo. 21 February 2012.

Plus ça Change? Observing the Dynamics of Morocco's 'Arab Spring' in the High Atlas

SYLVIA I. BERGH[*] & DANIELE ROSSI-DORIA[†]

*International Institute of Social Studies, Erasmus University Rotterdam, The Hague, The Netherlands, †The Hague, The Netherlands

ABSTRACT *This contribution focuses on the 'Arab Spring' in Morocco and on the interactions between the mainly urban-based activists that made up the 20 February Movement (F20M), and the population in rural areas. Based on six weeks of fieldwork between November 2013 and March 2014, mostly in the areas in and near Marrakech, we find that while the urban F20M events stimulated and inspired protests in rural areas, in practice there were only sporadic contacts based on the activists' personal feelings of belonging rather than their organizational membership. This is mainly due to discursive disconnects between the centre and periphery. As for the outcomes, in particular the new constitution, many respondents believe that nothing has changed so far.*

Introduction

This contribution focuses on the 'Arab Spring' in Morocco and on the interactions between the mainly urban-based activists that made up the 20 February Movement (F20M), and the population in rural areas. The 'Arab Spring' in Morocco is mainly represented by the F20M, which led a wave of protests against the widely perceived social ills (such as considerable levels of poverty, inequality, unemployment and widespread corruption) and raised the political consciousness of the average Moroccan citizen. However, the F20M did not lead to a revolution and to the overthrow of the regime as happened in Tunisia, Egypt and Libya. This is mainly due to the swift constitutional response by the king,[1] who announced a new constitution in March 2011, and the subsequent referendum in July of the same year. The new constitution includes important provisions for 'advanced regionalization' as well as the recognition of *Amazigh* as an official language. The case of Morocco is interesting because, together with most of the Gulf States and Jordan in particular, it can be considered an exception on the 'Arab Spring' scene because the defensive democratization strategies that brought about limited reforms (Kamel & Huber, 2015) defused the opposition while the power bases of the central regime remained intact.

The monarchy and the power structures surrounding it called the *makhzen* (Willis, 2002: 7) are key actors in Morocco. The 2011 constitution did not change the fact that the king holds a powerful role as arbiter between the various forces in the population, intervening from time to time to (re)define the rules of the game (Desrues, 2013: 414). However, civic activism against authoritarian rule does know a long history in Morocco, including the 'bread riots' in June 1981 when the bread price rose due to IMF conditions. Since the mid-2000s, the number of riots and protests has increased sharply, thanks to the more liberal political climate. For example, local groups (called 'co-ordinations') affiliated with national human rights associations have regularly mobilized people to protest against increased costs of living as a result of cuts in subsidies, unemployment, or the privatization of water and sanitation services, both in urban and rural/peripheral areas (see Bennafla & Emperador, 2010; Bogaert, 2015; Lahbib, 2011: 18; Saadi, 2012). Some of these groups were or are still part of the coalition that came to be known as the 20 February Movement. The F20M is thus the 'heir to earlier demonstrations and the culmination of a broad process in which a space of protest was formed' (Desrues, 2013: 416).

While quite a few studies have examined the F20M, its strategies and outcomes (see Benchemsi, 2012; Dalmasso, 2012; Desrues, 2012, 2013; Fernández Molina, 2011; González Riera, 2011; Hoffmann & König, 2013; Pace & Cavatorta, 2012), this article focuses on centre–periphery relations, in terms of the organizational and ideological linkages and commonalities as well as on the divergences between activists in urban and rural areas. It also examines the main means of communications between these groups, and considers their perceptions in terms of outcomes, in particular certain provisions in the new constitution.

By analysing the differences between urban-based activism and rural protest, this article finds that while the F20M tried to mobilize rural populations for its purposes, the rural populations did not try to mobilize the F20M for theirs. As will be shown below, this divergence has its origin in the different understanding of what the demand for social justice represented in the two areas: while the urban-based activists focused on the constitutional arrangements and demanded mainly political change, the population in the rural areas prioritized access to basic infrastructures and services and economic development issues. Hence, peripheral populations did not discursively connect their mainly socio-economic demands to the civic democratic struggle of the central movement.

The article is organized as follows: the next section presents the methodology, followed by an analysis of the rural periphery's opportunity structure. The F20M's main actors, demands and local organization are then introduced, before addressing the main topic – the mobilization strategies deployed by the urban activists in rural areas and the constraints they faced in doing so. The article then discusses the perception of the outcomes of the F20M before concluding.

73

Methodology

This article is based on qualitative fieldwork. The aim was to interview at least one member of each of the most representative F20M associations, political parties and trade unions both in urban areas, namely Marrakech and Rabat, and in a rural area in the High Atlas, namely the Al Haouz province between the town of Ait Ourir and the Zat Valley, in particular in the municipality of Tighedouine. This area was chosen for two reasons. First, the town of Ait Ourir and the Zat valley can be considered part of a marginalized 'periphery' characterized by limited economic activities, dependence on the Marrakech urban area, as well as weak basic infrastructures in terms of transport and social services. The main sources of income are small-scale agriculture and small enterprises, and many young people work in Marrakech or on the large farming areas near Agadir.

Second, we chose this area because both of us have previously conducted fieldwork there (Bergh in 2005–06 and Rossi-Doria in 2012), and this has facilitated our access to local associations and people. This allowed us to gather data on the rural people's perspectives and the linkages between urban- and rural-based activists and activities.

This research is based on six weeks of fieldwork conducted during November 2013–March 2014 by the second author. In total, the second author conducted semi-structured interviews[2] with 26 activists and respondents representing 17 organizations, as well as participant observation of some association meetings. The respondents were of various age groups, both male and female, and diverse professions. The interviews were conducted in French, English, Spanish and, with the help of an interpreter, in Arabic and *Amazigh*, mostly one-on-one but sometimes also with small groups.[3]

In order to select respondents for the interviews, a purposive sampling and snowball sampling strategy was used during the research fieldwork (Patton, 1990: 169–176; Albridge & Levine, 2001: 94–123). The choice of this sampling strategy was due to the structure of the F20M, composed of different socio-political groups in touch with each other, often in the same political area (trade unions, leftist parties and associations), or united by the same religious–political militancy (Islamist parties or groups), or by a common identity and cultural claims (*Amazigh* associations). This sampling strategy has been useful to identify the respondents among the F20M urban-based activists as well as those in the rural area and permitted us to get in touch with the village and town associations thanks to the previous contacts that the authors had made.

The Opportunity Structure of a Southern Moroccan Periphery

For this study, we chose the area south of Marrakech, including a municipality at the foot of the High Atlas (Tighedouine). The main village, where the municipal 'town hall' (*commune*) is located, could be understood as a centre to the other villages within its administrative borders, some of which are situated at very high altitudes or deep inside the Zat valley, and are difficult to access due to the lack of all-weather roads.

For our purpose, though, we consider the main village to be part of the periphery, dependent economically and politically on several centres: Ait Ourir, a larger town about 30 km away on the way to Marrakech, then the city of Marrakech itself where many villagers work or own property, and finally the capital Rabat, where important decisions on public services and development projects are made that impact on the village. Hence, rather than a linear centre–periphery relationship, we prefer to think in terms of concentric circles or spheres of influence at various scales which villagers can both act upon but are also impacted by. The notions of centre and periphery are thus always relational and relative.

Based on Rokkan (1999: 114), we adopt the notion of vertical peripherality (in addition to horizontal peripherality, which understands a periphery only in geographical terms) which draws our attention to the interactions between groups of actors.[4] A periphery can thus also be described as an opportunity structure that offers various possibilities of action to its inhabitants (Rokkan, 1999: 115). These possibilities are constrained or enabled by the periphery's distance from the dominant centre(s), by differences in resources and feelings of identity, and by dependence on the centre(s) in political decision making, economically and with regard to culture. These factors can combine to create uncertainty, ambivalence and even division within the periphery's population as they may feel part of the system, yet are marginal to it, and feel that their sense of separate identity is being threatened by central agencies (Rokkan, 1999: 115).

This last point refers to the (real or imagined) boundaries between the periphery and the remainder of the territory controlled from the centre, and the degree to which they can be penetrated by transactions across them. According to Rokkan (1999: 116), such transactions can be of an economic nature (imports/exports of goods, services, labour, credits, investments and subsidies); cultural (transfers of messages, norms, lifestyles, ideologies, myths, ritual systems – we would also add communication technologies), and political (conflicts over territorial rights, blockades, alliances and conflicts or accommodations between elite groups). Going back to the idea of an opportunity structure, we can ask, 'how far do peripheral actors remain dependent on the resources of the centre and how can they realistically become more independent?' (Kühn & Bernt, 2013: 315).

In the Moroccan case, the opportunity structure of the periphery studied here (namely the mountainous areas south of Marrakech with a relatively high level of poverty[5]) was and still is limited in the sense that 'the power of the Moroccan state is thoroughly insinuated into mountain life' through officers employed by various ministries, notably the Ministry of the Interior (Crawford, 2013: 647–648, quote on 647).

Rural Morocco has historically been a de-politicized area, at least since 1960. As Hart (2000: 84) notes, apart from a series of three rural, mainly tribal revolts immediately after independence in 1956, all other riots were urban-based. Furthermore, Hart (2000: 86) argues that 'none of the post-independence tribal uprisings really threatened the Moroccan monarchy in any way'. This is probably also due to King Hassan II's strategy of preventing the emancipation of rural areas that at the time represented between 60 and 70 per cent of the Moroccan population, keeping the rural areas less developed and disconnected from the urban centres. The strategy to control the rural population included co-operation with local notables, big landowners and local elites, as well as the threat and actual use of force by the king's local representative (the *Caid*) and the local police at the earliest signs of protests.[6] As a respondent put it, 'the *makhzen* wants to keep the civic development out of the rural world'.[7]

This explains to some extent why political parties have historically had their major activity in the urban areas. Even today, according to the rural respondents but also critical party members (Union socialiste des forces populaires (USFP), Parti de l'Avant-garde démocratique et socialiste (PADS) and Union nationale des étudiants marocains basistes (UNEM), see below) political parties are not present in the rural areas except during election campaigns, and voting decisions are based on the person and not on the party (see also Allaoui, 2010: 88; Bergh, 2010: 745). Leftist party and student union members argued that the high illiteracy levels in the rural areas (61 per cent in rural areas, compared to 29 per cent in urban areas)[8] prevented their discourses taking root and limited their possibilities of engagement in the 'peripheries'. Another reason they cited was that their young age did not allow them to have much influence in rural settings (where young people are generally less heard compared to older persons).[9]

However, since the early 1990s the presence of sections of political parties and national associations, the Moroccan Association of Human Rights (AMDH) in particular, has increased in rural areas in the context of a general political liberalization of the country, whereby the associations (rural development, *Amazigh* or youth) are much more politically active than the parties in the rural areas. Cultural assertion in the form of *Amazigh* activists mobilizing for regional (territorial) independence and for the official recognition of their language is growing.

It seems that in the High Atlas, and to a much greater extent in the Rif (see Suárez Collado, 2015) local identities that emerged during earlier and more recent protests became a cohesive factor that allowed for greater political participation and in some cases enabled local associations to formulate clear political–territorial demands.

Indeed, some *Amazigh* associations have in recent years been building important networks linking local to international levels in order to address their requests to the central government (see Oiry-Varacca, 2012; Silverstein, 2013; Suárez Collado, 2015). In Tighedouine, there are two associations representing *Amazigh* interests: *Yagour* and *Tamaynoute*. The latter is a national association with local branches; in fact, a local branch was established in Tighedouine during the fieldwork period without permission from the *Caid*.

Moreover, due to 'participatory' development programmes (such as the National Initiative for Human Development, known as INDH) that all require the setting up of local associations in order for the population to benefit from projects, there has been a rapid increase of such associations in rural areas; in Tighedouine, the number has increased from 26 in 2006 to 45 in 2013.[10] Since 2002, this development is also helped by a more liberal legal framework determining the right of freedom of association, even though the widespread refusal to apply provisions of the law on associations in effect transforms the law from what is, on paper, a declarative regime, to one that is, in practice, a prior-authorization regime. [... This indicates] that these practices emanate from a policy decided upon at a high level to weaken certain categories of associations whose methods or whose objectives disturb the authorities. (Human Rights Watch, 2009: 4; see also Bergh, 2009)

Similarly, according to an AMDH member,[11] the associations benefiting from the INDH are clearly an instrument of power in the hands of the regime meant to control the critical civil society emerging in the rural areas (see also Bergh, 2012).

The Islamist Justice and Charity (al-Adl wal-Ihsan) movement also has an increasing foothold in rural areas, as they are physically very present and rely on oral explanation of their political thoughts (see also Hamimaz, 2003). According to Fathallah Arslane,[12] leader and spokesman for al-Adl wal-Ihsan, another important factor is that the rural society understands and accepts with greater ease the movement's Islamic values and political vision than the more abstract discourse of the political parties, especially leftist ones.

Given this opportunity structure, apart from the Islamists, most of the associations and organizations involved in the F20M and whose representatives were interviewed for this article found it much more difficult to play their co-ordinating and mobilizing roles in rural areas (or small towns in the vicinity of rural areas) than in the cities.

Mapping of the Actors, Political Demands and Local Organization

Similar to other movements that mark the beginning and continuation of the 'Arab Spring' in Tunisia and Egypt, the F20M originated from an online movement – the movement for 'Freedom and Democracy Now' – that had successfully called for demonstrations in several towns beginning on 20 February 2011 (with 240,000–300,000 participants according to the organizers; 37,000 according to the Ministry of the Interior, in more than 50 cities; Fernández Molina, 2011: 437).[13] According to an AMDH member,[14] out of the 300,000 protesters on 20 February 2011, 26,000 were in Marrakech. the peak of the protest is considered to be 24 April 2011, with 110 demonstrations across the country, including the major urban centres as well as villages, with approximately 900,000 people taking to the streets.

The founding members of the F20M were mostly young urbanites who were already politicized as they had previously been active in one or several grassroots movements including the local co-ordinations that fought against the high costs of living and for better quality local public services; the Mouvement alternatif pour les libertés individuelles (MALI), which campaigns mostly for religious freedom; the struggles of the political left, trade unions, Islamist movements, the Amazigh movement or the Unemployed Graduates (Emperador Badimon, 2013; Desrues, 2013: 416; Hoffman & König, 2013; Sidi Hida, 2011).

Thus, thanks to their previous activism in these groups, the young instigators of the F20M earned support from a broad-based coalition made up of older activists from human rights associations, left-wing political parties and their and other parties' youth sections, trade unions, the Islamists of *Al-Adl wal-Ihsan* and *Al-Badil al-Hadari*, a significant part of the *Amazigh* movement, local 'co-ordinations', associations of emigrant communities in Europe, some noted intellectuals and even some big businessmen (Fernández Molina, 2011: 437).

The main actors in the F20M fall broadly into two camps. The first camp can be defined as traditional and reactionary, formed by Islamist and reactionary groups (mainly the Islamic group *Justice et Bienfaisance*, known as *Jamiat al-Adl wal-Ihsan*, and the *Parti Justice et Développement* – PJD), and the second as civic-democratic, aimed at the promotion of civic rights and rule of law, composed of student organizations and civil society associations,[15] *Amazigh* associations,[16] leftist parties[17] and trade unions,[18] among others.

The coalition of around 100 Civil Society organizations (CSOs) was soon structured under a 'National Council of Support for the 20 February Movement' (CNSAM20) in which the AMDH played a central role (Fernández Molina, 2011: 437). The CNSAM20 includes an executive committee of 16 members, and while it has no decision-making power, its main role is that of a financial backer (Hoffmann & König, 2013: 5–6).

The grievances and political demands voiced by the F20M through social media and demonstrations can be divided into those of a more socio-economic character and those that were aimed at political or democratic reforms. The first category includes grievances about the high costs of basic necessities and services, unemployment and low pay, poverty and exclusion, corruption and demands for social justice and rights, free education, housing etc. The more political demands included demands for the official recognition of the *Amazigh* language, profound constitutional and political changes to guarantee the rule of law and a free and independent legal system, embedded in a parliamentary (rather than executive) monarchy with a clear separation of powers. Many slogans called for the abolition of Article 19 in the then constitution, which stated that 'the King is the guarantor of the perennity and continuity of the State, ensures the respect of Islam and the constitution' and removes the king's decisions and actions from any judicial oversight (Faquihi, 2011; Madani et al., 2012: 11; Transparency Maroc, 2009: 9).

Indeed, activists of the 20 February movement have increasingly dared to denounce the king and the *makhzen* more broadly by framing them as 'predators' and 'mafia', and highlighting the undemocratic nature of the current system. Some elements even questioned the king's religious authority (Darif, 2012; Fernández Molina, 2011: 436–437; Hoffmann & König, 2013).

According to the representatives of the AMDH,[19] since the beginning of the protests, the movement refused to adopt a centralized structure, and the co-ordination between different groups was planned at the urban level by the different organizations. Even an association such as the AMDH did not have an overall plan, and the co-ordination between cities was limited to a national call for protest that was addressed to all the branches in the country.[20] The CNSAM20 operated at the national level, while the associations and the parties acted at the local level without a real centralization of the movement.

We can thus argue that the movement had an embryonic structure with some connection between a national centre and local realities. There were bodies of consultation both nationally and locally. The first were addressing the latter, which in total autonomy organized events locally. In Marrakech, the F20M protest was organized by the *conseils locaux* that co-ordinated 14 different organizations among which were associations, parties' sections and trade unions. Through these *conseils locaux* the various groups formed a network and organized the protest actions that took place regularly on Sundays in Bab Doukkala square as well as in the streets and in other neighbourhoods. However, the *conseils locaux* acted as a consultative body which co-ordinated only the groups that decided to join it, while others who did not participate pursued their own actions independently.

Indeed, the split between the two camps described earlier at the national level was mirrored at the local level, and even within the camps the various demands never gelled into a cohesive force. For example, the AMDH protest was mainly centred on separation of powers, on social justice, on the need for constitutional reform and on the violation of civil rights; the UNEM advocated for students' rights and for youth issues, trade unions focused on worker's rights and *Amazigh* associations demanded the recognition of their culture and their social political rights, etc.

Hence, even though most of the groups found common ground in issues such as social justice, the division of powers and constitutional rights, they did not become a unified political movement. Rather, our respondents argued that the movement created a unique momentum that each group tried to exploit for its own benefit.

Mobilization Strategies in the F20M

We now turn to the question of the extent of interaction and mobilization strategies between the urban-based activist middle class and the rural population during the F20M. This implies an assessment of the extent to which this interaction is based on common socio-economic and political grievances and shared values, and hence we present the analysis by actor.

As for the AMDH, the regime had accused it of being behind the outbreak of F20M protests (González Riera, 2011: 41). Our findings[21] show that the role of the association was significant but it cannot be considered the leader of the protest as the regime and some media have tried to show. According to the AMDH's activists interviewed,[22] the association's role was important with regard to the co-ordination of certain fringes of the movement in urban areas and supporting the demands emerging from the protests in rural areas. It was thanks to the AMDH's national network of 92 branches, five preparatory committees and nine regional sections[23] that the AMDH's militants were able to get news about protests, arrests and rights violations all over the country, thereby creating a system of counter-information to the official discourse. Of particular importance is the function of communication among rural and urban areas. In this sense, the AMDH militants had the triple function of activist, journalist and networker, alongside the organization's traditional role of defending arrested protesters.

The AMDH section in Ait Ourir supported the protest activities in the Zat valley by co-operating with an existing informal organization bringing together some of Tighedouine's youth, called *Tansikiyya Arbia Tighedouine*,[24] as well as local development associations. This is in line with Bogaert (2015: 131), who also stresses the importance of the *tansikiyya* (or *tansikiyat*) as a vital element in support of the F20M in small towns and the rural peripheries.

In two events in August and November 2011, these organizations managed to mobilize between 200 and 400 people in Tighedouine to claim better public infrastructure and services. The first protest held on 9 August 2011 was aimed at alerting the authorities about the fact that the unfinished sewerage network was polluting the irrigation waters, as well as pushing for the completion of the road between Tighedouine and Ansa. The second protest was held on 14 November 2011, again aimed at the same road issue. The protests were held at the commune headquarters (town hall) and led to the promise that the requests would be granted. While the sewerage network had been completed at the time of our fieldwork, the improvement and expansion works on the Tighedouine–Ansa road had not yet begun.[25]

However, due to the constraints in the opportunity structure outlined above, and the discursive disconnect between urban-based activists and the rural population, the AMDH was not able to mobilize rural populations on a large scale. For example, the AMDH section of Marrakech failed to organize significant demonstrations in Ait Ourir, which is only about 30km away from Marrakech, at best mobilizing 70 out of a total of approximately 20,000 residents. According to various local AMDH members, although education levels are fairly high, the local authorities kept a close watch on potential protesters.[26] The population also did not believe in the success of the F20M and therefore preferred not to take the risk of exposing themselves to the security forces. This difficulty in undertaking political activity in the rural areas was echoed by most of the leftist parties and other associations in our study.

Moreover, the contacts with rural areas were almost always facilitated by militants, usually young people, mostly students, who immigrated to the urban areas and tried to bring the discourses of protest to their rural homeland. Therefore, most of the actions were organized on the basis of the individual capacity of these militants, based on local feelings of belonging and 'social capital' rather than on the basis of their association membership. It could be argued that these activists exhibit multiple identities; while their activism in urban centres is based on membership in a group, in the peripheries their engagement is possible only on the basis of belonging to the area. Their support is often reduced to negotiating with the authorities and helping with technical-bureaucratic and legal matters, as in the case of Tighedouine.

This case is similar to many others in which urban-based activists have supported the protests in their native areas on a personal basis. A member of ATTAC had a similar role in trying to support and politically frame a protest in Kal'a M'Gouna, in the peripheries of Ouarzazate, where he comes from. According to him, 'peripheries remain such, marginalized and underdeveloped, forgotten until they become useful, as in the case of elections or the exploitation of resources'.[27]

The difficulty for associations such as the AMDH to mobilize rural populations also lies in the fact that while in urban areas the protest was based on issues such as civil rights, the separation of powers, freedom of expression, the rights of young people and the right to employment and fair wages – all strongly ideological and political issues – the rural protest was characterized mainly by material claims, such as infrastructural development or access to certain resources. Examples cited by a respondent[28] are protests against the exploitation of water in the province of Ouarzazate and Zagora. In Zagora (a town 330 km south-east of Ait Ourir), local people started to protest against the lack of drinking water due to high levels of salinity, pollution and priority given to irrigation (Bentaleb, 2012; and AMDH member[29]). In Ouarzazate (a town 170 km south-east of Ait Ourir), there were protests against a multinational company that is exploiting drinking water for commercial purposes, affecting local people's access to the resource.[30] As a member of the *Association Démocratique des Femmes du Maroc* (ADFM) stated, 'where the stomach is empty, it is difficult to talk about politics',[31] highlighting a lack of linkages between basic rural needs and the political parties' and human rights organizations' claims.[32]

Turning now to the *Amazigh* associations, their quest for recognition of *Amazigh* rights and culture can only be partially framed within the events of F20M, as some aspects go beyond the *Amazigh* groups' participation in the political uprising in the spring of 2011 and include an international dimension. During the fieldwork, we interviewed a member of the 'Réseau National *Amazigh* pour la Citoyenneté' (AZETTA), which is active in regional and international networks and has several local offices,[33] another member who was involved both in the national association *Tamaynaute* and the local association *Yagour* in Tighedouine, as well as an independent *Amazigh* activist.

These groups and individuals had different degrees of participation and involvement in the F20M. All maintained an equidistant position from both Islamist and leftist activists, using the space created by F20M to carry on their struggle for recognition of the *Amazigh* identity, language and culture, the fight against social exclusion, the demand for a democratic constitution that recognizes their rights, and the call for new elections on a democratic basis. The central bureau of the AZETTA left the choice of whether to participate in the F20M protests to its activists. According to its representative,[34] only one-third of its sections participated in the protest. The *Amazigh* activism was based on a shared sense of ethnic identity and on the widespread opinion among the *Amazigh* population that their social and cultural rights have been historically denied in Morocco. This allowed the *Amazigh* association to mobilize people both in urban and rural areas, enjoying a substantial degree of participation during the height of the F20M and afterwards.

As for the political party, trade union and student union members whom the second author interviewed, they are mainly engaged in urban areas, with the exception of the Islamist parties and movements, in particular Justice and Charity (*al-Adl wal-Ihsan*) which is also quite active in rural areas.

The two main Islamist groups that took part in the F20M are the *Parti de Justice et Développment* (PJD), since November 2011 part of the government, and the extra-parliamentary Justice and Charity (*al-Adl wal-Ihsan*) movement. *Al-Adl wal-Ihsan* was among the first to participate in the F20M, bringing a great number of participants into the movement and also qualifying themselves as one of the major forces.[35] But after the first four months, they abandoned the movement for two reasons. First, they felt distrusted by the organizations of the Left. While the Islamists accepted even the political lines of some atheist groups, they did not feel accepted as bearers of Islamic values. Moreover, often the slogans of other groups were also attributed to *al-Adl wal-Ihsan* both by the media and other F20M activists, and this was not acceptable to them. But the main reason is the fact that the constitutional response of the regime had weakened the F20M, and from that moment on, according to the Islamist leader, there were just two possible choices left: either the movement had to undertake a violent confrontation with the state, and this went against the non-violent principles of the organization, or it had to withdraw from the F20M. *Al-Adl wal-Ihsan* preferred to opt for the second choice.

Alongside the use of internet and of social networks such *Facebook* or *Twitter*, the diverse groups were organized through the massive use of mobile phones (the importance of which was underlined by all the respondents), as well as 'traditional forms' such as speeches in squares and leafleting. According to an AMDH member, given the still moderate penetration of ICT in Morocco, especially in rural areas, relying too much on the internet presented the danger of losing touch with the 'lower' and working classes who are less accustomed to these forms of communication and who prefer traditional means such as meetings and face-to-face discussion.[36] In the rural areas, therefore, the networking was based on personal contacts and the local and rural associations' capacity to mobilize people.

In sum, while F20M urban-based activists tried to mobilize and support rural protests, the rural population did not look for a strong connection with the urban F20M to promote their interests. This can be explained by several reasons. First, the low level of political engagement in the rural area is the result of the socio-political disconnect between centre and peripheries as explained above. Second, the divergences between literacy rates and the nature of demands created a discursive disconnect between the centre and the periphery. A third reason is the *makhzen*'s control over rural areas. While the urban population has over the last decades experienced a greater freedom to demonstrate, rural people fear and distrust the political activity coming from the urban areas; this is linked to their perception that the F20M would not achieve their objectives.

Perceived Outcomes of the F20M

Reflecting a common sentiment in the population, a young student respondent[37] stated: 'in Morocco, the constitution has prevented the protest becoming a revolt, and the revolt a revolution, like in other countries'.[38]

Our respondents agreed that the *makhzen* was the real 'winner' of the F20M mobilization, establishing itself as the main actor and the only one able to promote change, and therefore probably emerged stronger than before, or at least not much weaker. The analysis that the swift announcements of structural reforms defused the protests and kept the regime's power base mostly intact is shared by several external observers (Dalmasso, 2012; Kamel and Huber, 2015; Maghraoui, 2011; Pace & Cavatorta, 2012; Silverstein 2011).

The respondents attributed this to the F20M's strategic errors, which they see as being a lack of leadership, leading to divisions and contradictions within the movement, no clear demands for change, and the inability or unwillingness of the movement to become an actor in the constitutional drafting process. The absence in the advisory councils involved in drafting the constitution delegitimized the protest on the one hand and, on the other hand, the constitution itself. The respondents from the trade unions and political parties (UMT, USFP, PADS, CDT) were generally happy with the new constitution,[39] only expressing some doubts and complaints about the delay in its application, while others (mainly the AMDH members[40]) concluded that the F20M protests had been entirely in vain, given the contradictions in the constitution and the lack of its application. Nevertheless, most of them agreed that at least on paper, the new constitution is certainly an improvement compared to the previous constitutions. Only the UNEM rejected the 2011 constitution entirely since they do not consider it to be democratic or changing the actual political conditions, as it does not challenge the king's role. According to an AMDH member, the constitution 'is about everything but does not guarantee anything'.[41]

As for the recognition of *Amazigh* as an official language (article 5), it is mostly appreciated symbolically as an important first step for the recognition of *Amazigh* culture, although some respondents were sceptical about whether and how it could be made part of the national education system. The *Amazigh* groups recognized its importance, but they consider it mostly a populist move that will not end the marginalization of their culture, and this explained their boycott of the drafting process (with the exception of AZETTA that negotiated with the *makhzen*). They fear that their language will only be used in (propagandistic) official documents or alongside Arabic and French on certain road signs.[42]

With regard to the establishment of the Consultative council on youth and associative action (articles 33 and 170), it was considered by several respondents[43] as designed to conceal the parliamentarians' inefficiency as well as a dangerous means of co-optation of the best youthful human resources of the parties. A young member of the USFP[44] who had been nominated by his party as a candidate for the council refused to accept the nomination and preferred to continue his work in the Marrakech branch of the USFP because his life 'would have changed, being co-opted by the regime, with a very high monthly wage', and this would mean that he would soon lose touch with the people's needs. He was conscious though that with 'that wage the life of my family would have changed, and many young politicians are attracted by this possibility'.[45]

Finally, many consider the provisions for advanced regionalization (for directly elected regional councils, article 135) as a positive first step, but the fact that the fundamental law has still not been drafted suggests to them that this, like many other reforms, will remain on paper. It is also likely that most of the population in the rural periphery is not aware of these provisions.

More broadly, then, the articles proposed by the constitution are generally appreciated, but at the same time after almost three years with little sign of its application, many now believe that the new constitution will not bring the changes they hoped for. Opinions on the F20M legacy were divided between those who consider it a closed chapter and those who consider the movement to be latent and revivable. According to an *Amazigh* independent activist,[46] 'the persistence of the social, political and economic needs of the population which were not addressed by the new constitution will ensure that in the future something like the F20M will resurface'.[47]

However, it seems that at the time of writing (spring 2014), the level of political participation in rural areas has decreased to the levels registered before February 2011. Exceptions are the *Amazigh* associations. For example, in 2013, *Tamaynoute* founded the *Front Amazigh* in Meknes, a national network composed of more than 500 *Amazigh* associations for which it is the national contact point. In rural areas, the F20M has inspired a few protests, but mobilizations there started in the early 2000s and have continued afterwards as in the examples mentioned earlier, mainly to address urgent socio-economic needs. The number of localized rural/peripheral protests has increased over the last decade (see Bennafla & Emperador, 2010; Bogaert, 2015; Hadj-Moussa, 2013; Lahbib, 2011: 18; Planel, 2011; Suárez Collado, 2015), despite the fact that important national development programmes in the areas of rural roads, electrification and drinking water were implemented by the mid-2000s. In urban areas, the F20M has certainly left its mark. Many organizations are still active and use their networks to face the daily social struggles.[48]

Conclusions

Starting from the notion of vertical peripherality, this article has focused on the interactions between groups of actors in urban and rural areas in Morocco. We found that the F20M was a social movement characterized by a decentralized structure with some connections between the national centre and local, peripheral realities. The movement was composed of diverse social and political groups that created a unique political momentum in and through which each group, with different degrees of participation and involvement, could address their own demands to the regime. The protests assumed different characteristics in the urban centres compared to the rural peripheries, not least due to the limits posed by the opportunity structure of the High Atlas region. In contrast to other areas in Morocco such as the Rif and the Western Sahara, this region's opportunity structure did not include already existing well-organized and politicized structures of mobilization and opposition (see Suárez Collado, 2015; Fernández Molina, 2015; for the case of Syria, see Leenders & Heydemann, 2012).

In urban areas the protest was based on ideological and political issues such as civil rights, the separation of powers, freedom of expression, the rights of young people and the right to employment and fair wages, while the rural protest was characterized more by material claims, such as infrastructural development or access to certain resources.

Although the urban F20M events stimulated and inspired protests in rural areas, in practice there was a low level of interaction, limited to sporadic contacts between urban-based activists and citizens in the rural areas. This is due to the lack of engagement in the rural areas, particularly by political parties, and the difficulty that the more active associations such as the AMDH encountered in framing the socio-economic rural demands in terms of larger political grievances that matched their discourses in urban areas. The urban activists' attempts to support and politically frame rural protests were thus often reduced to negotiating with the authorities and providing help with technical-bureaucratic and legal matters.

The outcomes of the rural protests can be measured in terms of the increased demand for infrastructures, services and economic development in rural areas that has been, according to our respondents, partially inspired by the F20M. The protests started before the formation of the F20M and continued afterwards, but the rural peripheries continue to be marginalized and rural people do not have a very positive view, if any, of the constitutional achievements brought by the F20M.

Although many respondents stated that the F20M has failed in bringing about the hoped-for change, they admitted at the same time that the movement has created the conditions for the emergence of hitherto unheard popular demands. For this reason, most of our respondents declared that theoretically the new constitution is to be considered progressive compared to the previous ones. For example, the 'advanced regionalization' and many of the reforms contained in the 2011 constitution were deemed 'worthy of a modern country'.[49] But, at the same time, our respondents asserted that nothing had really changed for them, due to the lack of participation by representatives of the F20M in the constitutional drafting, the constitution's internal contradictions, and the long delays in passing the necessary implementing laws.

Notes

1. This is in line with Desrues' (2013: 421) argument that the main achievements of the F20M may lie in pushing the boundaries in the discursive sphere (the 'red lines' Hoffmann & König, 2013).
2. All interviews were conducted in person, except for one telephone interview (Interview 20, 2014).
3. All interview quotes in this article are the authors' translations. Most interviewees requested that we protect their anonymity.
4. This conceptualization is similar to that put forward by recent works in urban and regional sociology which emphasize the concepts of 'exclusion' and 'marginality/marginalization' and share an emphasis on the multidimensionality of group-related economic, political, educational and other disadvantages. This literature also focuses more on the processes that explain socio-spatial disadvantages (i.e. the 'peripheralization' processes), shifting from static to dynamic indicators and from attention to individuals and households to communities. Periphery is thus 'generally studied as a social relation with spatial implications' (Kühn & Bernt, 2013: 310), reflecting the horizontal and vertical dimensions in Rokkan's (1999) conceptualization.
5. The poverty rate in Al Haouz province (rural areas) was 15.8 per cent in 2007, according to the poverty map produced by the Haut Commissariat au Plan (see http://www.hcp.ma/Indicateurs-provinciaux-de-la-pauvrete-et-de-la-vulnerabilite_a648.html accessed on 1 May 2014).

6. Interviews with members of *La Voie Démocratique* (Interview 13, 2014) and USFP (Interview 14, 2014). Leveau (1985) shows convincingly how the monarchy restored the power of local elites to ensure it the support of the rural areas. See also Tessler (1981, 1982), and see Combs-Shilling (1989), Hammoudi (1997) and Garon (2003) on the importance of religious prestige and allegiance to explain the monarchy's survival. More recently, Hegasy (2007) shows how the habitus of youth is a major contributing element to the stability of the Moroccan monarchy.

7. Interview with a member of the AMDH central bureau (Interview 2b, 2013).

8. Data for 2004 for the population above 10 years of age, obtained from http://www.hcp.ma/Analphabetisme_a413.html (accessed on 25 March 2014).

9. Interview with a member of the AMDH (Interview 1b, 2013); interview with UNEM members (Interviews 4 and 5, 2014); and interview with an ATTAC activist (Interview 17, 2014).

10. Based on Bergh (2008) and according to the president of Tighedouine commune council during a brief visit in December 2013.

11. Interview 1c, 2013.

12. Interview 15, 2014.

13. For an elaborated article on how an online movement overflows to the 'real world', see Elghamry, 2015.

14. Interview 2a, 2013.

15. The most relevant F20M associations are the *Association pour la taxation des transactions financières et pour l'action citoyenne* (ATTAC), the *Association marocaine des droits humains* (AMDH), the MALI and the *Union nationale des étudiants marocains basistes* (UNEM).

16. Prior to the F20M, they were active in promoting the Amazigh language and culture in public arenas, such as schools and the media, calling for its official recognition as a national language in the constitution, and some even claimed regional autonomy (Layachi, 1998: 57–58). The fact that the king established a Royal Institute for Amazigh Culture (IRCAM) in 2001 can be seen as one of their most important achievements to date, but this arguably also led to the co-optation of their demands and discourse by the *makhzen* (see Silverstein & Crawford, 2004).

17. The main parties involved in the F20M are the *Parti Socialiste Unifié* (PSU), *Parti de l'Avant-garde démocratique et socialiste* (PADS); the *Jeunesse Ittihadi*, the youth branch of the *Union socialiste des forces populaires* (USFP) and *La Voie Démocratique*, an extra-parliamentary party that does not participate in national elections.

18. Mainly the *Union Marocain du Travail* (UMT) and the *Confédération Démocratique du Travail* (CDT).

19. Interview with AMDH members (Interview 1c, 2013 and Interview 2a and 2b, 2013).

20. See also Desrues (2013: 416) and Hoffman and König (2013).

21. According to various AMDH members (Interviews 1a, 1b, 2a, 2b, 2c, 3b, 19 and 23, 2013 and 2014) and other activists (Interviews 4, 5, 6, 7, 9, 12, 14 and 18, 2013 and 2014).

22. Interviews 1a, 1b, 2a, 2b, 2c, 3b, 19 and 23, 2013 and 2014.

23. See http://www.amdh.org.ma/en/about-amdh accessed on 20 March 2014.

24. Interview 23, 2014.

25. Interview 24, 2014.

26. Interviews 1a, 1b, 2a, 2b, 2c, 3a, 3b, 19 and 23, 2013 and 2014.

27. Interview 17, 2014.

28. Interview 1c, 2013.

29. Ibid.

30. Ibid.

31. Interview 21, 2014.

32. This resonates with the conclusion by Bennafla and Emperador (2010: 86). See also Oiry-Varacca (2012: 53) on this point for the Amazigh associations.

33. See http://www.reseauamazigh.org/?lang=fr, and Human Rights Watch (2009: 18–19).

34. Interview 10, 2014.

35. For strategic reasons and to avoid further control and repression by the authorities, the representatives of *al-Adl wal-Ihsan* did not want us to publish details about its organizational structure and mobilization strategy in rural areas. Interviews 15 and 16, 2014.
36. Interview 2b, 2013.
37. Interview 5, 2014.
38. Of course the constitution is only one of out of many dimensions of the regime's response to the protests (see Desrues, 2013; Fernández Molina, 2011; Hoffman & König, 2013).
39. Interviews 12, 14, 20, 25, and 26, 2014.
40. Interviews 1b, 2a, 2b, 2c, 3a, 3b, and 23, 2013 and 2014.
41. Interview 1a, 2013.
42. Interview 24, 2014.
43. Interviews 1b, 2a, 10, 11, 12, 13, 14, and 18, 2013 and 2014.
44. Interview 18, 2014.
45. The civic spirit expressed here confirms the findings by Desrues and Kirhlani (2013) on young people's activism in political parties in Meknes.
46. Interview 11, 2014.
47. See also Benchemsi (2012) for this point.
48. Interviews 1a–c, 2a–c, 3a–b, 4, 5, 6, 7, 8, 9, 10, 11, 12, 14, and 18, 2013 and 2014.
49. Interviews 10, 12, and 14, 2014. Quote from Interview 10, 2014.

Acknowledgements

We would like to thank the Zentrum Moderner Orient in Berlin for hosting the first author as a guest (sabbatical) researcher and providing a stimulating writing environment during February-March 2014, and all the respondents for their time and insights.

Funding

This work was supported by the International Institute of Social Studies in The Hague.

Disclosure statement

No potential conflict of interest was reported by the authors.

References

Albridge, A. & K. Levine (2001) *Surveying the Social World: Principles and Practice in Survey Research* (London: Open University Press).

Allaoui, O. (2010) Elections et production des élites locales: Cas de Ait Ourir, in: M. Tozy (Ed.) *Elections au Maroc: entre partis et notables (2007–2009)* (Casablanca: Centre Marocain des Sciences Sociales and Konrad Adenauer Stiftung).

Benchemsi, A. (2012) Morocco: outfoxing the opposition, *Journal of Democracy*, 23(1), pp. 57–69. doi:10.1353/jod.2012.0014.

Bennafla, K. & M. Emperador (2010) Le «maroc inutile» redécouvert par l'action publique: les cas de sidi ifni et bouarfa, *Politique Africaine*, 120(4), pp. 67–86. doi:10.3917/polaf.120.0067.

Bentaleb, H. (2012) Pénuries, salinité de l'eau et pollution: Zagora frôle la catastrophe écologique, *Libération*, 3 July, available at http://www.libe.ma/Penuries-salinite-de-l-eau-et-pollution-Zagora-frole-la-catastrophe-ecologique_a28672.html (accessed 20 March 2014).

Bergh, S.I. (2008) Decentralization and participatory approaches to rural development: assessing the scope for state-society synergies in Morocco, D. Phil, dissertation, University of Oxford.

Bergh, S.I. (2009) Constraints to strengthening public sector accountability through civil society: the case of Morocco, *International Journal of Public Policy*, 4(3/4), pp. 344–365. doi:10.1504/IJPP.2009.023496.

Bergh, S.I. (2010) Assessing the scope for partnerships between local governments and community-based organizations: findings from rural Morocco, *International Journal of Public Administration*, 33(12–13), pp. 740–751.

Bergh, S.I. (2012) 'inclusive' neoliberalism, local governance reforms and the redeployment of state power: the case of the national initiative for human development (INDH) in Morocco, *Mediterranean Politics*, 17(3), pp. 410–426. doi:10.1080/13629395.2012.725304.

Bogaert, K. (2015) The revolt of small towns: the meaning of Morocco's history and the geography of social protests, *Review of African Political Economy*, 42(143), pp. 124–140. doi:10.1080/03056244. 2014.918536.

Combs-Shilling, M.E. (1989) *Sacred Performances: Islam, Sexuality, and Sacrifice* (New York: Columbia University Press).

Crawford, D. (2013) Inventive articulation: how high atlas farmers put the global to work, *The Journal of North African Studies*, 18(5), pp. 639–651. doi:10.1080/13629387.2013.849891.

Dalmasso, E. (2012) Surfing the democratic tsunami in Morocco: apolitical society and the reconfiguration of a sustainable authoritarian regime, *Mediterranean Politics*, 17(2), pp. 217–232. doi:10.1080/13629395.2012.694045.

Darif, M. (2012) Morocco: a reformist monarchy? *The Journal of the Middle East and Africa*, 3(1), pp. 82–103. doi:10.1080/21520844.2012.675544.

Desrues, T. (2012) Moroccan youth and the forming of a new generation: social change, collective action and political activism, *Mediterranean Politics*, 17(1), pp. 23–40. doi:10.1080/13629395. 2012.655044.

Desrues, T. (2013) Mobilizations in a hybrid regime: the 20th February movement and the Moroccan regime, *Current Sociology*, 61(4), pp. 409–423. doi:10.1177/0011392113479742.

Desrues, T. & S. Kirhlani (2013) Activism under authoritarianism: young political militants in Meknes, *The Journal of North African Studies*, 18(5), pp. 753–767. doi:10.1080/13629387.2013. 849892.

Elghamry, K. (2015) Periphery discourse: An alternative media eye on the geographical, social and media peripheries in Egypt's spring, *Mediterranean Politics*, 20(2). doi:10.1080/13629395.2015.1033902.

Emperador Badimon, M. (2013) Does unemployment spark collective contentious action? Evidence from a Moroccan social movement, *Journal of Contemporary African Studies*, 31(2), pp. 194–212. doi:10. 1080/02589001.2013.781319.

Faquihi, F. (2011) Réforme constitutionnelle: Nouvelle formule du conseil pour juin, *L'economiste*, 11 March, Available at http://www.leconomiste.com/article/reforme-constitutionnellebrnouvelle-formule-du-conseil-pour-juin (accessed 15 August 2013).

Fernández Molina, I. (2011) The monarchy vs. the 20 February movement: Who holds the reins of political change in Morocco? *Mediterranean Politics*, 16(3), pp. 435–441.

Fernández Molina, I. (2015) Protests under Occupation: The Spring inside Western Sahara, *Mediterranean Politics*, 20(2). doi:10.1080/13629395.2015.1033907.

Garon, L. (2003) *Dangerous Alliances: Civil Society, the Media & Democratic Transition in North Africa* (London: Zed Books).

González Riera, J.M. (2011) Des années de plomb au 20 février: Le rôle des organisations des droits humains dans la transition politique au Maroc, *Confluences Méditerranée*, 78(Summer), pp. 35–48.

Hadj-Moussa, R. (2013) Les émeutes au Maghreb: Le web et la révolte sans qualités, *L'Homme et la société*, 1(187–188), pp. 39–62.

Hamimaz, M. (2003) *Elections et Communication Politique dans le Maroc rural: Une investigation dans une région du Moyen Atlas (Ribat el Kheir)* (Rabat: Fondation Konrad-Adenauer).

Hammoudi, A. (1997) *Master and Disciple: The Cultural Foundations of Moroccan Authoritarianism* (Chicago: The University of Chicago Press).

Hart, D. (2000) *Tribe and Society in Rural Morocco* (London: Frank Cass).

Hegasy, S. (2007) Young authority: quantitative and qualitative insights into youth, youth culture, and state power in contemporary Morocco, *The Journal of North African Studies*, 12(1), pp. 19–36. doi:10.1080/13629380601099443.

Hoffmann, A. & C. König (2013) Scratching the democratic façade: framing strategies of the 20 February movement, *Mediterranean Politics*, 18(1), pp. 1–22. doi:10.1080/13629395.2012.761474.

Human Rights Watch (2009) *Morocco: Freedom to Create Associations: A Declarative Regime in Name Only* (New York: Human Rights Watch).

Kamel, L. & D. Huber (2015) Arab Spring: The Role of the Peripheries, *Mediterranean Politics*, 20(2). doi:10.1080/13629395.2015.1033905.

Kühn, M. & M. Bernt (2013) Peripheralization and power – theoretical debates, in: A. Fischer-Tahir & M. Naumann (Eds) *Peripheralization: The Making of Spatial Dependencies and Social Injustice* (Wiesbaden: Springer).

Lahbib, K. (2011) La crise de la politique: quelles alternatives? in: A. Bouabid, K. Lahbib & M. Tamim (Eds) *La démocratie participative au secours de la démocratie représentative? Collection «les cahiers bleus» No. 16* (Rabat: Friedrich Ebert Stiftung).

Layachi, A. (1998) *State, Society and Democracy in Morocco: The Limits of Associative Life*, (Washington D.C.: Center for Contemporary Arab Studies, Georgetown University).

Leenders, R. & S. Heydemann (2012) Popular mobilization in Syria: opportunity and threat, and the social networks of the early risers, *Mediterranean Politics*, 17(2), pp. 139–159. doi:10.1080/13629395. 2012.694041.

Leveau, R. (1985) *Le Fellah Marocain: Défenseur du Trône* (Paris: Presses de la fondation nationale des sciences politiques).

Madani, M., D. Maghraoui & S. Zerhouni (2012) *The 2011 Moroccan Constitution: A Critical Analysis* (Stockholm: International Institute for Democracy and Electoral Assistance).

Maghraoui, D. (2011) Constitutional reforms in Morocco: between consensus and subaltern politics, *The Journal of North African Studies*, 16(4), pp. 679–699. doi:10.1080/13629387.2011.630879.

Oiry-Varacca, M. (2012) Les revendications autochtones au Maroc. Pour une approche postcoloniale pragmatique, *Espace, Populations, Sociétés*, 1, pp. 43–57.

Pace, M. & F. Cavatorta (2012) The Arab uprisings in theoretical perspective – an introduction, *Mediterranean Politics*, 17(2), pp. 125–138. doi:10.1080/13629395.2012.694040.

Patton, M. (1990) *Qualitative Evaluation and Research Methods* (Beverly Hills, CA: Sage).

Planel, S. (2011) Mobilisations et immobilisme dans l'arrière-pays de Tanger-Med, in: S. Ben Néfissa & B. Destremeau (Eds) *Protestations sociales, révolutions civiles: Transformations du politique dans la Méditerrannée arabe* (Revue Tiers Monde, Hors série, Paris: Armand Colin).

Rokkan, S. (1999) *State Formation, Nation-building, and Mass Politics in Europe: The Theory of Stein Rokkan (Based on His Collected Works)* (Oxford: Oxford University Press).

Saadi, M.S. (2012) Water privatization dynamics in Morocco: a critical assessment of the Casablancan case, *Mediterranean Politics*, 17(3), pp. 376–393. doi:10.1080/13629395.2012.725302.

Sidi Hida, B. (2011) Mobilisations collectives à l'épreuve des changements au Maroc, in: S. Ben Néfissa & B. Destremeau (Eds) *Protestations sociales, révolutions civiles: Transformations du politique dans la Méditerrannée arabe* (Revue Tiers Monde, Hors série, Paris: Armand Colin).

Silverstein, P. (2011) Weighing Morocco's new constitution, *Middle East Report Online, 5 July 2011*, Available at http://www.merip.org/mero/mero070511 (accessed 15 August 2013).

Silverstein, P.A. (2013) The pitfalls of transnational consciousness: amazigh activism as a scalar dilemma, *The Journal of North African Studies*, 18(5), pp. 768–778. doi:10.1080/13629387.2013. 849899.

Silverstein, P. & D. Crawford (2004) Amazigh activism and the Moroccan state, *Middle East Report*, 233(winter), pp. 44–48. doi:10.2307/1559451.

Suárez Collado, A. (2015) Territorial Stress in Morocco: From Democratic to Autonomist Demands in Popular Protests in the Rif, *Mediterranean Politics*, 20(2). doi:10.1080/13629395.2015.1033908.

Tessler, M. (1981) *Politics in Morocco. American Universities Field Staff Reports Africa* (Hanover, NH: American Universities Field Staff).

Tessler, M. (1982) Morocco: institutional pluralism and monarchical dominance, in: I.W. Zartman (Ed.) *Political Elites in Arab North Africa: Morocco, Algeria, Tunisia, Libya, and Egypt* (New York: Longman).

Transparency Maroc (2009) *Etude du système national d'intégrité: Maroc 2009* (Transparency International and Transparency Maroc) Available at http://www.transparencymaroc.ma/uploads/mab_rapport/13.pdf (accessed 6 February 2014).

Willis, M. (2002) Political parties in the Maghrib: the illusion of significance?, *The Journal of North African Studies*, 7(2), pp. 1–22. doi:10.1080/13629380208718463.

Interviews:

Interview 1a, Member of AMDH (anonymous n. 1). Marrakech, 5 December 2013.

Interview 1b, Member of AMDH (anonymous n. 1). Marrakech, 6 December 2013.

Interview 1c, Member of AMDH (anonymous n. 1). Marrakech, 9 December 2013.

Interview 2a, Member of AMDH (anonymous n. 2). Marrakech, 11 December 2013.

Interview 2b, Member of AMDH (anonymous n. 2). Marrakech, 12 December 2013.

Interview 2c, Member of AMDH (anonymous n. 2). Marrakech, 13 February 2014.

Interview 2d, Member of AMDH (anonymous n. 2). Marrakech, 14 February 2014.

Interview 3a, Member of AMDH (anonymous n. 3). Marrakech, 12 December 2013.

Interview 3b, Member of AMDH (anonymous n. 3). Marrakech, 14 February 2014.

Interview 4, Member of UNEM (anonymous. n. 1). Marrakech, 14 February 2014.

Interview 5, Member of UNEM (anonymous. n. 2). Marrakech, 14 February 2014.

Interview 6, Member of UNEM (anonymous. n. 3). Marrakech, 14 February 2014.

Interview 7, Member of UNEM (anonymous. n. 4). Marrakech, 14 February 2014.

Interview 8, Member of UNEM (anonymous. n. 5). Marrakech, 14 February 2014.

Interview 9, Member of UNEM (anonymous. n. 6). Marrakech, 14 February 2014.

Interview 10, Member of "Réseau National *Amazigh* pour la Citoyenneté" (AZETTA). Marrakech, 17 February 2014.

Interview 11, Independent *Amazigh* Activist. Marrakech, 17 February 2014.

Interview 12, Member of UMT. Marrakech, 18 February 2014.

Interview 13, Member of "La voie démocratique", Marrakech, 18 February 2014.

Interview 14, Member of USFP Marrakech branch, Marrakech, 19 February 2014.

Interview 15, Fathallah Arslane, spokesperson of *al-Adl wal-Ihsan*. Rabat, 21 February 2014.

Interview 16, Member of *al-Adl wal-Ihsan*. Rabat, 21 February 2014.

Interview 17, Member of ATTAC. Marrakech, 24 February 2014.

Interview 18, Member of USFP Youth section. Marrakech, 24 February 2014.

Interview 19, Former member of AMDH branch in Ait Ourir. Ait Ourir, 25 February 2014.

Interview 20, Secretary General of PADS. By phone, 25 February 2014.

Interview 21, Member of ADFM. Marrakech, 28 February 2014.

Interview 23, Member of AMDH branch in Ait Ourir. Ait Ourir, 1 March 2014.

Interview 24, Member of Association Yagour and Association Tamaynoute. Tighedouine, 1 March 2014.

Interview 25, Member of CDT (anonymous. n. 1). Marrakech, 2 March 2014.

Interview 26, Member of CDT (anonymous. n. 2). Marrakech, 2 March 2014.

Territorial Stress in Morocco: From Democratic to Autonomist Demands in Popular Protests in the Rif

ÁNGELA SUÁREZ COLLADO

Centre for Global Cooperation Research, University of Duisburg-Essen, Duisburg, Germany

ABSTRACT   *This article analyses the evolution of popular protest in the Rif within the Moroccan context of contention. It considers the specificity of the demands expressed and the strategies for mobilization adopted as a result of a long-term process of regional activism. The article finds that protesters in the Rif have had agency to conduct their own strategies, using the opportunity structure opened at state level to advance their own agenda. The pre-existing mobilizing structures and the reproduction of patterns of centre–periphery tension in the course of the contention have fostered a progressive localization of protest in the region, which has strengthened regional identity and regionalist activism in the Rif.*

Introduction

Since independence and the unification of the country, northern Morocco, and specifically the Amazigh (Berber) region of the Rif, have experienced an enduring peripheralization through the state, a factor which has strengthened Rifian regional identity and activism. For this reason, the term 'territorial stress', coined by Naciri (1999) to refer to the difficulties of the Makhzen in extending full control over its territory throughout the twentieth century, is used in this article to allude to the depth of penetration that centrifugal forces have had in Rifian civil society and the regional political realm in the last decade. It is also used to refer to the significant challenges they present to the Moroccan state, directly affecting some of its foundational pillars. Regionalist demands have ranged from the recognition of Rifian cultural and linguistic particularisms to demands for state investment in modernizing and transforming the region's economic structure and the establishment of a regional autonomous entity with power to manage its internal affairs.

Regionalism is not a new phenomenon in the Rif, but an evolution of the periphery's reaction to the expansion of the centre, its authority, the dominance of its administrative and political systems and the imposition of its culture and language.

Nonetheless, the increasing presence of regionalism in Rifian politics has been fostered by an array of different factors. These have permitted the consolidation of different mobilizing structures, which have led to popular protest in the region during the so-called Arab Spring. These factors include both the opportunity structure offered in the reconfiguration of the authoritarian system developed since the late 1990s in Morocco, and the agency of certain regional actors, such as local leaders of associations and political parties, in influencing the strategies to adopt in the centre–periphery relationship and within the Moroccan political system.

Local activist groups and elites in the Rif have therefore developed their own patterns of interaction with the centre and their own demands for political activism and politics at state level, deploying their strategies in both institutional and non-institutional spheres. In this special issue, the analysis of this progressive implantation of regional activism in the Rif is framed against a background that sees peripheries as dynamic structures, able to produce counter-hegemonic alternatives that challenge the centre in the long term, rather than as being submissive spaces under a dominant core. Moreover, peripheries are considered here not as monolithic spaces but as permanent sources of plurality.

These particularisms of Rifian politics and activism were present and apparent once the cycle of popular protest started in Morocco in 2011.Hence, despite the fact that the 20 February Movement's (M20F) general demands were welcomed by civil society and the Rifian population, over time the decentralized, heterogeneous and non-pyramidal nature of the M20F contributed to a progressive localization of the wave of protests, generating local discourses, demands and forms of contention. This tendency became more evident after the approval of the 2011 constitutional and regional reforms, which did not respond to Rifian demands. Thwarted expectations became the driving force behind some episodes of centre–periphery tension, in which old forms of conflict and state responses to them returned, showing the existence of a kind of path-dependency in centre–periphery relations in Morocco that the Arab Spring has not modified.

This article finds that the plurality of concerns among Moroccan protesters reflects the fact that popular protests in the country have been shaped by a concurrence of different visions about the change needed in the country and different conceptions about what the democratization of the state should entail, reinforcing the idea that uprisings in North Africa have consisted of diverse 'Arab Springs of different kinds' (Pace, 2013). In the case of the Rif, reactions and demands appeared in response not only to the evolution of popular mobilizations in Morocco but also to changes in Moroccan political life prior to the beginning of street protests in the country. Furthermore, they also displayed the persistence of old and new postcolonial problems related to issues such as transitional justice, territorial imbalances and the impacts generated by the neo-patrimonial system. The argument put forward here is therefore that peripheral actors had agency to conduct their own strategies, using the opportunity structure opened at state level to advance its own agenda, and that they were empowered with the idea that peripheral opposition was necessary for pressuring the centre to pursue political and social change. In the case of the Rif, the previous existence of rooted mobilizing structures around regional demands at meso level, especially local associations and groups and regional forums of civil society, permitted regional protesters to develop an active and independent role.

The article is divided into three sections. The first provides an overview of centre–periphery relations in Morocco, with a focus on the opportunity structure opened in the Rif during the reign of Mohammed VI for the strengthening and consolidation of a regionalist movement and awareness within Rifian activism. The mobilizing structures developed in the same period are also examined. This analysis proffers the context for the second section, which centres on the evolution of protests in the Rif during and after the Arab Spring, exploring the question why the actors involved adopted different behaviour in comparison with other parts of the country, such as the High Atlas, where hardly any mobilization took place (see Bergh & Rossi-Doria, 2015). Finally, the third section analyses the outcomes of protests, arguing that these have largely resulted in new forms of political participation, the politicization of local youth and the fostering of the regional identity.

This article is based on a period of in-depth research into Amazigh activism in Morocco and the Rif, which formed the basis of my doctoral thesis. The methodology used in the study draws on close-proximity fieldwork carried out between April 2007 and May 2011 using ethnographic observations, repeated participation in social movement campaigns, mobilizations and meetings in the Rif, semi-structured in-depth interviews, life-story compilations, the reconstruction of militant memories and discourse analysis. Regarding the territorial space of study, what this article terms 'the Rif' are the current provinces of Nador, Driouch and Al Hoceima.

Centre–Periphery Relationships and the Constitution of a Regionalist Movement in the Rif

Even in the pre-colonial period, the Rif has been historically portrayed as a region in tension with the central authority and a main focal point of rebellion and contestation. Its resistance to colonial rule during the Spanish protectorate helped to strengthen this image, which was perpetuated throughout the postcolonial history of Morocco (Madariaga, 2010), inasmuch as the region has been the source of different episodes of contention since independence was granted in 1956. The enduring asymmetries within the country and the state's repression of the territory have been the seed of several centre–periphery conflicts, which have reinforced regional disaffection with the Makhzen[1] and the emergence of different regionalist tendencies in Rifian activism over the years.

The Rif's relationships with the central power can be analysed through Lipset and Rokkan's (1967) centre–periphery model, in which the centre attempts to gain control over the periphery through the processes of state and nation building, while the periphery tries to resist this expansionism and defend its own interests. Within this frame, regionalism is considered a natural reaction to the expansion of central authority (Rokkan & Urwin, 1983), and its origins and relations with the state can be understood through the lens of this centre–periphery model (Dahl, 2009). Nevertheless, the relationship between both poles must not be seen in a linear mode, but subsumed in a dynamic structure, which expands and contracts, giving rise to cycles of shifting hegemony that peripheries can use to change their situation and obtain a position of 'central periphery' in the system (Ghosh-Schellhorn, 2006).

Following this comprehensive framework, the Rif can be viewed as a periphery from a fourfold perspective: from its difference in geographical, economic, ethnic and political terms; from its economic and political distance from and dependence on the centre; from its horizontality with regard to the core which controls it; and from its verticality, which permits it to establish interaction between groups. These features have shaped the Rif's peripheral situation, but they have changed over time, modifying the region's opportunity structure and consequently its patterns of action and interaction with the centre in a given context.

From independence to the late 1990s, the Rif's economic, cultural and political difference and distance from the central government were determinant for the emergence of different episodes of centre–periphery tension. The first reaction against the Rif's peripheral situation was the 1958–59 revolt, caused by the collapse of the regional economy, the under-development of education, infrastructure and employment in the region, the relative neglect by the state during the early years of independence and the assignment of official positions to people from outside the region (Ashford, 1961; Marais, 1969). That uprising gave birth to a proto-regionalist experience in which the centre's attempt at colonization and the periphery's resistance both came to the fore. State control of the revolt resulted in the imposition of central Moroccan state institutions throughout the country (Seddon, 1981). Nevertheless, the 1958–59 rebellion, the way it was stifled and the personal involvement of Prince Hassan sowed the seeds of distrust that the Rifian population has continued towards the Makhzen over subsequent decades (López, 2000; Madariaga, 2010). That feeling was consolidated due to the perpetuation of region's economic, political and cultural distance from and dependence on the centre. For example, there was no Rifian representation in the Moroccan government until the mid-1990s (López, 2000), besides economic oblivion and *laissez-faire* state policy, which left the region outside formal economic circuits, resulting in emigration, the cultivation and commerce of *kif* (hashish) and smuggling as the main sources of wealth (Planet, 1998). Moreover, the relationship between the monarchy and the Rif during Hassan II's reign was mainly characterized by public disdain, as illustrated by the king calling Rifians 'despicable people' (*aubach*) after the 1984 disturbances, which were especially strong in the Rif (López, 2000). The combination of all these features yielded particular forms of subjectivity and structures of feeling, with, as Hart (2000) asserted, the Rifians considering themselves to be somewhat apart from the rest of Morocco.

Regionalism in the Rif, like other movements committed to the national affirmation of sub-state entities, is rooted in both historical practice and in the assessment of the opportunities offered by the state (Keating, 2001). Reminiscent of typical cyclical patterns of regionalism (Hooghe, 1992) – and indeed also similar to the activism of other peripheries, as for example becomes evident in Edwige Fortier's article on expanding and contracting spaces for activism – regionalism in the Rif has undergone periods of expansion – in the distension junctures of late

1970s and from the late 1990s onwards – and contraction, forced by state cycles of repression. Considering its progression, it has presented an evolution that can be described as 'stages of escalation of peripheral aims' (Rokkan & Urwin, 1983) which have moved from integration petitions in the early years after independence to cultural demands in the 1970s and the final demand for political autonomy, broadly taken up after Mohammed VI took the throne in 1999.

Before the beginning of the new king's reign, certain regionalist awareness groups consolidated in the Rif's social and political realms, mainly thanks to the activity developed by Amazigh associations. These organizations were responsible for reintroducing the regionalist debate through a renewed interest in organizing events and debates related to the historical past of the region and the recovery of Rifian heroes. The détente process that began in the early 1990s, in which the monarchy was trying to establish a stable path towards succession, opened a favourable opportunity structure at the meso level to introduce new social and political demands in the public sphere. However, this was not contrary to persistence of state's surveillance over activism in the Rif. Notwithstanding, in spite of being banned or dispersed by the authorities, the associative work paved the way to the consolidation of the regionalist movement in the Rif that took place in the following decade and involved new generations in it.

The Political Realm in the Rif under Mohammed VI: Co-optation and Changes in Centre–Periphery Relations

The accession of Mohammed VI to the Moroccan throne introduced changes in the opportunity structure in the Rif, in both its socio-economic and political dimensions, opening new scenarios, spaces and means to interact with the central power. It was in the reign of Mohammed VI that the feeling of economic and political isolation was partly transformed as a redefinition of centre–periphery relations was initiated. Thus, Mohammed VI attempted to bring an end to the bitterness between the monarchy and the population in the Rif and to stabilize his legitimacy in the territory by renewing the social contract between the Makhzen and the region through three principal measures: manifold development plans,[2] the monarch's symbolic personal closeness to the Rif, exemplified by frequent trips to the region,[3] and the co-optation of new Rifian elites. Nevertheless, this latter issue has become a double-edged sword for both the regime and the new elites, as has been revealed in the course of popular protests.

The integration of new Rifian elites into state circles of power is related to Mohammed VI's great ability since his accession to preserve and even enhance his monopoly over the exercise of political and economic power in the country (Boukhars, 2010). To that end, different processes of political deactivation have been undertaken which the Moroccan regime has used to better control the political process as a whole and dissident forces in particular (Catusse, 2002; Sater, 2010; Hibou, 2011). Some of the strategies adopted have included the technocratization of politics, the co-optation of groups in civil society through governmental and semi-governmental institutions and financing the activities of selected associations, as well as the marginalization of the government and parliament as policymakers. All these political manoeuvrings have been frequently employed in Moroccan history to drive the organization of internal pluralism from above (Ojeda & Suárez, 2015). Nevertheless, their use has been increased during Mohammed VI's reign since they align with the monarch's preference for technocratic government and his idea of authority: an executive monarchy that governs and controls the limit of what is politically permissible (Ojeda & Suárez, 2015).

Notwithstanding the resilience of the Moroccan authoritarian system, some changes have occurred in Moroccan political life, especially the greater freedom of civil society to organize itself and operate in the public arena (Cavatorta & Durac, 2010). Social and political actors have seized these new opportunities to create associations and initiatives that have not only been targets of repression, but have also created a distance between the traditional forms of representation and the way politics is practised now (Catusse, 2002; Desrues, 2005). Thus, associations currently provide an alternative channel for political participation and for expressing preferences for new political ideas and values that the Moroccan political system did not previously represent (Desrues, 2005). Nevertheless, the consolidation of associations as a new form of doing politics has generated a paradoxical situation given that these associations have become platforms to implement not only different strategies of contestation, but also to be a means of potential co-optation or accommodation in the social and political realm with which to legitimize mediation and negotiation with local authorities and peers (Suárez, 2013a). Both functions of these new associations have played an important role in the transformations in the Rif's political realm in the last decade, especially in the frame of the monarch's initiatives for reconciliation and regionalization. Both processes have encouraged Rifian civil society and local elites to establish their positions as peripheral stakeholders and have constituted important parts of the inner workings of the development of the regionalist movement in the Rif.

The national initiative for reconciliation and the institution responsible for accomplishing that task, the Equity and Reconciliation Instance (IER), encouraged Rifian civil society to co-ordinate and establish a common stance among local political forces and activists through a multi-political force platform, the Rif Declaration Committee (CDR). Rif–state reconciliation was a sensitive point within the process at state level, so leading the regional reconciliation project became a means to achieve and exert a mediating role in centre–periphery relations (Suárez, 2013a). Despite the fact that the committee's activity ceased due to internal differences, certain sectors of Rifian civil society, which had been part of the committee, integrated into central Moroccan circles of power as secondary elites.[4] They occupied posts in some para-state institutions and formed new national associations in Rabat, from which they contributed to the formation of the Movement for All Democrats, later the Authenticity and Modernity Party (PAM), created by Fouad Ali El Himma, the king's closest friend (Suárez, 2013a). The PAM, which received the most votes in the Al Hoceima province in the 2009 legislative elections,[5] has served as a platform for developing a moderated regionalism within the system for these regional elites (Suárez, 2013a).[6]

Nevertheless, the CDR was also an important forum in terms of preparing the ground for the creation of outside pressure groups and for fostering a new regionalist debate, as did the so-called 'Rif Declaration' (2005). The declaration contained a series of demands considered essential for achieving real reconciliation with the past between the central power and the Rif, including an apology from the state for its repressive practices committed against the Rif population, economic reparation of victims, respect and recognition of the region's political, social and cultural rights, as well as a comprehensive development plan to stop the deliberate economic marginalization of the region.[7]

The IER's final report was strongly rejected by large sectors of the Moroccan opposition, including the CDR, which was dissatisfied with the limited attention given to the Rif (Suárez, 2013a). The report did, however, expose the need for regional agency and an evolving mobilization structure in the Rif. Opportunities for such agency were opened up by the presentation of the Moroccan initiative for Western Saharan autonomy and the king's declared interest in reforming the regional model in 2007. Both factors increased the number and widened the type of actors involved in the regionalist debate.

The regionalist movement in the Rif, according to the study by Belghazi and Madani (2001) on collective action in Morocco, is made up of formal organizations, informal networks and unaffiliated individuals engaged in a more or less coherent struggle which aims to consolidate the movement's position in the regional political and social realm. Its principal target is the recovery of some degree of autonomy over regional political life to protect its cultural legacy and identity, with demands ranging from advanced regionalization to a federal state or an autonomous region, with the latter being the most widely supported, not least since it is a term used by Morocco in its plan for Western Sahara. It is also the core demand of the Movement for the Autonomy of the Kabylie (MAK), the model and inspiration for those Rifian activists who constitute the Movement for the Autonomy of the Rif (MAR), the most popular group among Rifian youth (Suárez, 2010, 2013a).

Regionalist actors mainly came from the associative milieu and certain political parties and trade unions at the regional level,[8] other Amazigh associations and platforms at the national level,[9] and some activist groups from the Rifian diaspora.[10] They are characterized by their 'cross-militancy', that is, their multiple commitment and simultaneous participation in different organizations (political parties, associations or trade unions).[11] This particularity has produced ideological or programmatic clashes between local sections and their national branches in some political organizations, inasmuch as, in certain cases, they established alliances that do not follow the logic and dynamics of the policies adopted by those organizations at state level.

A second window of opportunity for Rif activism opened in January 2010 with the formation of the Consultative Commission for Regionalization (CCR), which increased the interest in the regionalism debate in the Rif and spurred the creation of a new organization, the Northern Morocco Forum for Human Rights (FDHNM). This new structure has been something of a continuation of the CDR, and its fundamental target – the creation of a regional political organization – challenged the expressed prohibition of regional parties by Moroccan law. This goal was already pursued by the CDR and the MAR (Suárez, 2013a).

Most of the actors and organizations involved in regional activism have neither clearly articulated the polity of their regionalist projects,[12] nor provided a clear territorial definition of regional borders.[13] Nonetheless, they do share certain aims, such as the creation of a regional political organization to represent regional rights and interests and to exert political pressure on the central power. The establishment of an autonomous entity is considered the only way to solve the Rif's under-development and social and economic deficits and to guarantee the full exercise of the region's democratic rights.[14]

Among all regionalist groups operating in the Rif, only the MAR has developed a structured political blueprint, proposing a complete regional administrative organization with a presidency, parliament, government and judicial system and a detailed distribution of powers between the state and the Rif autonomous region, establishing Rifian as the official language in the region (Suárez, 2010, 2013a).[15]

Even though neither the FDHNM nor the MAR have been legalized by the Moroccan authorities, both have been allowed to operate in a restricted environment, being monitored and pressured by the authorities (Suárez, 2013a). This has permitted them to shape discourses, which have progressively penetrated the young local population, as could be seen during the course of popular protest in Morocco to which this article will now turn.

The 'Autonomist Spring' in the Rif within Popular Protest in Morocco

The population and associations in the Rif joined the protests in Morocco, taking ownership of the grievances expressed and participating actively in the first wave of mobilization. But as the cycle of protests progressed, new and specific demands started to emerge in the region related to its political, economic and social particularities. As occurred in other territories, such as the Western Sahara, as shown in Irene Fernandez's article in this special issue, in the Rif, contention underwent a progressive localization in terms of demands, with a focus on political–territorial demands, as well as in terms of mobilization and collective action patterns, which included a cycle of violent confrontation with the security forces and symbolic defiance of the pillars of the Moroccan state.

Moroccan protests began on 20 February 2011 in a march that was organized by a group of young Moroccans using social networks, who, inspired by the uprisings across the region, decided to take to the streets to denounce the country's situation and demand changes in the country's political, economic and social spheres.[16] The Rifian population joined the mobilizers because the general feeling was that the uprisings in neighbouring countries had opened a window of opportunity to demand change, as a Rifian Amazigh activist declared to the author: 'It is a moment in which we are not afraid of demanding things' (Interview I).

The so-called 'Day of Dignity' passed completely normally across the country except for some riots in northern Morocco, especially in the Rif, as well in other places, such as Sefrou, Marrakech and Guelmine. The first day of protests in the Rif mobilized between 10,000 (according to certain digital media, such as *Mamfakinch*) and 50,000 people (according to the data estimated by the organizers, the M20F) (López, 2011). Whilst demonstrations in Nador developed peacefully, violent clashes took place in the Al Hoceima province, which ended with the burning of several institutional buildings, the headquarters of the Istiqlal (PI) and PAM parties, two bank offices and a hotel – without any police intervention.[17] Nevertheless, there were 38 arrests on the evening of 20 February and five bodies were found inside one burnt bank. The scant and contradictory official information about the situation in which the bodies were found and the authorities' refusal to open an investigation increased people's outrage, as testimonies circulated which corroborated the practice of illegal detention and torture in the Al Hoceima police station on the night of 20 February and during the following days.[18]

The incidents that occurred on 20 February were a watershed in the development of protest in the Rif. On the one hand, the intense unrest caused old local political conflicts to reappear and so also brought the issue of co-optation to the fore. New political elites, such as Ilyas El Omari,[19] became an issue in the protests. For part of the Rifian population and protesters in other parts of the country, he represented the parallel government of advisers, friends and palatial technocracy that controls or directly promotes all major decisions within the government, leading to the vast system of looting and favours available to those closest to the palace (Cohen & Jaidi, 2006; Desrues & López, 2008; Liddell, 2010). In this vein, a local leftist activist stated that the 20 February violent clashes in Al Hoceima had been fuelled by 'local groups opposed to the control that the PAM had over the Rif' (Interview II). Meanwhile, for other sectors, El Omari was part of the core that had approached the Rif and the monarchy, had created a Rifian lobby within the system and, via the PAM, had benefited from having some informal authority, which allowed his entourage to exercise political influence and pressure on certain areas of the country's political realm. Following this argument, a supporter of the PAM asserted to the author: 'The king is always here since 1999 and he has a great success every time he comes. Without the Rifian political lobby the reconciliation with the Palace had not occurred' (Interview III).

On the other hand, a particular pattern of contention appeared in the region after 20 February, in part derived from the horizontal and decentralized structure of the M20F (Suárez, 2013b), formed by day-to-day improvisation (Desrues, 2012), and in part from the 'defensive reaction–offensive action' strategy adopted by protesters in the Rif. This latter tactical approach was embraced by protesters as a means to respond to local events, the state's treatment of protest in the Rif and to challenge the central power with new forms of resistance. The 20 February turmoil triggered new demonstrations across the region, in both urban and rural areas, over the following days,[20] aimed at denouncing the violent clashes, reaffirming their commitment to the M20F's demands, condemning the death of the five young men – who became honoured 'martyrs of the M20F in the Rif'[21] – and demanding investigations into the crime. This response resulted in an increase in the number of police and army forces deployed in the region, prompting new confrontations between the population and security troops. Through this militarization, old centre–periphery tensions and resentments reappeared on both sides, encouraging civil society in Al Hoceima to mobilize and adopt common positions to de-escalate the situation while insisting on local demands. These included putting a halt to pressuring and monitoring activists and the intimidation and insulting of the population. The 'lack of ethics and commitment of security forces in their relationship with the citizens'[22] was lambasted, as was the 'lack of respect to the collective identity of the region and its national symbol, above all Abdelkrim Al Khattabi'.[23] Also demanded was a 'serious, responsible and impartial' investigation into the 20 February incidents and the liberation of all prisoners.[24]

On 4 April, 38 activists under arrest were freed in Al Hoceima and ten days later Chakib Al Khayari, the well-known president of the Rif Association for Human Rights, who had been imprisoned for denouncing drug smuggling and corruption in northern Morocco, was given a reprieve.[25] These measures were too few and too late to calm tensions. Individual confrontations between local and security forces intensified and ancient sensitivities came to the fore.[26] New types of regionalist resistance on the everyday level emerged, such as demonstrations in front of the police headquarters and threats to renounce Moroccan national identity if members of the security forces involved in the altercation remained unpunished.[27]

Between the summer of 2011 and the end of the year, other forms of collective action developed whilst tensions continued to rise and the army gathered in the interior areas of the Rif. Meanwhile, the cycle of protest was declining in the rest of the country. M20F local committees in Ait Bouayach, Imzouren and Driouch started to organize strikes against maintenance services, sit-ins in squares, blocking roads and boycotting the payment of electricity bills.[28] Rifian university students, looking for innovative forms of protest, also incorporated other grassroots activities which also increased their visibility and impact abroad, such as the march organized from Nador to Melilla to apply for political asylum in Spain and protest against the Moroccan state's Arabization policy.[29]

By autumn 2011, protests in Morocco had lost their initial homogeneity, and the demands and methods of Rifian protests differed from those adopted by the M20F at state level. They had acquired their own independent character, which contributed to making contestation in the Rif increasingly local. Demands addressed to the central power and local authorities included the end of the marginalization and exclusion of the Rifian population, improvement of health services, education and living conditions, acceptance of local cultural identity, as well as improvements to services and infrastructure – for example, the sewerage system, street lighting and refuse collection and the extension of the electricity grid and potable water system at the local level.[30] Demands and activities reverted to prior policies of contention, and protesters viewed their situation through the lens of old centre–periphery tensions, looking back to the militarization of the popular uprisings that occurred in the Rif in the late 1950s and mid-1980s, when there was 'a fierce siege, a bloody military retaliation and repression in the form of impoverishment and marginalization, displacement and deprivation [in the region]'.[31]

This localization of contestation reached its zenith in spring 2012 when protests in villages in the interior were radicalized, especially in Ait Bouayach, where the political and social demands of both activists and the population were focused on the situation generated by local protests[32] and local living conditions.[33] This radicalization of protests at the local level was accompanied by a withdrawal from the national political sphere. The Rif had one of the lowest levels of participation in the national legislative elections in 2011, which reflected the peripheral dissatisfaction that had accumulated in the region during the previous months.[34]

Regionalism after Regionalization in the Rif: The Strengthening of Regional Political Identity and Collective Action

The final draft of the advanced regionalization project was made public on 9 March 2011, and whilst it went largely unnoticed by most political actors and became a policy of secondary interest at the state level, it reactivated the debate over the territorial model and the autonomist aspirations of certain sectors of Rifian activism.

The territorial reform created a region basically built around economic criteria, focused on achieving integrated development in the regions, but without giving the population greater political independence from the central power. The project maintained the unitary nature of the system, did not legalize the constitution of regional parties, and the territorial demarcation it proposed did not accord with any of the regionalist movement's territorial projects for the Rif (Ojeda & Suárez, 2015).

From April, both the regionalist groups, especially the MAR and the FDHNM, and the local sections of the M20F organized meetings and events to protest against the reform, and demands for autonomy in the Rif were introduced as part of general demands for political change in Morocco.[35] Furthermore, as a means of protesting and reaffirming regional interest, the MAR announced in April 2011 the creation of its own political party, the Rifian Party for Solidarity, a decision also taken regarding internal differences within the organization, which tried to convince diaspora branches, which were reluctant to constitute a regional party without any prior unification of regionalist currents (Suárez, 2013a). According to this logic, the MAR co-ordinated meetings to establish a new Rifian multi-political force, despite the difficulty of integrating the PAM, something that was not accepted by all the regionalist stakeholders.[36] No decision was taken after two separate meetings, but the MAR achieved a greater capacity for dialogue and communication with local institutional powers (Suárez, 2013a).

The prohibition of regionalist parties also encouraged younger sectors of the population to take part in the protests, and in April they announced their intention to set up the Party of Nationalist Rifian Youth (Suárez, 2013a). That reinforced regional resistance to the Moroccan political system and the extension of regionalist demands among young people. The Rifian youth turned into the main driving force behind the symbolic challenges to the state through collective action. Their activities ranged from holding meetings with the image of Abdelkrim Al Khattabi instead of the ubiquitous portrait of the monarch – which far from being considered anecdotal by the authorities generated great nervousness among them[37] – to Rifian youth waving the Republic of the Rif flag in demonstrations. In particular, the flag waving has had an important effect on politics in the region since it appeared on 16 October in the course of a demonstration in Ait Bouayach, when it was seen as an act of courage both by other activists in the region and the diaspora.[38]

After that date, the presence of the Republic of the Rif flag in demonstrations and meetings has increased and spread to other Rifian locations and the diaspora, and a former government building from the times of the Republic of the Rif was taken over during the course of a youth march from rural areas to Al Hoceima city on 7 March 2012 (Suárez, 2013a). Once a complete taboo in the public sphere in the region, the flag emerged within the cycle of contention as a symbol that reinforced the identity of protest in the Rif and the regional political demands to the central power and expressed regional dissatisfaction with the results of the constitutional reform and the new territorial policy. For the banner-waving Rifian youth, the flag represented not only an expression of communitarian identity, but also their political commitment outside the traditional channels and values of the Moroccan political system.

During spring 2012, the protest and clashes between the population and security forces increased again in interior villages – especially Ait Bouayach, but also in Imzouren and Boukidam – which remained under curfew for weeks.[39] During that time, the army and police made arrests and regional courts imposed more prison sentences on protesters, despite the wave of solidarity with the Rif both within and outside Morocco,[40] including the M20F national co-ordinator, expressing support for local protesters in the Rif during protests.[41]

Regional defiance of the central authority drew a harsh response from the state. Harsh penalties were imposed on 24 youth protesters from Ait Bouayach, including on those who demanded autonomy for the Rif and waved the Republic of the Rif flag during the local uprisings.[42] From that moment onwards, the level of confrontation between protesters and security forces was restricted to critical junctures, mainly related to the commemoration of historical events important in Rifian collective memory, such as the official celebration of the Annual Battle on 21 July 2013.[43]

The radicalization of protest towards a regionalist tendency that occurred during the cycle of contention was favoured by the opportunity structure in the region in a twofold way. On the one hand, the state tried to control the level of repression in order to maintain its 'state of exceptionalism' within the Middle East and North Africa (MENA) region. On the other hand, the mobilizers counted on important resources to activate the population, especially the use of sympathizers to support the regionalist demands, primarily the young population, who had adhered to the regionalist debate, in both online and offline public spheres, during recent years (Suárez, 2013a).

The Aftermath of Popular Protests in the Rif: Outcomes and Conclusions

The evolution of popular protest in the Rif has important subjective and objective outcomes. The objective outcomes have been minor, but it is necessary to mention the state's decision to implement the IER's recommendation of creating a museum recording the Rif's material and non-material heritage and regional history. This initiative can be viewed as a central power's awareness that reconciliation between the Rif and the state is not final, and its transitional justice policy remains limited.[44]

Concerning subjective outcomes, the most noteworthy point is the end of the perception of threat among the Rifian public regarding its commitment to regionalist activism, above all among local youth which – as other articles in this volume also show – has been politicized and activated by the Arab Spring. Young people have mobilized more than ever in favour of regionalist demands, even from outside the regionalist organizations and groups that had been operating before the protests started. A regional sense of belonging among Rifian youth has been further promoted by the way in which protests developed in the region. Being – and standing up for being – Rifian in Morocco now represents a new form of political commitment. It also constitutes a commitment to a social project and a source of new cultural codes and is associated with a set of values including authenticity, citizenship, modernity and democracy. Thus, as Irene Fernández argues in her contribution to this issue, the Arab Spring protests have strengthened and crystalized local feelings of identity.

Moreover, the regionalist mobilization structures have also become denser and more diverse, including the diaspora, whose implication in the regionalism debate has also increased, encouraging the formation of new regionalist groups, such as the Rif Independence Movement.[45] This organization has been working on establishing new alliances with pro-self-determination and independence pressure groups and parties abroad, such as the National Liberal Party and Nations without States, through meetings such as that organized in Roosendaal on 30 November 2013.[46]

It follows from this article that the peripheries have contributed in a distinct way to popular protests, showing their own tempos and features. Political contention in the Rif has presented its own particularities in terms of space, time, substance, strategies and actors. In contrast to what occurred in other parts of Morocco, such as the High Atlas (see Bergh & Rossi-Doria, 2015), urban and rural populations have participated in popular demonstrations in the Rif, being even stronger and more radical in the rural and interior areas. In these parts of the region different strategies from those used in the cities were adopted, such as violent actions against representative spaces of central authority and security forces, economic boycott and symbolic challenges to the state's unity.

Protest in the Rif, still ongoing, has been mired by the existence of previously established mobilizing structures which provided the region with its own opportunity structure and resources to be an independent actor within the contention. The prior emergence of a regional political space was critical in the development of protest in the Rif and in the progressive localization of demands and modes of resistance. This has encouraged the incorporation of new types of socialized participants into the regionalist movement. These activists have also readjusted the repertoire of collective action and mobilization patterns, contributing to the consolidation of regional identity as a politicized identity and to regionalist discourse as a political project in the regional political realm.

Disclosure statement

No potential conflict of interest was reported by the author.

Notes

1. The Makhzen has been described by Cavatorta and Durac (2010: 57) as an 'informal governing alliance between the monarch, his advisers, selected businessmen, high-ranking bureaucrats and tribal chiefs operating as the unelected and unaccountable decision-makers in the country beyond the control of the elected government'.
2. Development plans and agencies have been central in the state's strategy for territorial reinforcement and functioned as a cornerstone of Mohammed VI's approach to the Rif, where the promotion of economic development has been implemented via a large number of projects to activate the regional economy and unlock the region from the rest of Morocco geographically. The monarch has personally followed the evolution of this development programme, visiting the Rif on a frequent basis for both official visits and personal holidays (Suárez, 2011).
3. Because of the continuity of his presence in the region, the local population has started to view the king as a bulwark there, breaking the barrier between the northern provinces and the Makhzen that existed for decades (Suárez, 2011, 2013a).
4. For Parejo and Feliu (2009), 'secondary elites' are made up of secondary figures of the army and intelligence services, state agents in charge of the machinery of repression, members of para-state institutions, the government, leaders of political parties and parliamentary elites, administration elites, businessmen and certain members of the media.
5. Detailed information about the constitution process of the PAM in the Rif, its electoral strategies and results in Al Hoceima province can be found in Suárez (2009).
6. For more about the participation of Rifian political elites in the constitution of the PAM, see Suárez (2013a).
7. 2005 فيلجنةﭐالريفلجنةﭐإعلان 29:يناير. See Suárez (2013a).
8. Despite the fact that Amazigh associations represent the core of regionalist activism, other local associations have also been integrated, such as local development associations and the so-called associations of memory as well as the local sections of the AMDH and UMT (Suárez, 2010, 2013a).
9. The Amazigh sectors in favour of the establishment of autonomy or federalized entities in Amazigh regions are the Amazigh Cultural Movement in Moroccan universities and some political organizations linked to Amazigh activism, such as the Amazigh Democratic Party, the Moroccan Amazigh Democratic Party and the Federal Democratic Party (Suárez, 2010, 2013a).
10. Amazigh associations in Spain, Belgium, Holland and Germany, the European branch of the MAR and associations of Rifians abroad in different European cities (Suárez, 2013a).
11. See the example of Annahj Addimocrati's section in Al Hoceima in Suárez (2013a).
12. However, an 'ethno-territorial mimesis' was observed in some of these projects with the political systems of certain European countries, especially those with important Rifian communities, such as Spain, Germany and Belgium. These communities have contributed to diffusing the particularities of the political systems where they live (Suárez, 2010, 2013a). For clarification, 'ethno-territorial mimesis' refers to the way that certain regions try to imitate the model of the state–region relationship, powers, institutions and symbols previously adopted by others (Moreno, 1997).
13. Proposals fluctuate from the territory defined as the 'Greater Rif' (from the Atlantic to the Algerian border and from the Mediterranean to the Rif Mountains), to the area considered as the 'Strategic Rif' (territory formed by the Al Hoceima, Driouch and Nador provinces along with certain parts of Taza and Berkane and Melilla) (See Suárez, 2010, 2013a).
14. In this respect, the political discourse rests on the consideration of the Rif as a nation, the idea that history has provided the Rifians with a democratic consciousness and its existence as a region with a historical identity and rights. It defies the ideological state apparatus sustaining the Arab and Islamic nationalist character of the modern nation-state, its policies and the dominant historiography of Morocco (Suárez, 2013a).

15. The MAR political project has been analysed through different documents issued by the organization, such as 'Le Rif stratégique' (2008), مشروع أطروحة فكرية لـ 'حركة سياسية ريفية' (2009) and 'Communiqué pour une large autonomie dans le Rif' (2008) (see Suárez, 2013a).

16. The reform of the constitution, the resignation of the Abbas Al Fassi government, the dissolution of parliament, an effective separation of powers, the prosecution of persons and authorities responsible for human rights abuses and corruption, the liberation of political prisoners, the official recognition of Amazigh language and identity and sanitary and education equality.

17. 'Une enquête au pays de Khattabi', *Mamfakinch*, 22 July 2011. Available at http://www.mamfakinch. com/une-enquete-au-pays-de-khattabi/ (accessed 22 July 2011).

18. 'Más pruebas acusan a la policía marroquí de la muerte de 5 personas el 20 de febrero en Alhucemas', *Kaos en la red*, 11 April 2011. Available at http://old.kaosenlared.net/noticia/mas-pruebas-acusan-policia-marroqui-muerte-5-personas-20-febrero-alhuc (accessed 2 May 2011).

19. Ilyas El Omari had been one of the Rifian activists who led the Rif Declaration Committee and has political experience in the GSU and local and national associations.

20. New mass demonstrations took place on 21 February in Imzouren, with the participation of 7,000 people and on 25 February across the Al Hoceima province with 10,000 participants. Rifian youth organized their own gatherings both in the secondary schools in Imzouren, Ait Bouayach and Ajdir on 23 February and at Oujda University where Rifian students received the support of all sections of the UNEM. See http://www.youtube.com/watch?feature=player_embedded&v=ulvuBQ3gcbw#t=0s; http://asenti. blogspot.com.es/2011/02/blog-post_22.html and احداثالحسيمةتساهمفيتوحيدطلبةالريفبجامعةوجدةرغمالاختلافاتالسياسية, Dalil Rif, 22 February 2011. Available at http://www.dalil-rif.com/home/-hoceimaunemoujda (accessed 22 February 2011).

21. بيان:ساكنة ايت بوعياش تستمر في مسيراتها النضالية بعد 20 فبراير and بلاغ لحركة 20 فبراير موقع تماسينت (Statements of local associations in Ait Bouyach and Tamassint) (see Suárez, 2013a).

22. الحسيمة إقليم الهيئات والفعاليات الشبابية ب (statement of organizations and youth of Al Hoceima province), 8 March 2011.

23. Ibid.

24. Ibid.

25. 'Chakib El Khayari libéré', Bladi, 14 April 2011. Available at http://www.bladi.net/chakib-el-khayari-libere.html (accessed 11 April 2011).

26. In this context, two remarkable events took place at the beginning of the summer when, first, on 13 June, a policeman, after attacking a taxi driver with a bladed weapon, uttered insults toward Rifians, including *aubach*, the word Hassan II had used to refer to the Rif population after the 1984 uprisings and 'sons of Spaniards'. Some days later, other policeman attacked and insulted four young men who were participating in a popular demonstration. The local population reacted in both cases by organizing protests, resulting in increased tension with the security forces and the ending of the king's visit to the region. See مدينةالحسيمةوسطاحتجاجليليعارم, *Hespress*, 14 June 2011. Available at http://hespress.com/permalink/32901.html (accessed 15 June 2011) مواطنينيشعلغضببالساكنة, إعتداءبعضالمحسوبينعلىالشرطةبالحسيمةعلى, *Rifnow*, 13 June 2011. Available at http://www.rifnow.com/index.php?option=com_content&view=article&id=3214%3A2011-04-13-15-07-04&catid=39%3A2009-04-12-16-06-34&Itemid=87 (accessed 15 June 2011).

27. 'Miles de manifestantes colapsan el centro de la ciudad marroquí de Alhucemas', Alhucemas Press, 15 June 2011. Available at http://www.alhucemaspress.com/index.php?option=com_content&view=article&id=2134:miles-de-manifestantes-colapsan-el-centro-de-la-ciudad-marroqui-de-alhucemas&catid=36:noticias-del-rif&Itemid=126 (accessed 15 June 2011).

28. ساكنةايتبوعياشتستجيبللاضرابالعامومسيرابالمحتجين Central Committee Ait Bouayach, 22 May 2011. Available at http://bouayach-comite.blogspot.com.es/ (accessed 20 April 2012); علىإهانتهلكرامةالمحتجين ساكنةآزلافتتحافقاجدياتهم،وتطالببمحاسبةرئيسمجلسالجماعة, Rifnow, 29 June 2011. Available at http://www.rifnow.com/index.php?option=com_content&view=article&id=3276:2011-06-24-18-45-15&catid=39:2009-04-12-16-06-34&Itemid=87 (accessed 1 July 2011).

29. See http://www.youtube.com/watch?feature=player_embedded&v=D_OBZAVIzUk#t=126s.

30. Tamsmunt n twengint n Arif gi Lhusima (Statement of Association of Rif Memory), Al Hoceima, 7 March 2011.

31. Ibid.
32. E.g. the immediate demilitarization of the area, the release of all detainees and political prisoners, the suspension of arrest warrants against the militants who had not been arrested and investigation into corruption at City Hall. See ساكنة ايت بوعياش تستجيب للاضراب العام ومسيرة حاشدة تطالب, *Bouayach Comite*, 22 May 2011. Available at http://bouayach-comite.blogspot.com.es/ (accessed 20 April 2012).
33. E.g. the transformation of the local health centre into a hospital, the rehabilitation of irrigation canals, installing fences on the banks of the Nekor and Souftoula rivers and the cancellation of electricity and water payments for two years in compensation for abuses committed. See ساكنة ايت بوعياش تستجيب للاضراب العام ومسيرة حاشدة تطالب, Bouayach Comite, 22 May 2011. Available at http://bouayach-comite.blogspot.com.es/ (accessed 20 April 2012).
34. National participation in the constitutional referendum was 75 per cent of registered voters, and in the case of Al Hoceima city 55 per cent of registered voters. National participation in the legislative election was 45.5 per cent whilst in the Al Hoceima province it was 37.2 per cent, 41.2 per cent in Driouch and 33.9 per cent in Nador (Suárez, 2013a).
35. بيان صادر عن مجلس التنسيق في شأن مستجدات الوضع الحقوقي والديمقراطي بالمغرب, Northern Morocco Forum for Human Rights, 3 December 2011.
36. الياس العماري يهدد بالحكم الذاتي للريف للعودة إلى دائرة القرار بالبلاد Arrifinu, 24 May 2011. Available at http://www.arrifinu.net/?p=46008 (accessed 26 May 2011).
37. Observed by the author in the course of a meeting organized by local section of M20F in Nador, 3 April 2011.
38. محتجون بنيبوعياشيرفعونعلمجمهوريةالريف, Maghress, 16 October 2011. Available at http://www.maghress.com/dalilrif/5982 (accessed 16 October 2011).
39. 'Ce Rif si rebelle', Telquel, 24 April 2012. Available at http://www.telquel-online.com/Le-mag/Reportage-ce-rif-si-rebelle/519 (accessed 2 May 2012).
40. 'Rassemblement de solidarité avec les populations du Rif victimes de la répression au Maroc', Tamazgha, 21 March 2012. Available at http://tamazgha.fr/Rassemblement-de-solidarite-avec,3317.html (accessed 3 April 2012). فعاليات ريفية تخلد فاتح ماي بمدريد, Midar 24, 1 May 2012. Available at http://www.midar24.com/?p=5933 http://www.midar24.com/?p=5933(accessed 3 June 2012).
41. Statement of National Council for Support of the Feb 20 Movement, Rabat, 12 March 2012 (distributed by e-mailing list Presse Maroc on 14 March 2012).
42. 'Duras penas de prisión contra militantes del 20F de Ait Bouayach', AlhucemasPress, 1 May 2012. Available at http://www.alhucemaspress.com/index.php?option=com_content&view=article&id=2496:duras-penas-de-prision-contra-militantes-del-20f-de-ait-bouayach-rif&catid=50:ultimas-noticias-slide-show (accessed 2 May 2012).
43. 'Les activistes Rifains réclament l'indépendance du Rif à l'occasion du 92e anniversaire de la bataille d'Anoual', Siwel, 23 September 2013. Available at http://www.siwel.info/Maroc-Les-activistes-Rifains-reclament-l-independance-du-Rif-a-l-occasion-du-92e-anniversaire-de-la-bataille-d-Anoual_a5245.html (accessed 12 October 2013).
44. 'Lancement du projet pour la création du musée du Rif en vue de promouvoir la réconciliation et de préserver le patrimoine de la région'. Available at http://www.cndh.org.ma/fr/bulletin-d-information/lancement-du-projet-pour-la-creation-du-musee-du-rif-en-vue-de-promouvoir-la (accessed 1 November 2014).
45. It was created in 2013 by Rifians in the diaspora, after the spring uprisings in rural areas and subsequent state repression. The organization's main concern is the Rif Republic's Self-Determination Cause. See http://rif.livenations.net/ (accessed 19 November 2014).
46. لقاءروزندال: الريفيحتاجلتحريرالعقولقبلتحريرالأرض Anoual.Net, 2 December 2013. Available at http://www.anoual.net/archives/5091 (accessed 5 January 2014).

References

Ashford, D.E. (1961) *Political Change in Morocco* (Princeton, NJ: Princeton University Press).
Belghazi, T. & M. Madani (2001) *L'action Collective au Maroc: De la Mobilisation des Resources à la Prose de Parole* (Rabat: Publications de la Faculté des Lettres et des Sciences Humaines).

Bergh, S. & D. Rossi-Doria (2015) Plus ça change? Observing the dynamics of Morocco's 'Arab Spring' in the High Atlas, *Mediterranean Politics*, 20(2). doi: 10.1080/13629395.2015.1033900.

Boukhars, A. (2010) *Politics in Morocco. Executive Monarchy and Enlightened Authoritarianism* (London: Routledge).

Catusse, M. (2002) Le charme discret de la société civile. Ressorts politiques de la formation d'un groupe dans le Maroc ajusté, *Revue Internationale de Politique Comparée*, 2, pp. 297–318.

Cavatorta, F. & V. Durac (2010) *Civil Society and Democratization in the Arab World: The Dynamics of Activism* (London: Routledge).

Cohen, S. & L. Jaidi (2006) *Morocco. Globalization and Its Consequences* (New York: Routledge).

Dahl, R. (2009) *The Rise of Regionalism. Causes of Regional Mobilization in Western Europe* (London: Routledge).

Desrues, T. (2005) La sociedad civil marroquí: indicador de cambio y modernización del autoritarismo marroquí, *Awraq: Estudios sobre el mundo árabe e islámico contemporáneo*, 22, pp. 393–424.

Desrues, T. (2012) Moroccan youth and the forming of a new generation: social change, collective action and political activism, *Mediterranean Politics*, 17(1), pp. 23–40.

Desrues, T. & B. López (2008) L'institutionnalisation des élections et la désertion des électeurs: le paradoxe de la monarchie exécutive et citoyenne, *L'Année du Maghreb*, 4, pp. 281–307.

Ghosh-Schellhorn, M. (2006) Revisting centres and peripheries: anglophone India and its diasporas(s), in: M. Ghosh-Schellhorn & V. Alexander (Eds) *Central Peripheries: India and Its Diaspora(s)* (Berlin: LIT Verlag).

Hart, D.M. (2000) *Tribe and Society in Rural Morocco* (London: Frank Cass).

Hibou, B. (2011) Le Mouvement du 20 février. Le Makhzen et l'antipolitique. L'impensedes reformes au Maroc, *CERIM*, Available at http://www.ceri-sciencespo.com (accessed 18 July 2012).

Hooghe, L. (1992) Nationalist movement and social factors: a theoretical perspective, in: J. Cockley (Ed.) *The Social Origin of Nationalist Movements. The Contemporary West European Experience* (London: Sage).

Keating, M. (2001) *Plurinational Democracy. Stateless Nations in a Post-Sovereignty Era* (Oxford: Oxford University Press).

Liddell, J. (2010) Notables, clientelism and the politics of change in Morocco, *Journal of North African Studies*, 15(3), pp. 315–331.

Lipset, M. & S. Rokkan (1967) *Party Systems and Voter Alignments: Cross-National Perspectives* (Toronto: The Free Press).

López, B. (2000) *Marruecos en Trance: Nuevo Rey, Nuevo Siglo, ¿nuevo régimen?* (Madrid: Biblioteca Nueva).

López, B. (2011) Marruecos ante el proceso de cambios en el mundo árabe, Real Instituto Elcano, *Real Instituto Elcano*, Available at www.realinstitutoelcano.org (accessed 4 March 2011).

Madariaga, M.R. (2010) El Rif y el poder central: una perspectiva histórica, *Revista de Estudios Internacionales Mediterráneos*, 9, pp. 17–25.

Marais, O. (1969) Les relations entre la monarchie et la clase dirigeante au Maroc, *Reveu française de Science Politique*, 19(6), pp. 1172–1186.

Moreno, L. (1997) Federalization and ethnoterritorial concurrence in Spain, *The Journal of Federalism*, 27(4), pp. 65–84.

Naciri, M. (1999) Contrôler ou développer, le dilemma du pouvoir depuis un siècle, *Maghreb Machreq*, 164, pp. 8–34.

Ojeda, R. & A. Suárez (2015) The project of advanced regionalisation in Morocco: analysis of a Lampedusian reform, *British Journal of Middle Eastern Studies*, 42(1), pp. 46–58.

Pace, M. (2013) An Arab 'spring' of a different kind? Resilience and freedom in the case of an occupied nation, *Mediterranean Politics*, 18(1), pp. 42–59.

Parejo, M.A. & L. Feliu (2009) Marruecos: la reinvención de un sistema autoritario, in: F. Izquierdo (Ed.) *Poder y Regímenes en el Mundo árabe contemporáneo* (Barcelona: Fundación CIDOB).

Planet, A. (1998) *Melilla y Ceuta. Espacios- frontera Hispano-marroquíes* (Melilla: UNED Melilla).

Rokkan, S. & D.W. Urwin (1983) *Economy. Territory. Identity. Politics of West European Peripheries* (London: Sage).

Sater, J.N. (2010) *Morocco. Challenges to Tradition and Modernity* (London: Routledge).

Seddon, D. (1981) *Moroccan Peasants. A Century of Change in the Eastern Rif 1870–1970* (Kent: Dowson).

Suárez, A. (2009) La inesperada desbalcanización de la vida política. Elecciones comunales en la ciudad de Alhucemas, *OPEMAM Observatory on Politics and Elections in the Arab and Muslim*, Available at http://www.opemam.org (accessed 3 November 2014).

Suárez, A. (2010) La sociedad civil frente al proceso de regionalización: el caso del Rif, *Revista de Estudios de Internacionales Mediterráneos*, 9, pp. 142–151.

Suárez, A. (2011) El regreso de la monarquía al norte de Marruecos. Una década de desarrollo económico en una reconciliación política inacabada, in: T. Desrues & M.H. de Larramendi (Eds) *Mohamed VI. Política y Cambio Social en Marruecos* (Córdoba: Almuzara).

Suárez, A. (2013a) El movimiento amazigh en el Rif: identidad, cultura y política en las provincias de Nador y Alhucemas, PhD thesis, Universidad Autónoma de Madrid.

Suárez, A. (2013b) The amazigh movement in Morocco: new generations, new references of mobilization and new forms of opposition, *Middle East Journal of Culture and Communication*, 6, pp. 55–70.

Interviews

Interview I, Amazigh activist, Al Hoceima, 7 April 2011.
Interview II, leftist activist, Al Hoceima, 12 April 2011.
Interview III, supporter of PAM, Al Hoceima, 8 April 2011.

Protests under Occupation: The Spring inside Western Sahara

IRENE FERNÁNDEZ-MOLINA
European Neighbourhood Policy Chair, College of Europe, Natolin Campus, Warsaw, Poland

ABSTRACT *The emergence and empowerment of Sahrawi civil protests and pro-independence activism inside the Western Sahara territory under Moroccan occupation have to be seen in the context of varying sets of opportunity structures which this peripheral movement has actively seized in the past two decades by symbiotically combining domestic non-violent resistance and international 'diplomatic' activities. Different forms of recognition received from the two reference centres – the Moroccan state and the Polisario Front – plus the international community have been crucial in this process, with the last representing the most significant achievement of the movement. The Arab Spring has been a particularly fruitful window of opportunity in this regard.*

Sahrawi civil protests in the Western Sahara territory under Moroccan control intensified just before the Arab Spring broke out in Tunisia. Indeed, the Sahrawi protest camp set up at Gdeim Izik, Laayoune, in October–November 2010 was described by some observers in hindsight as the first chapter of the Arab uprisings (Errazzouki, 2012). Not only was this protest based on the physical occupation of a public space in a non-violent but resolute way ('occupy' tactic) (Dann, 2014), but also the demands made brought together socio-economic grievances and an all-encompassing non-material call for 'dignity' ('karama') in a similar manner to other Arab Spring revolts. Nonetheless, there were also quite distinctive features resulting from a context of mixed decolonization and identity conflict,[1] along with Moroccan occupation of the territory. These peculiarities included the Sahrawi nationalist framing that was to be gradually imposed on events and the camp's distance from the city centre of Laayoune, where the level of security control would have never allowed it to be established. The unique political environment of Western Sahara certainly shaped an 'Arab Spring of a different kind' (Pace, 2013), in which popular demands for dignity, justice and freedom revolved more around the consequences of the protracted conflict than around primarily anti-authoritarian claims.

   This Sahrawi protest appears to be peripheral in three ways. Besides being marginal in both geographical and political terms – physically remote from any plausible state/ regional 'centre' and usually out of the international media's focus and political agenda – it remains exceptional because of the persistent constraints inflicted by protracted conflict and occupation. Hence both *distance* and *difference* (Huber & Kamel, 2015) feature prominently in this periphery. At the same time, it should be noted that the centre of gravity of the conflict has gradually shifted 'inwards' over the last two decades: from the international/diplomatic arena – the UN-led negotiations between Morocco and the exiled Polisario Front[2] – to the disputed land where it started, that is the now Moroccan-occupied territory, where the Sahrawi population has been transformed over the years into a demographic minority. The Arab Spring period represents the latest, albeit unique, phase in this process.

   What seems somehow more problematic to establish is in relation to which specific centre(s) this periphery has defined itself and constructed its identity over the years. This is a crucial question because of the inherently relational and relative nature of the notions of centre and periphery, which are dependent on interaction and also subject to change (Huber & Kamel, 2015). Unlike other territorial peripheries studied in this special issue which define themselves in relation to a distinct state centre (Suárez Collado, 2015) or a set of concentric circles (Bergh & Rossi-Doria, 2015), the protest actors inside Western Sahara have built their political identity and struggle upon relations and transactions with two disparate – and indeed opposed – centres: Rabat and Tindouf, i.e. the capital of the occupying and administering state and the refugee camps in south-western Algeria where the pro-independence Polisario Front established its headquarters and proclaimed the Sahrawi Arab Democratic Republic (RASD) in exile in 1976. Moreover, both of these centre– periphery relationships are dynamic structures: the intensity and content of interactions which determine distance in each of them have varied since the start of the conflict. Administrative and economic dependence on the Rabat centre has not prevented distance from the Tindouf centre being reduced in terms of communication and political identity over the last two decades.

   This article tries to *understand* how the 'inward turn' of the conflict was achieved by pro-independence Sahrawi activists operating inside the occupied territory; in other words, how such a politically peripheral community – even in the context of the Sahrawi camp – was able to become relatively empowered and central to the conflict. From the viewpoint of these actors, this counter-hegemonic process can be analysed as a *struggle for recognition* (Taylor, 1994; Honneth, 1996) vis-à-vis three significant others: the two reference centres – the Moroccan state (Rabat) and the Polisario Front (Tindouf) – plus the international community. Thus, the argument put forward is that the empowerment of this periphery was made possible not only by variations in the opportunity structure, mainly at the Moroccan state level, which were actively seized by the internal Sahrawi activists[3] through a novel combination of domestic non-violent resistance and international 'diplomatic' activism, but also that the recognition achieved through these strategies was crucial in this process.

   Research has tended to overlook the central issue of recognition. While some recent works have focused on Sahrawi non-violent resistance (Stephan & Mundy,

2006; Mundy & Zunes, 2014; Dann, 2014), they have not fully disentangled two aspects: first, the role played by Morocco's partial and flawed recognition policies in enabling and fuelling such activism and, second, the symbiotic relationship between this domestic struggle and recognition from the international community, which is the necessary 'mirror' that has allowed it to come into existence and gain significance. This article therefore argues that the achievements of internal Sahrawi activists should be assessed primarily in terms of recognition. The Arab Spring context, in the wake of the local protest of Gdeim Izik, was particularly conducive to this process as it broadened opportunities at Moroccan state level while reviving the international community's interest in human rights in Western Sahara.

In addition to social movement theory (McAdam et al., 1996: 1–17; Tarrow, 2003: 19–25) and Eduard Azar's (1990) theory of 'protracted social conflict', these arguments draw on Hegel-inspired theories of recognition, which underscore how any individual or collective agent depends on social interaction with (and feedback from) other subjects in order to gain self-consciousness – that is to create and preserve its own identity. Self-descriptions or self-interpretations always need to be acknowledged and validated by external others. Alongside (1) the most elementary sense of recognition as acknowledgement of an agent's very existence and distinct identity (cognitive recognition), this strand of literature distinguishes between three key psychological or emotional dimensions: (2) respect (recognition of equal status and rights), (3) esteem (recognition of difference) and (4) empathy (recognition through understanding and affection) (Taylor, 1994; Honneth, 1996; Thompson, 2006; Lindemann & Ringmar, 2012: 7). Thomas Lindemann (2010: 2–3) further adds an instrumental or strategic component found in cases in which recognition entails some kind of material advantages – which is also reminiscent of Nancy Fraser's emphasis on the connection between recognition and redistribution (Fraser & Honneth, 2003).

The bulk of the fieldwork for this article was conducted in June 2013 in a 'peripheral centre' (Huber & Kamel, 2015): the city of Laayoune, which is the capital of the territory under occupation, remains largely isolated and is hardly accessed by foreigners. This is, on the one hand, a particularly unfavourable and under-researched environment (Zunes & Mundy, 2010: xxxiii) where the movements and contacts of any visitor are constantly controlled by the Moroccan security services, while widespread fear and paranoia among the local population (of all political leanings) creates a tense and charged atmosphere. On the other hand, Sahrawi activists are extremely welcoming and eager to meet any external observer or supporter as a result of their political strategy and pressing need for recognition. The work mainly involved semi-structured individual or group interviews with representatives from some ten independent Sahrawi civil society organizations based in this city, most of which broadly supported the independence of Western Sahara.

This article is structured as follows. The next section will place the Sahrawi 'Arab Spring' in the context of a continuously evolving inward shift of the conflict. It will show how changing opportunity structures – specifically five windows of opportunity of which the Arab Spring represents the latest – were seized by internal Sahrawi activists. The following section will then turn to a deeper examination of how Sahrawi strategies capitalized on existing mobilization structures at the local, inter-Sahrawi, Moroccan and international levels during the Arab Spring. It will show that, in contrast to other peripheries treated in this volume, these comparably developed mobilization structures enabled internal Sahrawi activists to achieve a relatively important subjective outcome. This result is discussed in the concluding section, stressing the relevance of the recognition obtained from the Moroccan state, the Polisario Front and the international community.

Changing Opportunity Structures and the Sahrawi 'Arab Spring'

Five windows of opportunity can be identified within the chronology of the internal Sahrawi pro-independence movement, which Sahrawi activists have seized over the last three decades. The Arab Spring was the last of them, and while it might not necessarily have been the most important, it provided unique opportunities for a transforming Sahrawi activism. While the contingent empowerment of Sahrawi activism has been facilitated in each phase mainly by different recognition policies of the occupying state, the exceptional feature of the aftermath of the latest protest cycle has been the relative easing of the level of Moroccan repression, accompanied by a revived interest on the part of the international community in human rights in Western Sahara.

A Short Chronology of a Conflict Shifting 'Inside': 1991, 1999, 2004, 2009

The situation in the occupied Western Sahara territory in the 1980s and even the 1990s was one of virtual isolation, including a deep disconnect between Sahrawis who had remained there and the Tindouf centre of pro-independence struggle: 'This created a real break-up. We had a society that was divided into two and each part evolved separately' (Interview III, 2013). However, a first window of opportunity opened at the beginning of the 1990s, facilitated by the UN-sanctioned ceasefire and Settlement Plan (1991) accepted by Morocco and the Polisario Front, which provided for a referendum on self-determination (Mohsen-Finan, 1997), as well as a state-wide process of political liberalization launched by the Rabat authorities. Although it was a far cry from genuine democratization, the significant broadening of civil liberties and expansion of the public space witnessed in the 1990s did have a tangible impact on the development of civil society in Morocco and, albeit in a far more limited and slower way, in occupied Western Sahara.

This mix of factors led to two novel developments on the ground. First, UN involvement in the conflict and the establishment of the UN Mission for the Referendum in Western Sahara (MINURSO) in Laayoune encouraged a part of the Sahrawi population that had stayed silent under Moroccan occupation to express its grievances timidly. Second, in June 1991, a number of Sahrawi political prisoners and 'disappeared' were for the first time released – and thus acknowledged to exist, entailing recognition by the Moroccan regime in the most elementary sense. Some of them seized the opportunity of a 'fully transformed social context' (Gimeno, 2013: 13) and created informal groups, which merged into the so-called Co-ordination

Committee of Sahrawi Victims of Enforced Disappearances in 1994. Furthermore, first attempts at networking with Moroccan and international actors started with a clandestine expedition from this periphery to the Rabat centre (Martín Beristain & González Hidalgo, 2012, vol. 2: 229, 444).

A second window of opportunity related to changes in the Rabat centre opened in the run-up to the succession to the throne in 1999, which was surrounded by an all-pervasive discourse of change and had a deep impact on the perceptions of political opportunities: 'I think this opening-up exists. Mohammed VI is not Hassan II, it must be said. If we say that both are the same, it means that we are not "historical"' (Interview III, 2013). Memory policies and redress for human rights abuses during the 'years of lead'[4] took centre stage in the promised 'democratic transition' and unleashed unintended dynamics within Moroccan civil society. At the same time, after the historic wave of protests which started in Laayoune in the autumn of 1999, when the disproportionate repression of a peaceful sit-in by Sahrawi students expressing social demands led to violent riots lasting several weeks (Shelley, 2004: 115–121; Smith, 2005: 557; Stephan & Mundy, 2006: 11–13), a new era of appeasement and conciliation with the Sahrawi population was announced, coinciding with King Mohammed VI's tacit disengagement from the Settlement Plan roadmap. The idea of a 'third way' (autonomy under Moroccan sovereignty) towards the resolution of the conflict also made headway in Moroccan society. In sum, the Sahrawis were the target of first-time recognition measures in the sense of both respect (equal rights) and esteem (difference).

Within this climate, the Forum for Truth and Justice (FVJ), founded in 1999 by the most militant Moroccan human rights defenders, was unprecedentedly open to Sahrawi activists. This initiative of independent civil society within the Rabat centre had a significant impact on the Western Sahara periphery and on centre–periphery relations. In August 2000 a Sahara Section of the FVJ was established in Laayoune, thus becoming the first formal, fully operational and legal independent civil society organization in the occupied territory to be made up of Sahrawis, simply 'because the FVJ was an association of victims, that is the difference' (Interview III, 2013).[5] In parallel, strictly Sahrawi groups also continued to arise, seizing the opportunity. The Co-ordination Committee sent a vanguard group to Rabat in 1998 to build networks with representatives of foreign embassies and some Moroccan media, political parties and civil society organizations (Interview VI, 2013) and, one year later, submitted a joint application detailing some 1,200 files of human rights violations to the Independent Arbitration Committee set up by Mohammed VI (Martín Beristain & González Hidalgo, 2012, vol. 2: 267–269).

The third turning point in the evolution of the internal Sahrawi pro-independence movement came in 2003 at a particularly critical juncture at the diplomatic level when the Moroccan regime rejected the Baker Plan II,[6] which was interpreted as a sign of its fear that the independence option might win in a final referendum (Hernando de Larramendi, 2008: 191–192; *Le Journal Hebdomadaire*, 8–14 November 2003). The acceptance of this plan by the Polisario Front turned the tables (Zoubir & Benabdallah-Gambier, 2004: 68) and placed Rabat in the awkward position of being seen as a 'spoiler' by the international community. From this moment onwards, Morocco changed strategy and started openly to promote a solution of permanent autonomy that excluded the holding of a self-determination referendum. This substitute step towards recognition of Sahrawi difference within a Moroccan state framework was coupled with a more supposedly equal cross-Moroccan form of recognition of rights, namely the establishment of a widely publicized Equity and Reconciliation Commission (IER) in 2004. However, in the end the gap between the victims' expectations and the results of this flawed experience of 'transitional justice' proved to be large (Suárez Collado, 2015), especially for the Sahrawis who accounted for 23 per cent of complainants, and a precious opportunity for recognition was lost: 'We were treated like numbers' (Interview VI, 2013).[7]

The reaction by Sahrawi victims/activists to this new and paradoxical opportunity structure enabled by the Rabat centre was to create the Sahrawi Association of Victims of Gross Human Rights Violations Committed by the Moroccan State (ASVDH) in early May 2005, as well as strong protests and riots which came to be called the Sahrawi 'Intifada'.[8] Apart from its magnitude in terms of participation, extension over time and geographical scope, what made this protest cycle in the Western Saharan periphery different was the open use of pro-independence symbols and slogans and the unusual degree of attention received from the international media (Gimeno, 2013: 23). Both novelties were crucial for the elementary cognitive recognition of internal Sahrawi groups by the two significant others besides Morocco: the Polisario Front (the Tindouf centre) and the international community. In face of this, the Rabat centre chose to resume and upgrade the previous combination of the autonomy roadmap plus the spirit of 'reconciliation' (recognition of difference) by establishing a Royal Consultative Council for Saharan Affairs (CORCAS), which drafted a formal Autonomy Plan for Western Sahara.[9] On the ground, the post-'Intifada' stage was characterized by a relative decrease in repression and reduction in the isolation of the occupied territory as a result of the activists' growing use of new technologies and media, more frequent visits by foreign observers or supporters, as well as invitations to prominent internal Sahrawi leaders to participate in events abroad – the last constituting indications of recognition in the form of empathy. In October 2007, some figures from this well-connected associative elite (and former members of the dissolved FVJ-Sahara) officially founded the Collective of Sahrawi Defenders of Human Rights (CODESA), which would subsequently become a key organization (Interview X, 2013).

In 2009, two changes at international level opened up a fourth window of opportunity: the appointment of a new personal envoy of the UN secretary-general for Western Sahara, the American Christopher Ross, and the election of Barack Obama as president of the United States; while these changes represented a source of uncertainty for Morocco, they were viewed as an opportunity by the Sahrawi camp. Domestically, a dramatic tightening up was observed in Moroccan security control and rhetoric towards the Western Sahara population in response to unprecedented inter-Sahrawi reconnection between this periphery and the Tindouf centre. The first 'official' visit by seven Sahrawi pro-independence figures from the occupied territory to the Tindouf refugee camps in September 2009[10] confirmed and formalized their equal recognition (in the sense of respect) by the Polisario Front. The Rabat centre's repressive turn and the ensuing contraction of public space were explicitly reflected in Mohammed VI's warning on the anniversary of the Green March (6 November): 'There is no more room for ambiguity or duplicity: either a citizen is Moroccan or he is not. ... Either one is a patriot or one is a traitor' (Mohammed VI, 2009).[11] The most immediate consequence was the crisis that erupted in mid-November when the Moroccan authorities refused to allow Aminatou Haidar (CODESA) to enter Laayoune on her return from a trip abroad, expelling her to the Canary Islands (Spain). Her hunger strike challenging her deportation was not only successful in prompting US diplomatic intervention and reversing the Moroccan decision, but also highly profitable in terms of international recognition since it brought the internal Sahrawi activists an extraordinary level of external attention (cognitive recognition) and recognition in the form of empathy.

2010–11: Local and Arab Springs

The fifth and last turning point in this chronology can be associated with the protest cycle of the Sahrawi camp of Gdeim Izik in October–November 2010 and the subsequent regional political transformations following the Arab Spring. Some international commentators such as Noam Chomsky went so far as to argue that peripheral Gdeim Izik had been the first chapter of the Arab Spring (Errazzouki, 2012), while others maintained that the Arab Spring did not affect Western Sahara, judging by the 'semblance of stability and calm' that prevailed there for some time after this protest cycle (Boukhars, 2012: 4–5). The latter assessment, however, underestimates three issues which closely linked Gdeim Izik to the Arab Spring and which will be discussed below: first, the similarity of demands and type of activism of Gdeim Izik with those of other Arab Spring protests; second, the significance of Gdeim Izik for the Moroccan Arab Spring and vice versa; and third, the use of the Arab Spring by Sahrawi activists as a way of framing their ongoing protests in order to garner international attention and recognition.

The camp on the outskirts of Laayoune was originally set up by a group of disgruntled Sahrawi youths and unemployed graduates as a reaction to the irregular distribution of hundreds of plots of land for construction by the city council, which was criticized as having clientelist and electoral purposes (in the run-up to local elections in 2009). In the middle of a restrained but fierce power struggle between the 'wilaya' (provincial administration) and the Laayoune city council, not only did the 'wali' (provincial governor) first encourage unrest against the mayor, but he also later turned a blind eye to the rapid expansion of the camp, thus creating an unexpected and precious political opportunity for protest at local level. The number of 'khaimat' (tents) and demonstrators swiftly multiplied.[12]

The camp founders cautiously avoided displaying flags or giving it an explicit nationalist or pro-independence flavour, although they linked their complaints concerning housing and employment to alleged discrimination against 'true Sahrawis' indigenous to the territory. The Moroccan Ministry of the Interior agreed to negotiate with the protesters' Dialogue Committee and a basic agreement was reached which addressed their socio-economic demands. However, the limit of politicization seemed to have been exceeded and the camp was forcibly dismantled overnight on the following day (López García, 2011; Desrues & Hernando de Larramendi, 2011). The justification provided by Rabat authorities was, as stated in a parliamentary report, that 'the instrumentalization of social demands served outside political agendas seeking to generate violence and thus internationalize and perpetuate the camp' (*Au Fait Maroc*, 13 January 2011; see also Lakmahri & Tourabi, 2013). This intervention by the security forces provoked chaos, rioting and violence which spread to the city of Laayoune, resulting in 13 casualties (11 Moroccan policemen), acts of vandalism and reprisals between Sahrawis and Moroccans. The 'fragile coexistence' between the two communities appeared to have been broken by mounting 'ethnic tensions' (Gómez Martín, 2012). Thus, while the Gdeim Izik protest was similar to other Arab Spring protests in the appearance of the demands (socio-economic grievances which seemed quickly 'politicized')[13] and the forms of collective action (the 'occupy' tactic), it ended up reinforcing the unique nature of the conflictual context within which it took place.

At the same time, peripheral Gdeim Izik arguably played an indirect role in the Arab Spring in the Rabat centre. Sahrawi activists did not get involved in the pro-democracy protests organized by the 20 February Movement in Morocco in 2011, which represents a major difference and draws a dividing line with the behaviour of more indisputably 'Moroccan' peripheries such as the Rifian one (Suárez Collado, 2015). Conversely, the 20 February Movement did not engage with the Western Sahara issue in its political agenda because of its highly sensitive and divisive nature. However, if only as a pretext, the process of accelerated constitutional reform launched by Mohammed VI in response to new domestic and international pressures was officially justified by the long-promised process of 'advanced regionalization', which in turn largely resulted from the Sahara autonomy project and growing unrest in Western Sahara. A Consultative Commission on Regionalization (CCR) had been established in January 2010, charged with drafting and submitting this regionalization project to the king. Nonetheless, neither the new constitution approved by referendum in July 2011 (Theofilopoulou, 2012) nor the CCR plan (Interview IV, 2013),[14] which soon became deadlocked, brought about substantial institutional changes beyond the declaratory effect.

Conversely, the 2011 reform at the Rabat centre that had a more concrete impact on the ground in the Western Sahara periphery was the transformation of the old Consultative Council on Human Rights (CCDH) into the National Council on Human Rights (CNDH), which was formally more independent and prepared to propose measures towards the equal recognition of rights (respect) for the Sahrawis. The first recommendations of the new body included the grant of a royal pardon to 190 prisoners considered to be political, including Sahrawi pro-independence activists. Furthermore, the CNDH set up regional commissions all over the country, three of which were located in the Western Sahara territory (Boukhars, 2013: 4). The aim was to mitigate the 'problem of lack of intermediaries' between the Moroccan authorities and the Sahrawi population (Interview II, 2013), that is, in centre–periphery relations. When interviewed, the president of the CNDH Regional

Commission acknowledged the special situation of dealing with human rights violations occurring within a context of 'political conflict' and emphasized the difficult intermediary role played by his institution, not least since it lacked the power to enforce its own recommendations (Interview XIV, 2013).

Apart from that, the Arab Spring stage in this periphery was characterized by the recovery of previous levels of freedom of movement and a new expansion of public space, following the obstacles faced in 2009 and 2010. An increasing number of delegations of internal Sahrawi activists was able to travel to the Tindouf camps and to international meetings, just as more foreign observers, journalists, non-governmental organizations (NGOs), parliamentarians and supporters arrived in Laayoune (Gimeno, 2013: 40). Most importantly for the international recognition of internal actors, in November 2012 Christopher Ross became the first personal envoy of the UN secretary-general for Western Sahara ever to visit the specific territory in dispute – and not only Rabat, Tindouf and Algiers as his predecessors had done (*Lakome*, 21 December 2012). This generated an extraordinary pride as well as mounting expectations among the activists who met him (Interview VI, 2013; Interview VII, 2013). In all of these interactions, Sahrawi activists appropriated the Arab Spring label and used it as a universalistic framing for their protests (Interview VI, 2013; Interview X, 2013), which might have helped them at the international level to strengthen the demand to extend the mandate of MINURSO to monitor human rights in both Western Sahara and the refugee camps, as (unsuccessfully) proposed by the US to the UN Security Council in April 2013. Several Sahrawi interviewees of different political persuasions positively stressed the greater, 'never expected' US involvement in these human rights issues. 'The US Embassy knows more about our work than the Moroccan authorities themselves', said the president of the CNDH Regional Commission (Interview XIV, 2013). Thus, the regional Arab Spring context helped Sahrawi activists to increase international recognition of their positions, making up for continuing strain in relations with the Rabat centre.

The Capitalization of Existing Mobilizing Structures during the Arab Spring

This transformed structural context sat well with the type of activism which the transforming Sahrawi movement had followed over the past years, and indeed strengthened it. Two prominent strategies and repertoires of collective action stand out in the recent development of the internal Sahrawi pro-independence movement: non-violent resistance and protests inside the occupied territory on one hand and 'international diplomatic activities' (Taras & Ganguly, 2006: 32) on the other. This was enabled by the availability of pre-existing mobilizing structures within/for this periphery – meso-level groups, organizations and informal networks (McAdam et al., 1996: 3) – which can be located on four different levels: Sahrawi civil society operating locally in the peripheral Moroccan-controlled territory itself; the larger transnational inter-Sahrawi sphere also encompassing actors from the Tindouf centre, the Polisario Front and the diaspora; a limited part of civil society and institutional actors from the Rabat centre; and international civil society.

Within the Western Saharan periphery, the basis for the mobilizing structures was provided by civil society organizations which share the characteristic of operating without legal recognition, as their bids for legal status have been irregularly rejected by the Moroccan authorities under different pretexts (Human Rights Watch, 2008: 97–108). This lack of equal status does not mean that their activity is strictly clandestine, but does make them subject to regular harassment and arbitrary repression. Another prevalent trait is the focus on the universalistic sphere of human rights, with the two most relevant human rights organizations being ASVDH and CODESA. ASVDH, which claims to be the civil society organization to develop the broadest grassroots activity in the occupied territory (Interview XVI, 2013),[15] devotes its everyday work to documenting and spreading information on human rights violations, which is often supplied to foreign NGOs and governments (the annual human rights reports the US State Department regularly acknowledge this source). Therefore, its most significant contribution within the Arab Spring context was a thorough report on the Gdeim Izik events (ASVDH, 2011) which helped to set a Sahrawi narrative on this contested episode and was given credibility and relayed by international NGOs and the media. In the case of the CODESA, the focus was rather placed on 'elite work' (Interview X, 2013) and international advocacy and denunciation,[16] although a similar report needed also to be drafted on Gdeim Izik (CODESA, 2011).

Beyond the human rights sphere, politically relevant and active internal Sahrawi organizations include the Committee for the Defence of the Right to Self-Determination for the People of Western Sahara (CODAPSO),[17] the Committee for the Support of the UN Settlement Plan and the Protection of Natural Resources of Western Sahara (CSPRON) and the Trade Union Confederation of Sahrawi Workers (CSTS). CODAPSO and CSPRON share an explicitly 'political' pro-independence stance and an emphasis on (or specialization in) the issue of the Moroccan exploitation of Western Sahara's natural resources, which occupies an increasingly prominent place on the diplomatic agenda of the broader Sahrawi movement and benefits from the effective international support of the NGO Western Sahara Resource Watch (Interview VIII, 2013; Quarante, 2014). Major efforts by these organizations include the campaigns organized in 2011–12 against the fisheries and agricultural agreements between the EU and Morocco. The trade union CSTS, which was officially created in 2007 by former mine workers from Fos Boucraa but is open to members from other sectors and unemployed graduates, is also heavily involved in this international 'economic' struggle (Interview XV, 2013).

An effective division of labour exists between all of these groups (focusing on international advocacy, human rights, victims and their families, natural resources, unemployed graduates or other specific social problems) and, besides a dense social fabric and key individual networks, formal co-ordination occurs between organizations at local level within the so-called 'tansikiyat' (co-ordination committees). The Laayoune 'tansikiya' is made up of some 15 groups which meet with essentially two purposes: the preparation of joint demonstrations and planning of the reception of foreign delegations (Interview VI, 2013).[18] In fact, both kinds of action have been strategically related in recent years, with local protests being staged to coincide with foreign visits, as well as key diplomatic junctures such as the annual renewal of MINURSO's mandate by the UN Security Council. For example, a significant protest cycle took place in different Western Saharan cities in April–May 2013 not only in protest against the failure to extend MINURSO's mandate to human rights, but also encouraged by the unusual arrival of foreign observers and journalists.

Furthermore, the pro-independence groups from occupied Western Sahara are no longer isolated from the exiled population in the Tindouf centre and the Polisario Front. Technological and communicational factors, and more specifically the spread of mobile phones and internet connections, contributed more than anything to 'breaking the wall' and reducing the distance between this periphery and this centre, as well as with the Sahrawi diaspora.[19] This and other increasingly frequent transnational contacts and exchanges of all kinds (human rights associations, trade unions, youth organizations, media, family visits) have arguably helped to consolidate a shared 'Sahrawi political identity and political project' (Barreñada, 2012). At least at the societal level, they have fostered a growing recognition of hitherto peripheral internal Sahrawis by their compatriots in exile in the sense of empathy. Nonetheless, concrete 'political' inter-organizational links with the Polisario remain opaque and ambiguous (Gimeno, 2013: 36). Unlike the Moroccan official discourse which maintains the absolute identity of the external 'enemy' and its domestic 'fifth column' (Interview IV, 2013), activists from internal Sahrawi groups largely emphasized their organizational autonomy.[20] The bottom line is that there is 'sympathy and harmony on goals' (Interview V, 2013), or a broad identity-driven 'political alignment' (Interview III, 2013), but no organizational or dependency relationship between Sahrawi actors in Laayoune and Tindouf (Interview X, 2013). Despite this, the 2009 visit to Tindouf certainly broke a taboo by officializing the recognition of internal activists by the Polisario. The growing formalization of contacts was to turn into equal participation in political bodies two years later, when the 13th Polisario Popular General Congress, held in Tifariti in December 2011, for the first time officially included a delegation of activists from occupied Western Sahara.[21]

The role played by this transnational inter-Sahrawi network with regard to internal Sahrawi activists in the context of the Arab Spring involved recognition, backup and framing. Different signs of recognition were given in the sense of respect (recognition of equal status) and empathy (recognition through understanding and affection), yet always avoiding esteem (recognition of difference) for the sake of the unity of the larger Sahrawi movement. Backup was visibly provided by the spread of information and the placing of a growing official emphasis on human rights violations and resistance in the occupied territory, which were now established by the Polisario as a major bone of contention with Morocco at diplomatic level, together with the demand to extend MINURSO's mandate to human rights. Although they should not be fully dismissed outright, Moroccan suspicions of material support or funding for internal Sahrawi activism have not been backed by evidence. Framing entailed placing all manifestations of internal Sahrawi activism within the unifying framework of a single Sahrawi nationalist struggle, as happened for the Gdeim Izik protest.

As regards the interaction between the peripheral internal Sahrawi movement and the Rabat centre, the activists' relations with a limited number of Moroccan, 'Moroccanized' or somehow intermediary actors, placed halfway between Rabat and Laayoune, have also proved to be relevant. Among civil society organizations, the pioneering Moroccan Association for Human Rights (AMDH) stands out as a taboo-breaking exception due to its simultaneous work at Moroccan state level and in the occupied territory, which has however come at the expense of constant internal rifts. The AMDH branch in Laayoune is open to activists of all political persuasions, but is in practice mostly made up of Sahrawis, many of whom combine this membership with parallel engagement with other associations, most notably the CODESA. As a result, it has been subject to official harassment akin to that of pro-independence groups (Interview XI, 2013). In practice, the AMDH is used as a 'node' or interface between Sahrawi and Moroccan civil society, for example, in the context of the follow-up committee on the recommendations of the Equity and Reconciliation Commission or campaigning against the military trial of 25 Gdeim Izik activists in February 2013.

At institutional level, the main intermediary actor in these centre–periphery relations since the Arab Spring has been the CNDH Regional Commission in Laayoune (Interview XIV, 2013), even though Sahrawi activists perceive their access to this Moroccan consultative body as a double-edged sword. Some of them refuse all co-operation since the CNDH does not meet the international standards for national human rights institutions (Paris Principles) and its Laayoune branch is led by co-opted Sahrawis, while others maintain personal contacts with its officials, recognizing their good faith but limited room for manoeuvre (Interview X, 2013) in securing practical improvements for the human rights situation in the territory (treatment of detainees, prison conditions, replacement of certain security officials). At a more individual level, an also widely recognized 'nodal' or bridging role is that played by former Polisario dissident and member of the Moroccan parliament Gajmoula Bint Ebbi (Progress and Socialism Party, PPS) who, despite her involvement in Moroccan institutional politics, is said by some to have 'always been with the Sahrawis' (Interview VI, 2013). Interviewees acknowledged her positive contribution as part of the official team that negotiated with the Gdeim Izik protesters in November 2010, her subsequent bold denunciation of the forcible dismantling of the camp and her personal support for the activists who faced military trials along with their families (Interview I, 2013).

The specific international connections and networks that can be viewed as integral to the mobilizing structures of the internal Sahrawi movement include most notably foreign advocacy groups and NGOs. Some relevant state diplomatic representatives, in particular those of the US, British and Swedish embassies in Rabat, have shown a growing willingness to establish direct contact with Sahrawi human rights activists. However, their job is largely limited to that of observers or interlocutors. More active or overt support work is carried out at the level of civil society through international networks which partially overlap but do not conflate themselves with those backing the Polisario and the Tindouf refugees. The more visible and effective partners nowadays are the international human rights organizations Amnesty

International and Human Rights Watch, the US-based Robert F. Kennedy Center for Justice and Human Rights (RFK Center) and the network Western Sahara Resource Watch. These advocacy groups serve as interfaces between local activists and international institutions, and lobby in three crucial arenas: the UN Human Rights Council (HRC), the US Administration and Congress, and the European Parliament.

For instance, CODESA co-drafted with the RFK Center and five other international organizations a joint report on the human rights situation in Western Sahara which was submitted to the 'troika' in charge of the HRC's Universal Periodic Review of Morocco in May–June 2012.[22] At the end of that year, the UN special rapporteur on torture, Juan E. Méndez, visited Morocco and Western Sahara to prepare another report for the HRC which was in no sense indulgent of the Rabat authorities (OHCHR, 22 September 2012). The lobbying of the RFK Center, Amnesty International and Human Rights Watch was instrumental in pushing the Obama Administration and its UN ambassador to circulate a draft Security Council resolution in April 2013 seeking to extend MINURSO's mandate to human rights monitoring (although it was ultimately unsuccessful). One year later, Aminatou Haidar again requested the same measure in the US Congress (SPS, 24 March 2014). As regards WSRW, it played a decisive role in the campaign that ended with the European Parliament's rejection of the protocol of extension of the EU–Morocco fisheries agreement in December 2011 due to, among other things, persistent legal doubts regarding the inclusion of the territorial waters of Western Sahara.[23] In 2012, another resolution of the European Parliament expressed 'concern at the deterioration of human rights in Western Sahara' and called for the 'release of all Sahrawi political prisoners' (European Parliament, 2012).

Outcomes and Conclusions

Assessments of the results to date of the internal Sahrawi pro-independence movement's domestic and international strategies vary greatly depending on the point of view. As in the cases of most of the peripheries addressed in this special issue, the outcomes seem meagre from a structural and 'objective', ultimately *external* perspective (Huber & Kamel, 2015). Protests in occupied Western Sahara have certainly not led to better socio-economic conditions or greater political autonomy for the territory, nor have they increased the chances of a global resolution of the conflict according to these actors' preferences (self-determination) in the international diplomatic sphere. The Gdeim Izik protest and the subsequent Arab Spring developments stopped short of changing the foundations of Moroccan regional and local governance. Neither the new 2011 constitution nor the regionalization project that accompanied it at the Rabat centre brought about substantial institutional changes. The reform of the Political Parties Act approved in October 2011 did not lift the existing ban on the formation of parties on an ethnic or regional basis. The below-average abstention rates recorded in these 'southern provinces' in 2011 in both the July constitutional referendum and the November legislative elections could well be used to legitimize the status quo (Boukhars, 2012: 4–5).

Nonetheless, there is also some room for optimism, as the international pressure on the Moroccan authorities obtained by internal Sahrawis has lately brought about some tangible changes in centre–periphery relations. As recently confirmed by leaked confidential documents of the Moroccan diplomacy, President Obama put forward three specific demands to King Mohammed VI during their meeting in Washington in November 2013: to put an end to military trials for civilians, to allow the UN high commissioner for human rights to visit Western Sahara and to legalize Sahrawi associations such as ASVDH and CODESA.[24] Steps towards the fulfilment of the first two requests were taken in March and May 2014, respectively (*Yabiladi*, 14 March 2014; OHCHR, 29 May 2014). As regards the legalization of associations, it was the subject of a recommendation by the CNDH according to a trial balloon issued in late 2013 (EFE, 20 November 2013), but it has not materialized to date.

The strategies of the internal Sahrawis during the Arab Spring appear to be most successful when one considers these actors' 'subjective' accounts and the extent to which they perceive that their self-descriptions or self-interpretations have been acknowledged and validated by external others. That is to say, their outcomes as a periphery need to be judged first and foremost in terms of the recognition gained – or seized – from three significant others: the Moroccan state, the Polisario Front and the international community. The Rabat centre might have been the most prolific promoter of policies of recognition towards this periphery, from equal human rights initiatives to recognition of difference and material reparations. However, as they have taken place against the backdrop of structural misrecognition of the Sahrawis entailing an essential lack of respect or equal status (human rights violations, repression of pro-independence activists, no legal recognition for Sahrawi civil society organizations), these partial actions have been flawed by an inherent mismatch with the self-identity of the target actors. They have thus been largely ineffective if not ultimately counterproductive for Moroccan interests.

Conversely, the internal Sahrawi activists have achieved growing cognitive recognition (attention) and respect (equal status) from the Tindouf centre and relevant international actors, including the UN and the US, as well as considerable empathy from inter-Sahrawi and foreign civil society. Cautious optimism prevailed in the responses provided during the author's interviews, based above all on the movement's successes in the Arab Spring context in making its voice heard and achieving a certain impact in international fora, hand in hand with its international support and advocacy networks. However excessive the activists' expectations of future influence on the US Administration and the European Parliament may seem, their 'subjective' views do reveal the invaluable significance of these international connections and achievements, if only for their coming into existence and the assertion of a long-denied identity. This suggests some parallels with the internationalization strategy followed by the Palestinians since 2011, with the UN statehood bid as the most emblematic measure, although the extent of this inspiration is qualified by the Sahrawis' more peripheral position, lack of an internationally recognized state-like 'authority' and less developed foreign networks.

While the larger and complex reconstruction of Sahrawi communal and/or national identity which appears to have been underway since the turn of the millennium falls beyond the scope of this article, it seems clear that each of the above-mentioned forms of (mis)recognition has had a distinct impact on the dynamics of identity construction of the internal Sahrawis. Most conspicuously, the Moroccan (depoliticized) recognition of Sahrawi cultural difference has accidentally fostered an ethnicization that transcends colonial territorial demarcations, while the international recognition of internal Sahrawi civil society has encouraged the latter to concentrate on universalistic issues such as human rights and the exploitation of the natural resources of the occupied territory, even more so since 2010–11 in order to accommodate and capitalize on the Arab Spring framing.

Altogether, this article has shown that the emergence and empowerment of internal Sahrawi pro-independence activism has to be seen in the context of varying sets of opportunity structures actively seized by this peripheral movement over the last two decades through the symbiotic combination of domestic non-violent resistance and international 'diplomatic' activities. The Arab Spring has offered the latest window of opportunity in this chronology and Sahrawis have successfully been able to frame their protests within this paradigm. Building on comparatively rich mobilization structures at the local, inter-Sahrawi, Moroccan and international levels, internal Sahrawis have been relatively more effective than other peripheries treated in this volume at garnering international recognition, which has helped to strengthen and crystallize their own identity.

Acknowledgements

In memory of Lahcen Moutik who passed away in December 2013, a few months after our interview. Thanks to Miguel Hernando de Larramendi and Michal Natorski for their feedback on the empirical work and the theoretical hints, to the editors of this special issue and to all of the interviewees from Laayoune and Rabat (also those who asked for confidentiality).

Disclosure statement

No potential conflict of interest was reported by the author.

Notes

1. See the classification of conflicts in Ramsbotham et al. (2011: 76).
2. Sahrawi national liberation movement fighting against Moroccan presence in Western Sahara and recognized by the UN General Assembly in 1979 as 'the representative of the people of Western Sahara'.
3. In this article the term 'internal Sahrawi' is applied to civil society, organizations, groups, activists and leaders operating inside Western Sahara occupied territory, which self-define as 'Sahrawi' and broadly favour independence, in order to emphasize the distinction between them and their counterparts in the refugee camps of Tindouf or the diaspora, which is central to the argument. For an overview of Sahrawi civil society in the Tindouf camps, see Darbouche & Colombo (2011).
4. A period of heightened state violence against political opposition under the reign of Hassan II, from the 1960s to the 1980s.
5. The Moroccan Association of Human Rights (AMDH) had also opened a pioneer office there shortly before, but at that time only included members of Moroccan origin. Viewed as increasingly menacing by the Rabat authorities, the FVJ-Sahara was eventually dissolved by the Laayoune Court of First

Instance in June 2003 on the grounds that it used 'human rights as a cover to pursue both violent and diplomatic "separatist" activities' (Human Rights Watch, 2008: 99–101).

6. The Baker Plan II represented a polished proposal for a mixed solution combining a stage of transitory autonomy with a final referendum on self-determination.

7. Not only was the Western Sahara territory excluded from the collective reparation programme designed for some regions, but also the public hearing scheduled in Laayoune was eventually cancelled (Vairel, 2006: 243). 'The IER rather than addressing the particular breadth of violations suffered by Sahrawis, increased their feelings of marginalization' (Amnesty International, 2010: 269–275).

8. In late May, a small rally in Laayoune opposing the transfer of a Sahrawi prisoner to Agadir resulted in an unprecedented cycle of demonstrations, repression and riots after it was violently broken up by the Moroccan police (Mundy, 2007; Smith, 2005: 546, 558; Solà-Martín, 2007: 402; Interview XII, 2013).

9. The Autonomy Plan was to be submitted to the UN in March–April 2007, and was backed up by an ambitious diplomatic offensive.

10. The meeting organized in September 2009 stemmed from an initiative of internal groups later adopted by the Polisario (Interview III, 2013), which resulted in the arrest of the activists on their return to Laayoune, amid a climate of Moroccan patriotic outrage. In spite of the obstacles faced, this ground-breaking visit set a precedent and was to become the first of a handful of journeys to Tindouf in subsequent years.

11. This address was highlighted as a pivotal fact almost unanimously in the author's interviews (for example Interview XIII, 2013).

12. Some estimates refer to around 6,500–8,000 tents and 20,000–25,000 protesters (Gómez Martín, 2012).

13. The distinction between socio-economic and 'political' protest is widespread in the literature on the Arab Spring and social movements in this region (Bergh & Rossi-Doria, 2015). For a critique of the 'hierarchy of struggles' implicit within this dichotomy, see Bogaert (2014: 2–4) and, in the case of Western Sahara, see Veguilla (2009).

14. A draft regionalization bill following the recommendations of this Commission was presented by the Moroccan government in the summer of 2014.

15. Set up in 2005 by former members of the Co-ordination Committee, ASVDH is characterized by its self-definition as an 'association of victims'. Although all legalization procedures established by the Moroccan Association Law were followed, the Moroccan authorities continued to treat it as an 'unrecognized' organization. ASVDH has sections in several cities of Western Sahara as well as southern Morocco (Barreñada, 2012), but its failure to secure normalization has prevented it from having a proper membership record, so in principle 'any victim can consider himself/herself as a member' (Interview VI, 2013).

16. CODESA was formally created in 2007 as the successor of the former FVJ-Sahara, although the Moroccan authorities prevented its founding congress from being held and refused to legalize it, arguing that its principles undermined the state's 'territorial integrity' and that its focus on the Sahrawi population amounted to 'discrimination'. Due to this legal situation, the only internal body established within the organization is a 14-member secretariat (*bureau*). The three tasks performed are assisting the victims of violations to file both lawsuits and complaints with the CNDH, preparing annual and thematic reports concerning the human rights situation in Western Sahara, and carrying out international advocacy work (Interview X, 2013).

17. CODAPSO was founded in April 2005 by the renowned Mohammed Daddach, the longest Sahrawi prisoner of war held by Morocco (1976–2001) and former Polisario Front fighter, in response, he said, to 'the Moroccan propaganda regarding the Autonomy Plan' (Interview VII, 2013).

18. Another local 'tansikiya' was operating in the city of Smara at the time of Christopher Ross' visit in October 2013. The only relevant group that prefers to stay out of these inter-organizational networks is the CODESA (Interview X, 2013), which suggests a subtle strategic and tactical cleavage with the other leading organization, the ASVDH. The opposition between grassroots activity vs. 'elite work' and promotion vs. rejection of local inter-organizational co-ordination roughly describe the acknowledged differences between their respective approaches. This is coupled with some inevitable competition for domestic leadership and international attention and recognition at both individual

and organizational level, even though in general co-operation visibly prevails over tensions or fragmentation.

19. In the early 2000s, the use of mobile phones started to become widespread, rendering futile the previous restrictions on international calls from landlines in the occupied territory, while the internet entered the scene with the appearance of the first cybercafés. Later on, in 2009, another powerful vehicle for inter-Sahrawi reconnection in the media sphere came with the launch of regular RASD TV broadcasts from Tindouf, which soon became the most widely watched channel in the Moroccan-controlled Western Sahara (Interview IX, 2013).

20. Two vital yet somehow contradictory discursive red lines were at stake here for a mixture of pragmatic/tactical and principled/identity reasons. On the one hand, any questioning of the unity and unanimity of the broader Sahrawi movement is avoided as being detrimental to the nationalist struggle and the preservation of the legal self-determination framework, to which pro-independence Sahrawis of all sides remain attached. On the other hand, any acknowledgement of integral connections with the Polisario would play into the hands of the Moroccan authorities, giving them a pretext to justify harsher repression of internal activists. An additional more identity-related explanation is that the internal groups' own search for recognition also discourages them from blending themselves in with the Polisario.

21. The 54 members of this delegation, who belonged to organizations such as CODESA, CODAPSO, ASVDH and CSPRON, were involved in the so-called Commission of the Occupied Territories and the Intifada of Independence (SPS, 20 December 2011), and participated in all votes on an equal footing with the other congress delegates (Interview VII, 2013; Interview VIII, 2013).

22. http://www.cihrs.org/wp-content/uploads/2012/05/RFK-Center-Joint-UPR-Submission-Morocco.pdf.

23. However, a new fisheries protocol was signed and adopted by the European Parliament and Council at the end of 2013.

24. See, for example, Fiche USA-UK/Projet de lettre du MAEC au Roi du Maroc, Rabat, 3 February 2014, leaked document available at http://www.arso.org/Coleman/Fiche%20usa-uk.pdf.

References

Amnesty International (2010) *Broken Promises. The Equity and Reconciliation Commission and its Follow-up* (London: Amnesty International).

Association Sahraouie des Victimes des Violations Graves des Droits de l'Homme [ASVDH] (2011) *Rapport de l'ASVDH sur le campement de Gdeim Izik et les événements qui ont suivi son démantèlement* (Laayoune: ASVDH).

Azar, E.E. (1990) *The Management of Protracted Social Conflict: Theory and Cases* (Aldershot: Dartmouth).

Barreñada, I. (2012) Asociacionismo y cuestión nacional en el Sáhara Occidental, *Revista de Estudios Internacionales Mediterráneos*, 13.

Bergh, S. & D. Rossi-Doria (2015) Plus ça change? Observing the dynamics of Morocco's 'Arab Spring' in the High Atlas, Mediterranean Politics, 20(2). doi: 10.1080/13629395.2015.1033900.

Bogaert, K. (2015) The Revolt of Small Towns: The Meaning of Morocco's History and the Geography of Social Protests, *Review of African Political Economy*, 42(143), pp. 124–140.

Boukhars, A. (2012) Simmering Discontent in the Western Sahara, Carnegie Endowment for International Peace/Carnegie Middle East Program, March.

Boukhars, A. (2013) Western Sahara: Beyond Complacency, FRIDE, Policy Brief 163, September.

Colectivo de Defensores de Derechos Humanos Saharauis [CODESA] (2011) *Campamento Gdeim Izik* (Laayoune: CODESA).

Dann, N. (2014) Nonviolent Resistance in the Western Sahara, *Peace Review*, 26(1), pp. 46–53. doi:10.1080/10402659.2014.876312.

Darbouche, H. & S. Colombo (2011) The EU, Civil Society and Conflict Transformation in Western Sahara: The Failure of Disengagement, in: N. Tocci (Ed.) *The European Union, Civil Society and Conflict* (London: Routledge), pp. 126–146.

Desrues, T. & M. Hernando de Larramendi (2011) Initiatives souveraines, attentisme partisan et protestation au Sahara: une année politique transitoire au Maroc, in: *L'Année du Maghreb 2010* (Paris: CNRS), pp. 305–332.

Errazzouki, S. (2012) Chomsky on the Western Sahara and the 'Arab Spring', *Jadaliyya*, 30 October.

European Parliament (2012) Resolution on the Annual Report on Human Rights and Democracy in the World 2011 and the European Union's Policy on the Matter, 13 December.

Fraser, N. & A. Honneth (2003) *Redistribution or Recognition? A Political-Philosophical Exchange* (London: Verso).

Gimeno, S. (2013) Situación de los derechos civiles y políticos en el Sáhara Occidental: de 1999 a la actualidad, Seminario de Investigación para la Paz, 30 May.

Gómez Martín, C. (2012) Sahara Occidental: quel scénario après Gdeim Izik? in: *L'Année du Maghreb 2011* (Paris: CNRS), pp. 259–276.

Hernando de Larramendi, M. (2008) Intra-Maghrebi Relations. Unitary Myth and National Interests, in: Y.H. Zoubir & H. Amirah Fernández (Eds) *North Africa: Politics, Region, and the Limits of Transformation* (London: Routledge), pp. 179–201.

Honneth, A. (1996) *The Struggle for Recognition: The Moral Grammar of Social Conflicts* (Cambridge, MA: MIT Press).

Huber, D. & L. Kamel (2015) Arab Spring: The Role of the Peripheries, Mediterranean Politics, 20(2). doi: 10.1080/13629395.2015.1033905.

Human Rights Watch (2008) *Human Rights in Western Sahara and in the Tindouf Refugee Camps. Morocco/Western Sahara/Algeria* (New York, NY: Human Rights Watch).

Lakmahri, S. & A. Tourabi (2013) Le Maroc a-t-il échoué au Sahara? *Zamane*, 28, pp. 34–41.

Lindemann, T. (2010) *Causes of War: The Struggle for Recognition* (Colchester: ECPR).

Lindemann, T. & E. Ringmar (Eds) (2012) *The International Politics of Recognition* (London: Paradigm).

López García, B. (2011) Sahara-Marruecos: el miedo a la autonomía, *Política Exterior*, 139, pp. 38–46.

Martín Beristain, C. & E. González Hidalgo (2012) *El oasis de la memoria. Memoria histórica y violaciones de Derechos Humanos en el Sáhara Occidental* (San Sebastián: Universidad del País Vasco/Hegoa).

McAdam, D., J.D. McCarthy & M.N. Zald (Eds) (1996) *Comparative Perspectives on Social Movements: Political Opportunities, Mobilizing Structures, and Cultural Framings* (Cambridge: Cambridge University Press).

Mohammed VI (2009) Discours de SM le Roi à la Nation à l'occasion du 34ᵉ anniversaire de la Marche Verte, Available at http://www.maroc.ma/fr/discours-royaux/discours-de-sm-le-roi-%C3%A0-la-nation-%C3%A0-loccasion-du-34%C3%A8me-anniversaire-de-la-marche

Mohsen-Finan, K. (1997) *Sahara Occidental. Les enjeux d'un conflit régional* (Paris: CNRS).

Mundy, J. (2007) Western Sahara between Autonomy and Intifada, *Middle East Report Online*, 16(3).

Mundy, J. & S. Zunes (2014) Western Sahara. Nonviolent Resistance as a Last Resort, in: V. Dudouet (Ed.) *Civil Resistance and Conflict Transformation: Transitions from Armed to Nonviolent Struggle* (London: Routledge), pp. 20–44.

Pace, M. (2013) An Arab 'Spring' of a Different Kind? Resilience and Freedom in the Case of an Occupied Nation, *Mediterranean Politics*, 18(1), pp. 42–59. doi:10.1080/13629395.2012.745705.

Quarante, O. (2014) Si riche Sahara occidental, *Le Monde Diplomatique*, March.

Ramsbotham, O., T. Woodhouse & H. Miall (2011) *Contemporary Conflict Resolution. The Prevention, Management and Transformation of Deadly Conflicts*, 3ʳᵈ ed. (Cambridge: Polity).

Shelley, T. (2004) *Endgame in the Western Sahara. What Future for Africa's Last Colony?* (London: Zed Book).

Smith, L.E. (2005) The Struggle for Western Sahara: What Future for Africa's Last Colony?, *The Journal of North African Studies*, 10(3–4), pp. 545–563.

Solà-Martín, A. (2007) The Western Sahara Cul-de-Sac, *Mediterranean Politics*, 12(3), pp. 399–405.

Stephan, M.J. & J. Mundy (2006) A Battlefield Transformed: From Guerrilla Resistance to Mass Nonviolent Struggle in the Western Sahara, *Journal of Military and Strategic Studies*, 8(3), pp. 1–32.

Suárez Collado, A. (2015) Territorial Stress in Morocco: From Democratic to Autonomist Demands in Popular Protests in the Rif, *Mediterranean Politics*, 20(2). doi: 10.1080/13629395.2015.1033908.

Taras, R. & R. Ganguly (2006) *Understanding Ethnic Conflict: The International Dimension*, 3rd ed. (New York, NY: Longman).

Tarrow, S. (2003) *Power in Movement: Social Movements and Contentious Politics*, 2nd ed. (Cambridge: Cambridge University Press).

Taylor, C. (1994) Politics of Recognition, in: C. Taylor & A. Gutmann (Eds) *Multiculturalism: Examining the Politics of Recognition* (Princeton: Princeton University Press), pp. 25–73.

Theofilopoulou, A. (2012) Morocco's New Constitution and the Western Sahara Conflict – a missed opportunity? *The Journal of North African Studies*, 17(4), pp. 687–696. doi:10.1080/13629387.2012.686297.

Thompson, S. (2006) *The Political Theory of Recognition: A Critical Introduction* (Cambridge: Polity).

Vairel, F. (2006) L'Instance Équité et Réconciliation au Maroc: lexique international de la réconciliation et situation autoritaire, in: S. Lefranc (Ed.) *Après le conflit, la réconciliation?* (Paris: Michel Houdiard), pp. 229–253.

Veguilla, V. (2009) L'articulation du politique dans un espace protestataire en recomposition. Les mobilisations des jeunes Sahraouis à Dakhla, in: *L'Année du Maghreb 2008* (Paris: CNRS), pp. 95–110.

Zoubir, Y.H. & K. Benabdallah-Gambier (2004) Morocco, Western Sahara and the Future of the Maghrib, *The Journal of North African Studies*, 9(1), pp. 49–77. doi:10.1080/1362938042000292306.

Zunes, S. & J. Mundy (2010) *Western Sahara: War, Nationalism and Conflict Irresolution* (New York, NY: Syracuse University Press).

Interviews

Interview I, Abderrahman Zayou, Sahrawi activist, member of the Dialogue Committee of the Gdeim Izik protest camp subjected to military trial. Rabat, 5 June 2013.

Interview II, Rahal Boubrik, director of the Centre des Études Sahariennes and professor of Sociology, University Mohammed V Rabat, advisor of the president of the National Council for Human Rights (CNDH). Rabat, 6 June 2013.

Interview III, Lahcen Moutik, former Sahrawi leader of the Forum for Truth and Justice (FVJ). Rabat, 6 June 2013.

Interview IV, Abdelhamid El Ouali, professor of International Law and International Relations, University Hassan II Casablanca, and former member of the Consultative Commission on Regionalization (CCR). Casablanca, 7 June 2013.

Interview V, Brahim Elansari, research assistant at Human Rights Watch (Middle East and North Africa Division). Rabat, 7 June 2013.

Interview VI, Elghalia Djimi and Brahim Sabbar, respectively vice-president and secretary-general of the Sahrawi Association of Victims of Gross Human Rights Violations Committed by the Moroccan State (ASVDH). Laayoune, 9 June 2013.

Interview VII, Mohammed Daddach, president of the Committee for the Defence of the Right to Self-Determination for the People of Western Sahara (CODAPSO). Laayoune, 9 June 2013.

Interview VIII, Ali Salem Babeit, Abdelhay Toubali and Salha Boutenghiza, respectively vice-president and members of the Committee for the Support of the UN Settlement Plan and the Protection of Natural Resources of Western Sahara (CSPRON). Laayoune, 10 June 2013.

Interview IX, Hayat Hatari and Salha Boutenghiza, volunteer reporters of RASD TV in Laayoune. Laayoune, 10 June 2013.

Interview X, Ali Salem Tamek, Larbi Messaoud, Lidri Hussein, Mohamed Salem Lakhal and Mohamed Fadel Gaoudi, respectively vice-president, secretary-general and members of the secretariat of the Collective of Sahrawi Defenders of Human Rights (CODESA). Laayoune, 10 June 2013.

Interview XI, Hamoud Iguilid, president of the Laayoune section of the Moroccan Association of Human Rights (AMDH). Laayoune, 10 June 2013.

Interview XII, Group of former political prisoners arrested during the 2005 'Intifada'. Laayoune, 11 June 2013.

Interview XIII, Mohamed Boukhaled and Mohamed Lehbib Ergueibi, Sahrawi lawyers and defence counsels of many activists. Laayoune, 11 June 2013.

Interview XIV, Mohammed Salem Cherkaoui, president of the Regional Commission of Laayoune-Smara of the National Council on Human Rights (CNDH). Laayoune, 12 June 2013.

Interview XV, Sidi Ahmed Eddia, secretary-general of the Trade Union Confederation of Sahrawi Workers (CSTS), and four other members of its executive board. Laayoune, 12 June 2013.

Interview XVI, Brahim Dahane, president of the Sahrawi Association of Victims of Gross Human Rights Violations Committed by the Moroccan State (ASVDH). Laayoune, 12 June 2013.

Periphery Discourse: An Alternative Media Eye on the Geographical, Social and Media Peripheries in Egypt's Spring

KHALED ELGHAMRY

Associate Professor of Computational Linguistics, Ain Shams University, Cairo, Egypt

ABSTRACT   *The growing literature on the use of social media for social protests generally, and during the Arab Spring in particular, has generally failed to show a periphery-inclusive perspective. This article employs statistical data on the use of alternative media outlets (Facebook, Twitter, blogs and YouTube) in Egypt's spring to show how an alternative media structure was expanding which not only empowered social and geographic peripheral actors but was, in turn, also empowered by their contributions. YouTube videos and Twitter messages from peripheral areas exposed police brutality towards protestors in the backstreets that could otherwise have been unnoticed and saved lives in isolated areas in Egypt. Social media thus gained critical mass and expanded to the point that it had an overflow effect from the virtual sphere to the real world. Contrasting the roles of alternative and state-run media machines in different phases of the revolution, the article traces how peripheries could challenge the existing opportunity structure through alternative media, but also how their role has contracted again after the revolution reached its peak.*

Introduction

There has been increasing interest in studying different aspects of how social media outlets have been used in the protest movements that have erupted since late December 2010 in Tunisia, Egypt, Libya, Bahrain, Syria and Yemen.[1] Felix Tusa (2013), using an analysis of a few thousand sample Twitter messages and Facebook posts, has argued for the Egyptian case that the Internet and social media were far more effective tools for framing protest movements than for organizing them, and that the success of the movement was largely thanks to the Egyptian protesters' focus on traditional methods of organization rather than relying on the Internet. Analysing 3 million tweets, gigabytes of YouTube content as well as thousands of blog posts on the protest movements in Tunisia and Egypt, Howard et al. (2011) argued that social media played a central role in shaping political debates in the Arab Spring, where conversations about revolution often preceded major events on the ground, and that social media carried inspiring stories of protest across international borders.

Alex Scott (2012) used case studies from Egypt and Tunisia to demonstrate that the increased legitimacy given to social movements, through the use of social media as a legitimate tool for gathering reliable information, has enabled social media to act as a sounding board for dissenting opinions. This has acted as a catalyst for social movements to reach a tipping point where they have globally become the new means of engaging in civil unrest. Essam Mansour (2012) used material from two focus groups of individuals who participated in the 25 January protests to assess the potential role of social networking sites (SNSs) in the revolution. The findings of the study showed that (1) the users of these sites during the protests were likely to be male, under 30 years of age and educated; (2) university professors followed by engineers, lawyers, teachers and students were the most likely to use SNSs in this revolution; (3) participants were more likely to be experienced users of SNSs (more than half of them had been using these for about two years); and (4) all participants confirmed that the role of SNSs in the Egyptian revolution was very significant to them and that SNSs – especially Facebook, YouTube, blogs and Twitter – have played a major role in mobilizing and in connecting demonstrators and co-ordinating their efforts against the regime.

What has been lacking in these studies, however, is a large-scale quantitative description of the role that social media played as a periphery-empowering tool in protests. Thus, this contribution looks at peripheries from the media angle, which is crucial since the alternative media structure has both empowered peripheries and been empowered by them. This article is based on a detailed quantitative analysis of how and to what effect alternative media outlets such as Facebook, Twitter, blogs and YouTube were used by peripheries in the different phases of the Arab Spring protests in Egypt by examining their interaction with and influence on a repressive political core and its traditional media machine.

A fundamental assumption here is that a large-scale quantitative analysis of the role of the social media outlets in the Egyptian version of the Arab Spring provides enough data for exploring history from below of this part of Egypt's modern history. A possible and legitimate criticism of this approach is that the data sources are restricted to the users of social media and do not include peripheries that participated in the protests but did not use these outlets either in mobilization or in recording the details of their participation. However, the quantitative analysis presented here provides an approximation of a bottom-up history of this period for a two reasons. Furthermore, social media sample data is diversified in such a way that the perspectives of a good number of participating social, geographical, gender and religious peripheries are represented, and in quantitatively reasonable detail.

This contribution is divided into four sections: the next section details the methodology of data collection, preparation and analysis. The following section gives an overview of the Egyptian media structure before the 25 January protests – in other words of the existing opportunity structure in the media field. This is contrasted by a section that presents the emergence of an alternative media structure. To frame this within the conceptual framework of this volume, this should be seen as the meso structure (see introductory chapter by Huber and Kamel in this volume). The article then discusses the strategies of geographic and social peripheries within this evolving alternative structure and their achievements in six stages, arguing that this alternative structure on the meso level has not only empowered peripheries but has also been empowered by them as they provided it with a critical mass, so enabling an overflow effect from the virtual sphere to the 'real world'. To assess the outcome, the article then traces the expansions and contractions which the alternative media structure has witnessed after the peak of the Egyptian revolution in three phases (the SCAF, Morsi and El-Sisi eras), before concluding.

Methodology

The data for this chapter were collected from four alternative media sources: Facebook, Twitter, blogosphere and YouTube, using as search terms Arabic key words and phrases that are strongly related to the Arab Spring uprisings. In the case of Twitter, the hashtag #Jan25 was also used as a search term. A list of such terms was compiled and searches were conducted using Google, Bing and the search services in YouTube and Twitter. The search process was conducted on a daily basis during the period from 25 January to 12 February 2011. It is important to mention here that the list of keywords and phrases was updated daily in order to include new ones that emerged as events developed. Searches by date were also conducted for pre-25 January content so as to determine the exact time when the calls for the protests first began. Search results were then retrieved and the mark-up encodings stripped off. The output of these processes is a list of protest-related content units.

For every unit the following information was extracted: (1) the user who generated the content and his/her profile information, if available; (2) the timestamp which carries the exact date on which the unit was produced; (3) the number of views, comments and the length for YouTube videos; (4) the number of retweets for the short messages on Twitter; and (5) the number of comments for every Facebook and blog post.

The content of every unit was then analysed as follows. First, a sample of the content in each channel was manually analysed in order to determine the type and location of the event or topic in every unit described or discussed. The output of the analysis is a list of events and topics that summarize the major themes during the protests. This annotated sample was then automatically analysed in order to identify the linguistic signature that is strongly associated with every theme. The linguistic signature of a given topic is a set of words and phrases that are strongly related to this particular topic (Lin & Hovy, 2000; Zhou et al., 2007). These signatures were then used to automatically annotate the rest of the content for theme and location. The two processes of signature selection and automated annotation were repeated several times, where samples were manually checked and the signature modified and updated accordingly to guarantee the maximum level of annotation accuracy.

Three important points should be mentioned: (1) this annotation was also used to classify Facebook pages and groups in terms of the dominant interest of each; (2)

Twitter short messages and video captions on YouTube were assigned one topic; and (3) long Facebook and blog posts were assigned more than one topic.

The processes of data capturing and content analysis were performed using tools developed by the author of this article for web information retrieval, analytics and text analysis. These tools were used later in collecting and classifying the content for the Arabic Digital Content Statistical Database.[2]

The Media Landscape in Egypt before 25 January

The opportunity structure in the media field prior to the protests of 25 January 2011, was relatively limited as Egyptian media outlets were deeply implicated with the state. Newspapers and broadcast television in Egypt could be classified according to their distance from the state (this section is adapted from Peterson, 2011 and Abdulla, 2013). State newspapers were unreservedly pro-regime and served as the voice of the government. Their editors were appointed by the Ministry of Information and the newspapers were funded in part from the state treasury. State newspapers not only reported events from the government's perspective, but constructed heroic narratives around the persons of leading government figures, and the Mubarak family in particular. *Party newspapers* were published by officially sanctioned political parties. Fourteen of Egypt's political parties had the right to publish their own newspapers, receiving a small subsidy from the government and sometimes the use of government presses. Most of these were small, weekly publications, with the exception of the newspapers published by Al-Wafd, Al-Ahrar and Al-Ghad parties. Although by definition these newspapers took anti-government positions on many issues, state domination was exercised through control of subsidies, and journalists and editors were liable to prosecution under emergency law if they violated certain taboos, such as direct criticism of the president or his family.

Independent newspapers, also often called opposition newspapers, are for-profit newspapers licensed by the state. The most prominent then were *Al-Masry Al-Youm*, *Al-Dostor*, *Al-Youm Al-Sabie* and *Al-Shorouk*. Owners of independent newspapers were required to be cleared by several security and intelligence agencies in order to receive a state licence, and the State Information Service could revoke the licence at any time. Some were required to (pay to) use state presses to publish. Independent newspapers were not pre-censored but were subject to prosecution under vague laws that prohibited journalists and broadcasters from saying or writing things that might damage 'the social peace', 'national unity, 'public order' or 'public values'. Such laws were inconsistently enforced by the state. No journalist, blogger or television reporter knew exactly where the lines were drawn or when the police might show up because they had crossed an invisible line. This produced a self-censorship far more efficient and cost-effective than direct pre-censorship would have been, while allowing the regime to state truthfully that there was no state censorship of news. *International newspapers* can be subdivided into regional and international, the former consisting of other mostly Arabic-language newspapers (but including those published by Arab communities seeking press freedom in Europe), and the latter consisting of newspapers in languages other than Arabic and published from sites outside the Middle East. Although the international press is free from both censorship and prosecution, it is against the law to 'damage Egypt's reputation abroad' by criticizing the government in foreign media, making sources for stories on Egypt necessarily less forthright in speaking to foreign reporters than they might otherwise have been.

Broadcast television in Egypt followed a similar pattern of domination by the state. Since its establishment in 1960, Egyptian television has always been regarded as the voice of the Egyptian government. Terrestrial channels and Egyptian satellite channels are under direct government supervision, operation and ownership. The Egyptian Radio and Television Union or ERTU is the state agency that operates all terrestrially broadcast television in Egypt. Since 2009, ERTU has also included the Nile TV International satellite network. Both the ERTU and the television sector chairmen are appointed by the Minister of Information. A handful of private channels exist but continually face the dilemma of creating programming that will attract audiences without provoking the authorities. All private channels are subject to indirect control by ERTU, which is the main shareholder of Egyptian Media Production City (EMPC) and Nilesat,[3] services crucial to private broadcasting. Additionally, companies producing television shows in the EMPC require licences from the Public Authority for Investment and Free Zones, which can suspend or refuse to renew licences in the case of questionable content. Egypt's emergency law granted the government complete freedom to punish political criticism. Among other things, ERTU forbade rival television news programmes, so private channels had to make do with talk shows and political commentary. In 2010, Reporters Without Borders ranked Egypt 127 out of 178 in its Press Freedom Index, which evaluates both print and television news-making.

The Internet began in Egypt as a university intranet system that connected to the global Internet in 1993. At that time, there were only about 2–3,000 Internet users in Egypt. By the time protests began in January 2011, there were nearly 20 million Internet users in Egypt (CIA World Factbook). With the rise in Internet use came a rise in the importance of social media, especially between 2005 and 2010. The potential of social media outlets, Facebook in particular, as virtual platforms for political activism and mobilization already came to the fore in 2008 during the calls for the strike on 6 April of the same year (by what became known later as the 6 April Youth Movement). Its second period of rapid expansion came in 2010 with the creation of the *We are Khaled Said* Facebook page in the name of 'Khaled Said' who was killed by police personnel in Alexandria.

The Emergence of an Alternative Media Structure

The first call for people to protest on 25 January 2011 came from Facebook and was made on 10 January at 4.35 pm Cairo time on the *We Are All Khaled Said*, page. The English translation of the original (heavily sarcastic) post in Arabic was:

Any ideas for celebrating (Egyptian) Police Day? Those people (police officers) get tired humiliating, torturing and sometimes killing Egyptian citizens. It would be really improper that their 'day' passes without us making them realize that we will never forget. Please, put forward your suggestions and ideas, preferably shocking and different ones, to pay them back for their [the officers'] favours.

On the same day, similar calls for protesting on 25 January were posted on Twitter and the Egyptian blogosphere. On 15 January, the day Tunisian president Ben Ali fled to Saudi Arabia, the first video calling for protest against torture, poverty and corruption was published on YouTube. From this date on, the four outlets together constituted the components of a citizen media machine that was effectively used in the fight against a repressive regime and a manipulative state-run media machine. These outlets were also used as an alternative platform for a new discourse that challenged dominant social and cultural norms (see also the contribution of Khatib in this volume). Each of the four channels of this alternative media structure was 'collectively unconsciously' assigned a role that fitted its nature and utilized its potential strength in the management of the events. Facebook functioned as the core of this machine and a platform for mobilization and collective planning and discussion, Twitter as 'the battlefield communication tool', YouTube as the protestors' citizen TV and blogs mainly as a theorization and interpretation platform. The following subsections elaborate the features of this alternative media structure.

Facebook: The Virtual Core

Table 1 shows the volume of the protests on Facebook. There were 2,313 Facebook pages and groups that participated in the events. These pages and groups contributed 9,816 Facebook posts, photos, events, notes and videos that received 461,120 comments. The two politically oriented Facebook pages *We Are All Khaled Said* and *The 6th of April Youth Movement* were the core of the alternative media machine, not only within Facebook but also in relation to other channels:[4] Twitter, YouTube and blogosphere. The core status of these two pages was primarily attributed to their connectedness within this machine and to the geographical distributions of those who followed the pages. For example, *We Are All Khaled Said* had links to other 127 Facebook pages and groups, 116 YouTube videos, five 'influential' blogs, and nine institutional and state-run Egyptian news sites that published news and op-eds related to the protests. *The 6th of April Youth Movement* page, on the other hand, had

Table 1. The distribution of 25 January posts and comments on Facebook

Content source	Posts (%)	Comments (%)
We Are All Khaled Said	6.7	29.4
6th of April Youth Movement	10.6	5.8
18 cities other than Cairo	4.7	4.1
Far-from-politics groups	33.4	32.8

similar connectedness but with two qualitative differences: (1) it had links to Egyptian as well as foreign news sites that provided coverage of the events, particularly *Aljazeera* and *France24*, and (2) it was concerned with aligning the 'virtual planning' with the changing dynamics of the situation in the street. These differences could be attributed to the movement's tendency to act and to 'get things done, and fast' (Abdul-Rahman, 2012):

Based on the analysis of the Facebook profiles of a sample of the followers of *We Are All Khaled Said*, it was found out that those followers came from 14 cities and towns other than Cairo in different parts in Egypt. The followers from the North-Coast (e.g. Alexandria and Behira), Delta (e.g. Dakahlia and Gharbia), and the Suez Canal area in the east (Port Said, Suez and Ismailia) governorates were clearly present. The southern cities were also represented, yet with few numbers and mainly concentrated in Asiut and Beni Suef. The sample also included a few followers from European as well as US cities.

One relevant point in this context is that during this period these two pages developed a strong awareness of being the core of an alternative and peripheral media machine and the responsibility that comes with it. This awareness was clear in frequent posts on these pages calling upon Facebook users in cities other than Cairo to send their videos and photos of the protests and confrontations with the security forces where they are located. The role of this awareness and its realization in the way these pages used Facebook was central in bringing to the spotlight ongoing protests in geographical peripheries that received no coverage, either intentionally or unintentionally, from traditional media outlets. This strategy was crucial in providing a critical mass for the revolution all over the country and throughout diverse social strata.

Table 1 also shows the volume of participation by what might be called 'far-from-politics' and apathetic types of Facebook pages and groups. The content of these pages prior to 25 January 2011 reflected a clear and strong lack of interest in politics and issues of public concern, and evolved mainly around topics such as fashion, new films, jokes and sometimes drugs and sex. However, during the events the content shifted completely to posts of mobilization and information sharing of events and regular discussions concerning the unfolding protests, to the extent that these pages contributed more than 30 per cent of both the posts and comments related to the events on Facebook. Furthermore, on 23 January it was found that Facebook users from 18 different cities other than Cairo wrote posts declaring their participation in the protests on 25 January. Many of those users contributed posts, photos and videos covering the details of the events where they lived.

Twitter: The Battlefield Communication Tool

On Twitter, there were 12,039 short messages posted by 2,789 Twitter users which were retweeted 72,746 times. The distribution of these messages reflects three different features that clearly distinguish the role Twitter played during the events as part of the citizen media machine. It was found that 47.62 per cent of these messages were related to the confrontations with the security forces in the streets.

Using the location information and the 'sent via' feature for each of these tweets, it was found that 25.22 per cent of these messages were posted on Twitter via mobile phones by people in the locations mentioned in these tweets. Later on, messages were distributed on Twitter asking demonstrators to disable the location feature on their Twitter accounts after reports that some protesters were arrested by the police.

The second aspect highlighted the role played by Egyptian Copts, individually and institutionally, during the events. This role was documented in 5.73 per cent of the messages that (1) presented photos of a Copt human wall guarding Muslims during their prayers in Tahrir Square and (2) detailed the efforts of the Kasr Eldobara Evangelical Church, in the vicinity of Tahrir Square, in collecting medical supplies, treating the injured and allowing Muslim protestors, especially veiled and face-covered women, to conduct their prayers inside the church building as well as attend the Christian masses.

The third highlighted the role of Egyptian women in the protests, which was mainly done through using photos of women helping injured protesters and chanting slogans of protest and defiance. These messages constituted 3.18 per cent of the Twitter messages in the sample shown in Table 2.

YouTube: The Life-saving Citizen TV

On YouTube, there were 1,064 videos, 5,700 minutes, which were viewed more than 6 million times, and had 7,627 comments. Analysing the content of the YouTube videos revealed four main functions for this outlet during the events. The first and most dominant function was documenting the details of the different events of the revolution in different cities and areas in Egypt with 735 videos. There were also 118 videos that told the stories of the victims of police brutality. The third dominant function was mobilization and keeping the revolutionary spirit up through using emotional songs and poems. The last dominant function was following and commenting on mainstream media coverage of the events (88 videos). The remaining 16 videos covered miscellaneous issues that did not fit into clear categories or functions.

Geographically, about 45 per cent of the videos were about different events in Cairo, and Tahrir Square in particular. The remaining videos covered the protests and clashes with the security forces in 14 cities (Alexandria, Ismailia, Asiut, Mansoura, Beni Suef, Port Said, Demanhour, Demietta, Zagazig, Suez, Tanta,

Table 2. Sample of Twitter messages

'Security forces use gas bombs to disperse the demonstrators in Tahrir Square.'
'Clashes between security forces and demonstrators in Ismailia.'
'Demonstrators in Mansoura broke security cordons, and thousands in the streets.'
'The third martyr fell in Suez because of rubber bullet in the tummy. Down with Hosni Mubarak. Down with the military rule!'
'A march in the streets of Port Said, and security forces backed with bullies attack demonstrators.'

Note: The original Twitter messages in Arabic were translated into English by the author.

Manzala, Kafr Ezzaiat and Mehallah) that were out of the spotlight and received no media coverage. From among these videos, YouTube will be remembered through four videos in particular: the first was of a white van with a diplomatic plate speeding into protesters in a Cairo backstreet, reportedly killing at least 20 protestors.[5] The second video was of an unarmed male demonstrator in another backstreet (in Alexandria) who was shot dead by a police officer in charge of securing the roads to a police station in the area. That video was recorded by a girl on a balcony with her mother next to her. The two were shouting at the demonstrator to keep away from the security forces, and then burst into hysterical screaming after he was shot dead.[6] The other two videos showed similar police brutality against protestors in cities in Suez and North Sinai.[7]

Blogs: Theorizing the Right to Protest

Quantitatively, blogs were the least-contributing component in the alternative media machine. The analysis showed that there were only 1,129 blog posts contributed by 89 Egyptian bloggers, and that these posts received 3,900 comments. It was also found that the blog with the highest number of visitors and comments was that of the female blogger Nawara Negm.[8] That blog was already popular among young Internet users in Egypt before 25 January 2011, and was active in calling for protests on that day and in publishing regular and detailed updates of the ongoing protests.

However, the influence of these blogs was further amplified through links to them in Facebook and Twitter. These blogs presented (1) detailed personal diaries of the events; (2) narratives of encounters and clashes with the security forces;, (3) explanations concerning citizens' rights to protest and revolt against a repressive regime; (4) exposures of the tricks used by the state-run media to defame the protestors; and finally (5) interpretations of the events in Egypt in the context of the changes that had taken place in Tunisia.

The Use of the Alternative Media Structures by Peripheries and Core – Periphery Interactions in the Media Domain

This new, alternative media structure described above was both empowered by contributions from the peripheries and also empowered them. Political e-activists and protestors viewed the social media as their communication space since the regime and other institutions had their hands on the mainstream media space (Abdul-Rahman, 2012; Elghamry, 2014). The users of the social media saw it as their source of 'alternative' power in the face of an exclusive and manipulative mainstream and state-run media. In other words, the social media users, especially in the domain of political activism, seemed to have a one-sided agreement that 'alternative belongs to the periphery and the mainstream belongs to the core'. That was first stated explicitly after an Aljazeera interview during the Iranian presidential crisis in 2009 with Heikal,[9] a leading Egyptian journalist, commentator and a former editor-in-chief of the Cairo newspaper *Al-Ahram*. Heikal believed that thousands of Twitter accounts were created days before the presidential elections in Iran for the purpose of destabilizing the regime and inflaming anger against the results of the coming elections, and that many of these sites, according to Heikal, were initiated in Israel. Egyptian Twitter users reacted with sarcasm and anger at 'this very old man who is spreading his ignorance of Twitter', as was explicitly stated in a tweet in Arabic by @waelabbas on 9 July 2009.[10] Furthermore, during this period Egyptian Twitter users showed a similar 'leave us alone' attitude through their direct Twitter interactions with press and media figures they believed were pro-regime, who started using Twitter at that time.[11]

Generally speaking, the use of social media outlets in the context of the Egyptian version of the Arab Spring presents a clear example of the interaction and conflict between a periphery empowered mainly by technology and a core that has the traditional power of ideology in the form of social, cultural and religious traditions and norms, as well as the power of a state-run media machine. One important factor that had a significant effect on the final outcome of this conflict seems to have been the social media users' clear awareness of the power of social media and their maturity in using its different tools, on the one hand, and the political regime's time-honoured belief that there is no real power or threat outside the space of the conventional media machine, on the other.

So, while peripheries were aware of the empowering potential of these media, a 'sarcastic' political core initially saw no real power or danger in any form of media outside the space of the conventional, mainstream and state-run media. These two different and conflicting perceptions of social media had a clear impact on how both the core and periphery acted, reacted and interacted with each other during the unfolding of events. Elghamry and Gheitas (2011a: 27–31) identified six main parallel tracks that summarize the core–periphery dynamics before and during the protests (Table 3).

In Track 1 a mobilizing periphery was met with sarcasm from the political regime (especially the Ministry of Interior) and disregard from the state-run media. On Tracks 2, 3 and 4, protesters and activists were either on the streets engaged in expressing their anger against a repressive regime or on social media outlets defending their right to protest. The regime and its media machine, meanwhile, were trying to implement a technique of 'othering' and 'over-peripheralizing' through picturing the protesters as cultural and social outcasts and 'paid traitors'. The state-run media aired testimonies by what it described as 'eyewitnesses' accusing the protesters of immoral conduct (for example, full sexual relations and drug abuse in the protestors' tents in Tahrir Square)

Table 3. Paths of core–periphery dynamics

Track	Date	Social media	The regime	State-run media
1	1–25 Jan	Mobilization	Sarcasm	Disregard
2	25–28 Jan	Expression of anger	Police violence	Disinformation
3	21 Jan–3 Feb	Right to protest	Information war	Disinformation
4	28 Jan–3 Feb	Documenting	Mob violence	Justification
5	28 Jan–8 Feb	Focused	Manoeuvring	Justification
6	10–11 Feb	Challenging	Disintegrating	Loss of control

that violated the social, cultural and religious traditions and norms of the Egyptian society.[12] Another group of state-run media eyewitnesses said they saw people who spoke a foreign language and were distributing money in Tahrir Square. Amidst this 'othering' discourse, the state-run media justified the 'honourable' citizens' right to defend the 'values' of their society as well as their 'livelihood' against an 'immoral and disruptive minority'. On Track 5, while the protesting discourse in the different channels of social media was focused on the demands for change, the state-run media was trying to justify the regime's political manoeuvres through a mix of promises of 'limited changes' and implicit warnings that the alternative to the current regime is 'chaos'. And finally, on Track 6, there was an accelerating process of 'control switch' in operation, where a protesting and challenging periphery was accumulating more power by the minute at the expense of a disintegrating repressive core that was obviously losing control over the angry streets and its 'clueless' media machine. This was reflected in the clear increase in the number of protests and strikes in different parts of Egypt during this phase. According to Abdalla (2011), the number of protests jumped from a few on 7 February, mainly in Cairo, to 65 protests in 14 different governorates on 11 February 2011.

These phases reveal a clear juxtaposition of a dynamic citizen media machine maturing day by day and a traditional state-run media machine unable to accommodate the new state of affairs where its full control over 'mass communication' was weakening and its influence on a significant slice of the masses diminishing. Indeed, the process from Track 1 to 6 witnessed a continuously increasing phenomenon that can be called the overflow of a virtual critical mass to the real world. It was observed that the volume of the online presence and interactivity in terms of social media posts and comments had a threshold around which some online activities started to overflow from the virtual sphere and to have some real-world effects. This overflow followed two main patterns: the first is the direct one-stop overflow from the virtual to the real, and the second is the indirect two-stop overflow, where the volume of virtual presence attracted the attention of the mainstream media which then functioned as a bridge of the virtual to the real. A brief empirical case study on the *We are all Khaled Said* Facebook page highlights this phenomenon.

Facebook was first used in the mobilization for a public strike in Egypt on 6 April 2008. The strike was mainly called for by a group of political activists who, immediately after what they believed was a successful strike, decided to refer to themselves as 'The 6th of April Youth Movement'. The Facebook page that was started by the group gained the attention of about 70,000 Facebook users from across Egypt (Abdalla, 2009). In this context, Facebook began to function as a platform for virtual resistance that the political periphery could effectively use against a repressive political regime (Elghamry, 2014). During this period, the political regime's view of Facebook as a 'playground for "kids"' was also established and adopted later in January–February 2011. This view was reflected in the phrase 'the Facebook kids' that the state-run media machine used at the time to sarcastically refer to the political activists using Facebook as a tool of political resistance.[13] Since then, the e-activists' maturation curve in using social media has been noticeably rising. On 10 June 2010, the *We are all Khaled Said* Facebook page was created, which reached the 100,000 threshold in three days (the following section of this contribution draws on data and information from Ghonim, 2012), Before this threshold, the activities on the page were limited to virtual discussions and sharing of information and pictures related to the case, but as soon as the threshold reached 100,000 members, there were many calls on the page to take the case to a wider public through silent pro-Khaled Said protests, in black, in Cairo and Alexandria and through sending letters to newspapers and making phone calls to popular TV talk shows in Egypt to draw their attention to the case. The two procedures resulted in wider public awareness of the case, on the one hand, and a more aggressive and hostile discourse on the case in the state-run media outlets, on the other. Subsequently, the number of page members grew by thousands on a daily basis, and the virtual presence of the case expanded in the form of more page members living in geographical areas other than Cairo and Alexandria. By the end of June 2010, the number of page members jumped to over 183,000, with a parallel jump in engagement as reflected in the volume of comments and likes on the page. The number of street protests also gradually increased and the police handling of this growing wave of protest became harsher. On 10 January 2011, the first call for protests on 25 January was posted on the page, and the number of members then was around 365,000 (Ghonim, 2012). Thus, for the virtual critical mass to overflow, three issues appear crucial. First, the volume of the virtual presence has to pass the 100,000 member threshold. Secondly, this threshold seems to have been sensitive to the level of the members' engagement not only in terms of the number of likes and comments, but also in terms of using social media as a basis from which to organize an infiltration into the traditional media to inform citizens who do not use social media and who therefore were not aware of the virtual acts of protest. Thirdly, the members' age and geographical distribution were significant: wide geographical coverage is a necessary condition for a virtual protesting mass to turn critical and to overflow from the virtual to the real.

The Media Landscape in Egypt after 25 January – In a State of Fluidity

The outcome described above needs, however, to be qualified. While the six phases described an expansion of the alternative media structure with an overflow from the virtual to the real world, ensuing developments in the real world had an effect on the alternative media machine. Politicians have increasingly tried to control the virtual world. Since the stepping down of Mubarak on 11 February 2011, the media landscape in Egypt has been mostly 'fluid' and dramatically changing, strongly correlating with the 'fluidity' in the structure of power after Mubarak. Using this correlation, we can distinguish three major phases that could summarize a significant element of the post-January media path.

The first phase started with the Supreme Council of the Armed Forces (SCAF) as the interim ruler of the country. In the first few weeks of this phase, a wave of revolution-praising discourse was dominant in almost all media outlets, even by those that were previously known to be pro-Mubarak. In this phase, there was a strong emphasis on the role of the Egyptian armed forces, youth, as well as the social media outlets in the success of the revolution. It was clear that social media had taken on a whole new importance in post-Mubarak Egypt, not only among those who participated in the uprisings, but for Egypt's state media, for political parties and for SCAF as well (Peterson, 2011). Leaders of the protest movement continued to use social media as a tool to guide the ongoing revolution in the desired democratic directions. Blogs and Facebook pages such as *We Are All Khaled Said* continued to serve as forums for discussing social ills and the collective actions needed to redress them. Yet the interim rulers had also tested the power of the groups that used social media so effectively in setting off the 25 January protests. The social media youth movements could not swing a 'No' vote on the constitutional changes endorsed by the military; nor could they inspire much anti-military sentiment after the army arrested and tortured protesters on 9 March 2011 (Peterson, 2011). Yet in April 2011 these same sites proved able to help call 100,000 protesters back onto the streets to support the prosecution of Hosni Mubarak.

The role of social media in Egypt's changing political culture continued to evolve as it was used experimentally for a variety of forms of political communication.[14] The press also continued to transform itself. *Al-Ahram* newspaper apologized to the Egyptian people on 13 February 2011 for its decades of 'bias in favour of the corrupt regime' (Peterson, 2011).

In addition, state media underwent a complete reshuffling of leadership positions in late March 2011.[15] There were far-reaching changes in independent and state media that were dramatically illustrated on 2 March 2011 when the then prime minister Ahmed Shafiq was grilled mercilessly by novelist Alaa Al-Aswany on a television show and subsequently resigned.[16] Many in the national audience were deeply offended by Aswany's complete lack of reserve in confronting the head of the government, but after Shafiq's resignation the transformative agency of an open media could not be denied (Peterson, 2011).

However, the new independence of the media apparently did not extend to the military itself. While the military had been responsive to popular protest against the former regime, it was far less patient with criticisms directed at its own actions. For example, the seizure and torture of protesters on 9 March 2011 was underreported in the Egyptian press. Many of the stories that did appear were based primarily on army statements. On 23 March the interim cabinet headed by Essam Sharaf imposed a theoretical gagging order on the media, suggesting that news on military arrests, torture and secret trials would be even more deeply buried. Yet social media continued to serve as an alternative to mainstream media. On 9 March 2011, several victims gave public testimony about their experiences at Cairo's Press Syndicate. Given the scant attention Egyptian and international media paid to the event, some testimonies were videotaped, subtitled in English and posted to YouTube; others were posted to Facebook pages, sometimes in multiple languages. Only when Amnesty International issued a statement on a subset of victims – women subjected to 'virginity tests' – did these events receive significant mainstream media attention. Even here, many Egyptian news media quoted foreign news sources, to distance themselves from the reporting, or quoted only army spokespersons, without interviewing victims.

During this phase, the Muslim Brotherhood's (MB) power share was increasing and their influence on the political and media landscape was growing stronger. This influence reached its apex with the election of the group's presidential candidate, Muhammad Morsi, as President of Egypt, which signalled the beginning of the second phase. Two main features were dominant during this phase. The first was the MB's obvious and 'impatient' pursuit of media dominance through appointing pro-MB figures in as many media positions as possible. This pursuit resulted in a sporadic and short-lived pro-MB media discourse that tried to maximize the MB's role in removing Mubarak. The second was the rise of a strong anti-Ikhwan discourse that was,[17] according to non-Ikhwan, a reaction to the MB's attempts to dominate the media and political scenes, on the one hand, and the MB's ongoing Islamization and consequently the 'annihilation' of the national identity of Egypt, on the other. This discourse was mainly championed by (1) new TV channels (CBC, for example) owned by businessmen who were known to be influential members of Mubarak's National Democratic Party, and (2) 25 January revolutionaries who believed that the Ikhwan had betrayed the revolution through secret power-sharing deals with SCAF. The role of these channels was strong in the anti-Ikhwan mobilization and on 28 April 2013 this mobilization was materialized in the 'Tamarod' ('rebellion') grassroots movement that led to the removal of Muhammad Morsi as president, on 3 July 2013.

This date marked the beginning of the continuing third phase. Though it is still early to reach a full and deep understanding of this phase, it is characterized by a set of defining features. The first can be seen in the continuation of the strong comeback of the traditional media that had already begun in the second phase and that is paralleled by a decline in the social media's impact on public opinion and politics. The immediate and visible effect of this influence gap seems to be the return of the old dynamics in the media as well as the political landscape, where the traditional power and media structures are moving back to the pre-25 January core status, and the alternative (both in media and politics) to the periphery. In this atmosphere, finding a place for critical voices in established media outlets has become increasingly difficult. Much of Egypt's media has strongly supported the regime's narrative since the Muslim Brotherhood-backed president, Mohamed Morsi, was ousted from power in July 2013. Dissenting voices are almost absent from newspapers and television shows. Social media outlets continue to offer a platform for otherwise marginalized views.

The second feature is that social media reflect the growing polarization of Egyptian society –even though some social media platforms provide one of the few forums in which activists pursuing the middle ground can voice their opinions and document human rights violations (Abdulla, 2014).[18] Together with this polarization, there has also emerged a new level of aggressiveness in discourse in both the traditional and the alternative media outlets. There is, for example, an ongoing discursive battle on defining the events of 25 January 2011, 30 June 2013 and 3 July 2013. Though the present Egyptian constitution explicitly recognizes both 30 June and 25 January as revolutions, pro-regime media repeatedly and aggressively push for the conspiracy interpretation of the 25 January revolution and for bringing those behind it to justice.[19] Another polarizing debate in the social media has evolved around the person of El-Sisi.[20]

On 26 March 2014, an anti-Sisi Twitter hashtag in Arabic was created that can be translated as '#ElectThePimp'. According to some estimates, the volume of the hashtag so far, from its creation until 23 October 2014, is more than 1,445,000 tweets and around 2 billion impressions (the number of Twitter users that saw the hashtag on their timelines).[21] In addition to its virtual presence, the hashtag also gained some street presence in the form of stencils of El-Sisi's face with the hashtag painted on walls and metro stations in some locations in Cairo. The unprecedented popularity of the hashtag took the pro-Sisi media outlets by surprise and raised a large number of 'angry' reactions in mainstream media.[22]

Pro-Sisi social media users, on the other hand, showed their support in the form of two much less popular Twitter hashtags that can be translated as '#FinishYour-Favor' – calling upon El-Sisi to run for president, and 'IwillElectElSisi'.

The third and last feature that is dominant in this ongoing phase is the regime's repeated attempt to have more control over the virtual space of freedom of expression. On 1 June 2011, Elwatannews published what it called a 'scoop', detailing a so-called plan by the Egyptian Ministry of Interior with the code-name 'Electronic Fist' to monitor Internet users in Egypt.[23] According to the newspaper's website, the ministry mentioned 26 threats that it saw as 'reasonable justifications' for monitoring Internet use in Egypt, on top of which were: religious defamation, personal defamation, violation of established societal values, calling for violence and rebellion, and mobilizing for illegal demonstrations, sit-ins and strikes. The reactions to the 'leaked plan' ranged from the ministry's denial of the existence of such a plan, support and justification by pro-regime media figures, sarcasm by anti-regime social media users, to outright rejection and privacy concerns by human rights activists.[24] The media presence of the monitoring plan and the related privacy and freedom of expression issues gradually fell off. On 17 September 2014, the Ministry of Interior officially announced the beginning of surveillance of Facebook, Twitter and Skype.[25]

Conclusions

This article has looked at the periphery theme of this volume through a media perspective. It has examined the expansion and contraction of an emerging alternative media structure before, during and after the protests of 25 January 2011, and has shown that alternative media have empowered peripheries for which it provided a platform to make their voice heard. Peripheries have employed their strategies within this new emerging alternative media structure, not only through documenting events in geographically remote areas, but also by constituting a platform for bringing the role of ethnic and gender peripheries in the protests to the centre, and by engaging previously apolitical sectors of society.

At the same time, this alternative media machine has also been empowered by peripheries since they provided it with critical mass, contributing to the overflow from the virtual space to the real world. The existing opportunity structure has been deeply challenged, not only in the media sphere which has started to change, but also in the political realm. Initially, the core held onto its power with a state-run media machine through which it attempted to 'other' and 'peripheralize' protests, but it failed to do so in the January/February 2011 period. Following this, in the interim period, social media continued to serve as an alternative to mainstream media and to contribute to an opening of the general media landscape. In the long term, however, the alternative media structure may again contract. A marked comeback of the traditional media machine is likely, as can be seen in the current decline in the social media's impact on public opinion and the path of events in the political sphere where the alternative (both in media and politics) is returning to the periphery.

Disclosure Statement

No potential conflict of interest was reported by the author.

Notes

1. It should be noted that there has also been a growing general literature on the use of social media for current protest movements spanning across different regions of the world: see, for example, Garett (2007), Diani (2010) and Christensen (2011). None of this literature has, however, focused on the use of social media in peripheral areas.
2. http://arabdigitalcontent.org.
3. Nilesat is a state-owned company in charge of operating Egyptian satellites and their control stations.
4. This Facebook page was created in 2008 mainly to mobilize and call for a general strike in Egypt on 6 April of the same year.
5. http://www.youtube.com/watch?v=M4fSMaS7jSo.
6. http://www.youtube.com/watch?v=u5QLEBNlDWw.
7. http://www.youtube.com/watch?v=1dG1cWPUaLY.
8. http://tahyyes.blogspot.com.
9. http://www.aljazeera.net/home/print/0353e88a-286d-4266-82c6-6094179ea26d/5f074d16-84cb-4680-ab93-3dfdf359827f.
10. https://twitter.com/waelabbas/status/2432885242.
11. https://twitter.com/3eeb3aleek/status/5017907698, https://twitter.com/mrmeit/status/5181983990.
12. http://www.youtube.com/watch?v=VZVnHsUlqW8.
13. http://www.youtube.com/watch?v=VlBAzvX9Xw4.
14. In April 2011, the prosecutor general announced the detention of Hosni Mubarak on Facebook, rather than calling a press conference. The same month some 1,400 university professors used Facebook as a vehicle to demand the removal of Amr Ezzat, the then Higher Education Minister and demand reforms in higher education.
15. The government had earlier hinted that it might allow editors to be elected by members of the press syndicate, but eventually settled for a mere reshuffling of positions. These changes failed to appease many staff members, who were calling for more dramatic reforms. Staff pointed out that the new faces were mostly long-time players who were as comfortable with the traditional ways of doing things as the people they replaced, and many of the sacked leaders had been kept on as consultants (Peterson, 2011).
16. http://www.youtube.com/watch?v=z2NH-INW2GY.
17. 'Ikhwan' is the Arabic word for Muslim Brotherhood.
18. The degree of polarization seems to be affected by the nature of the event, figure or political entity that has triggered this polarization. Examples of major polarizing events include, but are not limited

to, 30 June, the subsequent ousting of Mohamed Morsi and the pro-Morsi sit-ins in Rabia and Nahda Squares and their dispersion. Abdel-Fattah El-Sisi, the current president of Egypt, and Mohamed Morsi, the former president, are examples of major polarizing figures. And finally, the Muslim Brotherhood and its Freedom and Justice Party are examples of polarizing political entities.

19. See, for example, this video of Ahmed Moussa, a talk show host on the pro-regime Sada Elbalad TV channel: https://www.youtube.com/watch?v = md7w3LDSrxA.

20. Analysing a sample of the social media content regarding El-Sisi since his appointment as the head of the Egyptian Armed Forces on 12 August 2012 shows him as 'the great polarizer'. Opinions of him ranged from 'a bridge to power', to 'a power seeker' or just a reincarnation of the old regime.

21. http://www2.keyhole.co/realtime/7Tn3bJ/.

22. This anger could be summarized in describing 'those behind the hashtag as lacking proper upbringing' and 'the possibility of the (Egyptian) government blocking Twitter – and maybe be YouTube as well – in Egypt'. See for example this video of Khairy Ramadan, a talk show host on the pro-regime CBC TV channel: http://www.youtube.com/watch?v=vbP-W-LzM0g.

23. http://www.elwatannews.com/news/details/495659.

24. See links to relevant news in http://www.elwatannews.com/news/details/495659.

25. http://www.buzzfeed.com/sheerafrenkel/egypt-begins-surveillance-of-facebook-twitter-and-skype-on-u.

References

Abdalla, Nadine (2009) *Labor Movement in Mahala El-Kobra City: Catalyst for Political Change?* (Cairo, Egypt: Arab Forum for Alternatives).

Abdalla, Nadine (2011) (in Arabic) *Understanding and Developing the Movements of Social Protest: a Socio-political Perspective* (Cairo, Egypt: Arab Forum for Alternatives).

Abdulla, Rasha (2013) *Mapping Digital Media: Egypt* (New York: Open Society Foundations).

Abdulla, Rasha (2014) *Egypt's Media in the Midst of Revolution* (New York: Open Society Foundations), (accessed 20 October 2014). Available at http://carnegieendowment.org/2014/07/16/egypt-s-media-in-midst-of-revolution

Abdul-Rahman, Amr (2012) (in Arabic) The Internet and the Egyptian revolution: democracy and the search for a place in this world, in: *Proceedings Non-Traditional Forms of the Youths' Political Participation in Egypt [Before, during and after the Revolution]* (Arab Forum for Alternatives), pp. 143–171.

Christensen, Christian (2011) *Twitter Revolutions? Addressing Social Media and Dissent*, Available at http://www.tandfonline.com/doi/abs/10.1080/10714421.2011.597235 (accessed 15 November 2014).

Diani, Mario (2010) *Social Movement Networks, Virtual and Real*, Available at http://www.tandfonline.com/doi/abs/10.1080/13691180051033333 (accessed 15 November 2014).

Elghamry, K (2014) (in Arabic) Technology and the clash of generations, *AlAhram Newspaper*, 46345(138), p. 12.

Elghamry, K. & G. Gheitas (2011a) (in Arabic) How Facebook and YouTube were used in the Egyptian Revolution, *Lughat Alasr Information and Communications Technology Magazine*, 123, pp. 14–42.

Garett, Kelly (2007) *Protest in an Information Society: A Review of Literature on Social Media and New ICTs*, Available at www.tandfonline.com/doi/abs/10.1080/13691180600630773 (accessed 15 November 2014).

Ghonim, Wael (2012) *Revolution 2.0: The Power of the People is Greater than the People in Power: A Memoir* (New York: Houghton Mifflin Harcourt).

Howard, P.N., A. Duffy, D. Freelon, M. Hussain, W. Mari & M. Mazaid (2011) *Opening Closed Regimes: what was the Role of Social Media During the Arab Spring? Project on Information Technology and Political Islam* (Seattle: PIPTI).

Lin, C & E. Hovy (2000) The automatic acquisition of topic signatures for text summarization, in: *Proceedings of 18th International Conference of Computational Linguistics, COLING'00, 2000*, Strasbourg, France.

Mansour, Essam (2012) 'The role of social networking sites in the January 25th revolution of Egypt', *Information Studies*, 14, pp. 128–159.

Peterson, M. (2011) Egypt's media ecology in a time of revolution, *Arab Media and Society*, 13. Available at http://www.arabmediasociety.com/articles/downloads/20110531103710_Peterson.pdf (accessed 19 October 2014).

Reporters without Borders (2011) Press Freedom Index 2010, Available at http://en.rsf.org/pressfreedom-index-2010,1034.html (accessed 29 April 2014).

Scott, Alex (2012) "From First Tweet to Final collapse – the dimensions of social media in regime collapse." Prepared for the International Studies Association Annual Convention, San Diego, CA, April 02, 2012. files.isanet.org/ ... /15b61bd4ac8a464f8de701ba03cd7faa.pdf

Tusa, Felix (2013) How social media can shape a protest movement: the cases of Egypt in 2011 and Iran in 2009, *Arab Media and Society*, 17. Available at http://www.arabmediasociety.com/articles/downloads/20130221104512_Tusa_Felix.pdf (accessed 19 October 2014).

Zhou, X.H., X.H. Hu & X.D. Zhang (2007) Topic signature language models for ad hoc information retrieval, in: *IEEE Transactions on Knowledge and Data Engineering*, 19 (9), pp. 1–12.

Arab Spring: A Decentring Research Agenda

LORENZO KAMEL[*,**] & DANIELA HUBER[***]

*Department of History, Cultures and Civilizations, Bologna University, Italy, **Center for Middle Eastern Studies, Harvard University, Cambridge, MA, USA, ***Istituto Affari Internazionali (IAI), Rome, Italy

ABSTRACT   *This article calls for a decentring research agenda and serves as a reminder to look beyond the centres when seeking to understand attempted or accomplished processes of transformation. The Arab Spring is not a unitary whole but part of a variety of processes which differs in terms of space (diverse countries, diverse areas in countries), time (the Ghedim Izik protests in Western Sahara started in October 2010, while protests in the Rif are still ongoing), substance (demands for civil and political rights, equality rights, material claims, autonomy), strategies (from violence to apathy), involved actors (social movements, civil society organizations or individual actors) and outcomes (from regime repression to empowerment of peripheries).*

More than four years after the so-called Arab Spring started, research on the region is increasingly turning once more to its traditional focus on authoritarian resilience and security issues, driven by dynamics which are perceived to be happening in the core. Research is thus returning to a focus which deals with issues that appear most urgent at first sight, but which did not permit a prediction of the uprisings, or an *ex post* understanding of them. After presenting the main findings of this collective volume, we therefore propose a decentring research agenda.

Main Findings in Comparative Perspective

The case studies in this volume show that peripheries play(ed) an important role in the Arab Spring; indeed they show that the latter consists of multiple 'springs'. They have varied not only across various countries but also across diverse sections of societies within countries. Several contributions to this work show that the Arab Spring has been used as a framing claim by peripheries to lend political weight to their own protests, which is one of the reasons why the uprisings accumulated a

147

critical mass to become a powerful political phenomenon. This volume therefore serves as a reminder to look beyond the centres when seeking to understand processes of transformation. The dynamics currently at work in the Middle East and North Africa (MENA) region are not part of a unitary whole but of a variety of processes which differed in terms of space (diverse countries, different areas in countries), time (the Ghedim Izik protests in Western Sahara started in October 2010, while protests in the Rif are still ongoing), substance (demands for civil and political rights, equality rights, material claims, autonomy), strategies (from violence to apathy), involved actors (social movements, civil society organizations or individual actors) and outcomes (from regime repression to empowerment of peripheries). The role peripheries could play more concretely in the Arab Spring and the impacts they achieved depended on diverse factors which are now discussed within the given analytical frame of this volume.

Opportunity Structure

Strategies of co-optation which the regimes have used towards peripheries have featured in almost all contributions. These strategies have taken different shapes. Morocco has employed defensive democratization before and during the Arab Spring – that is, the adoption of some reforms which aim at appeasing the opposition while leaving the central political structure intact. Regarding peripheries, this strategy has mostly focused on possibly de-politicizing peripheries by preventing the creation of (local sections of) political parties and civil society associations, by seeking to co-opt elites, and by some forms of limited repression of protests. As the contributions on Morocco show, however, the success of this state policy has crucially depended on accommodation or resistance to this strategy – thus on agency – by peripheries themselves. Most successful in containing resistance has been the Moroccan state in the Atlas mountains. This area hosts a comparatively depoliticized periphery, partially as a result of King Hassan II's policy of preventing the emancipation of rural areas and of King Mohammed VI's strategy of defensive democratization. This is contrasted by resistance in the Rif, where the Moroccan state similarly tried to co-opt an elite into its centre, but encountered strong opposition to this strategy during the Arab Spring.

In the case of Syria and Egypt, state strategies of co-opting peripheries can be framed less as defensive democratization, but rather as activating the support of specific peripheries for an autocratic state. Farha and Mousa (2015) show how the political and socio-economic inclusion of Syrian Christians into the elite has guaranteed their support for the regime before and during the Arab Spring protests from which Syrian Christians largely abstained. Egyptian Christians, in contrast, had little to lose from overturning a regime that compounded their status as a religious, political and socio-economic peripheral group. Egyptian Copts shared socio-economic grievances with the Muslim majority and identified mainly as Egyptians, hardly ever politically expressing themselves as a religious community. They affiliated with class rather than sect and participated in the Arab Spring protests together with their Muslim compatriots. Syrian Christians, in contrast, were socio-economically detached from the majority population and feared the religion-based, peripheral designation that may come with an Islamist-driven transition process.

A similar fear was shared by the LGBT community in Tunisia in a transition process in which – as Edwige Fortier (2015) shows – some public spaces expand rapidly, while others contract in terms of liberalization. While the Tunisian LGBT community could initially benefit from opening spaces at the political level, for example through founding an association, during later stages it has effectively become more peripheralized at the socio-cultural level. This is, however, not a necessary outcome and the role of agency also figured importantly here. Fortier sheds light on how political groups used tactics of scapegoating weak peripheries in a heated public discourse to demoralize opposite political forces, rally a constituency behind a political group and build a new national identity. LGBT communities were specifically exposed to this process since they are peripheralized in three ways – space, difference and distance – and on three levels: the political, religious and socio-cultural. This, however, does not mean that we should 'victimize' them: both Fortier (2015) and Khalid (2015) show the agency that has come from LGBT communities in terms of challenging dominant discourses through social media, participating in protests, fostering a mobilization structure through civil society groups and networks, but also through the daily practising of a certain lifestyle. As both Fortier and Khalid point out, practising such a lifestyle has been less sanctioned than speaking about it.

The mobilization structure has figured as an important feature of the opportunity structure in all articles and the three case studies on peripheries in Morocco are especially illuminating in comparative perspective here. As a result of Morocco's strategy of defensive democratization, the mobilization structure in the Atlas mountains has remained rather under-developed. Bergh and Rossi-Doria (2015) shed light on this aspect and suggest that this was one of the reasons why the 20 February Movement (F20M) was not successful in mobilizing larger protests in this periphery. The actions which did emerge were not based on a well-developed organizational structure but were organized by individuals based on local feelings of belonging rather than membership in an association. This was contrasted by activism in the Rif (Collado, 2015) and in Western Sahara (Molina, 2015). In both cases a strongly politicized regional identity existed and activists could rely on previously established mobilizing structures. The Rif is especially telling in this respect. While the demands of the F20M were supported, activists in the Rif also used the Arab Spring as a frame to advance their own demands. Over time protests localized in terms of demands, as well as patterns of action, reverting to previous policies of contention.

Strategies

Within this structural context, which strategies have been successful? Mobilizing international links has been a rather successful strategy, as the case of Western Saharan activists shows. Molina (2015) argues that Sahrawis were relatively empowered as they actively seized new strategies – concretely a combination of domestic non-violent resistance and international diplomatic activities. The protest cycle in Western Sahara started with the camp in Gdeim Izik in October/ November 2010 and while the F20M did not introduce the Western Sahara issue into its agenda due to its divisive nature, Sahrawis nonetheless could capitalize the international attention which shifted to the whole region with the Arab Spring by representing their protests as one of the first instances of this phenomenon. This framing helped these protests to draw international attention, which was seen as an important achievement by Western Saharan activists. The fostering of a regional network was also a meaningful strategy for Tunisian LGBT activists. It helped them to exchange experiences, learn from and support each other.

Another strategy was to seek alignment with the social movements which protested in the centre and the dominant tactic in this respect has been the use of framing. Homosexual communities quickly sought to utilize the opening by presenting their demands in the framework of the calls of the broader social movement in Tunisia: they participated in the protests with the rainbow flag and founded an online magazine, as well as an association called Association for Justice and Equality whose aim was to fight against stigma and for human rights. As the activists themselves pointed out, they sought to influence the discourse 'before it turned against us'. Nonetheless, while homosexual communities would adopt strategies of publicity and visibility at the political level, they used discretion and invisibility at the socio-cultural level. Due to restrictive socio-cultural norms and the use of the issue of sex and gender in a heated public discourse, however, they were hardly successful with this strategy of framing.

Bergh and Rossi-Doria (2015) also identify a discursive disconnect between protest in the periphery and the centre as an explanatory factor. The human rights discourse of the F20M in Morocco was disconnected from the local needs of the people in the Atlas mountains and thus constituted one of the reasons why F20M failed to mobilize rural populations. While the urban-based activists focused on political change in terms of constitutional arrangements and on political and civil rights, the rural population prioritized access to basic infrastructures and services and economic development issues.

Finally, social media feature as periphery-empowering tools in terms of mobilization and of contesting dominant discourses in almost all contributions, and Khaled Elghamry (2015) examines the issue in depth for the case of Egypt. He shows how Facebook, Twitter, YouTube and the blogosphere constituted an alternative citizens' media machine that was successful in challenging the state-run media machine and the dominant social and cultural discourse, at least during the revolutionary phase. Social media groups developed an awareness of their periphery-empowering role and actively called on users from geographical peripheries outside of the centres to post photos and videos; they were able to show the role of peripheral groups like women or Copts in the protests; and they succeeded in mobilizing previously apolitical communities, thus acquiring a virtual critical mass which eventually brought down the dominant discourse of a state-run media machine.

Outcomes

The picture in terms of outcomes of these strategies for peripheries is mixed. All authors draw a rather pessimistic picture when it comes to 'objective outcomes' in the opportunity structure. Some peripheries have reverted to pre-Arab Spring status: for instance, Elghamry (2015) argues that under the current political circumstances Egyptian traditional media are enjoying a strong comeback; Morocco adopted cosmetic changes which do not modify the situation in peripheries like the Atlas mountains, the Rif or in occupied Western Sahara. Other peripheries have significantly worsened their standing due to the identity conflicts which are proliferating in Arab Spring states: the Tunisian LGBT community, as well as religious peripheries in both Egypt and Syria are at risk of becoming more marginalized, finding themselves at the heart of complex discourses on socio-cultural and political identity in their countries. This discourse, it should be noted, has not been confined to the Arab world alone. As Maryam Khalid (2015) shows, western and Arab discourses illustrated the deployment of Arab women and LGBT as a means to debate issues such as citizenship, authenticity, tradition and identity.

But while our authors hardly found improvements in terms of the opportunity structure of peripheries, the picture changes when we look at their agency. In the wake of the Arab Spring, many peripheries have been and now remain politicized. This applies for example to the Copts in Egypt, where more political expression is emerging within and outside of the church (notably among the youth) as a result of a relatively recent strategy of creating political opportunity structures by engaging with the public sphere. In the Rif, the major consequence of the localization of protest has been the end of a perception of threat in the public commitment to regional activism, above all among local youth for whom activism, and a commitment to values like citizenship and democracy, represents a new form of expression. Indeed, one of the most important outcomes is the emboldening of young people. Thus, the Arab Spring – specifically in the peripheries – has not ended, but is an ongoing process.

Finally, international recognition has also been a form of success for peripheries. Firstly, in more general terms, the West had to acknowledge its distorted perception of the region. This has not meant, however, that the representations of the Arab Spring in western media have not perpetuated long-standing orientalist schemes. Maryam Khalid (2015) shows how the western discourse on gender peripheries during the Arab Spring and in its aftermath has victimized Arab women by focusing on their treatment, instead of their agency. Thus, it has continued to present the Arab world as the 'other', neglecting the fact that women remain discriminated against in many parts of the world including the West. Secondly, international recognition has also been important for the identity of peripheries, as Irene Fernandez Molina (2015) highlights. As internal Sahrawi activists achieved growing recognition from the Polisario Front and relevant international actors such as the UN and US, as well as considerable empathy from inter-Sahrawi and foreign civil society, this was perceived as a success and asserted a long-denied identity.

A Decentring Research Agenda

What do the findings of this collected volume mean for future research on the region? Several academic and journalistic publications which have appeared in recent years in the West have conveyed the idea that the uprisings did not pass through the peripheries. This special issue has powerfully rejected that assumption. At the same time, given that a large part of the population in Arab Spring states is made up by peripheries, many of them have not been covered in this issue and more research should go into rural areas specifically. Egyptian women, in particular in rural areas, for instance, played an important role in the dynamics at work in the region in these last few years. A relevant proportion of the most meaningful episodes that paved the way to the January 2011 and June/July 2013 uprisings in Egypt were linked to women's initiatives, notably also in rural areas. Women have been behind dozens of strikes and worker protests organized throughout Egypt in the past decade, as in the December 2006 Mahalla Textiles strike, when 3,000 women marched to protest against the unsafe and degrading conditions in which they were forced to work. 'Women are here, where are the men?' was written on the signs that they held on many such occasions. Mahalla's strike paved the way for dozens of other protests, including the national protest called on 6 April 2008, the founding event for the '6 April Movement'. As Manar El-Shorbagy has argued, 'at no point in the struggle for Egypt's freedom did women take the role of followers'. It was never the case that men took the initiative and women 'joined' (El-Shorbagy, 2013: 101).

Also in Tunisia, the uprisings started among marginalized groups in rural areas such as Sidi Bouzid. The first signs of a potential major shift in the local societal and political equilibrium could already be seen two years earlier, when the small town of Redeyef, situated 350ºkm south of Tunis, witnessed months of bloody protests at the Gafsa Phosphate Company. The turmoil was triggered by a phenomenon that was anything but new: the open call for jobs organized by that state-run enterprise was rigged and the available positions were offered to and filled by supporters of then-president Zine El Abidine Ben Ali.

The Syrian uprising of 2011 also erupted in an agricultural area, the province of Dara'a, where reportedly more than 100,000 people attended an anti-government demonstration on 25,March 2011 (CNN, 2011). Despite having been for decades a stronghold of the Syrian regime, Dara'a was one of the many areas that suffered most from the neoliberal economic reforms that reached their climax on 10 March 2009, with the launching of the Damascus Stock Exchange and the cut in economic support for agricultural areas implemented by Bashar al-Assad soon after succeeding his father in 2000. Due to the lack of transparency of the Syrian regime, the revenues of these neoliberal policies have essentially gone to the Assad clan and its associates only (Achcar, 2013: 175; Guazzone & Pioppi, 2012). On the other hand, Syrian markets were open to cheaper agricultural imports and, as a result, farming communities were increasingly unable to rely on agriculture as a source of stable livelihoods (Zurayk & Gough, 2014: 112).

The exclusion, marginalization and peripheralization (Kühn, 2015) of these and other areas and sectors of the local populations triggered some of the main conditions for the 'revolutionary moment' (Gerges, 2014: 2) and the 'epistemological break' (Bachelard, 1951: 25) that we are currently witnessing. One of the main reasons why these aspects have passed largely unnoticed and the Arab uprisings came as such a surprise are most likely connected to the fact that many observers spent (too) much time on understanding the dynamics of (apparently) resilient regimes,[1] while largely ignoring the marginalization of certain areas and sectors of the local populations where the social protests and dissent were rooted.

This research focus has arguably been rather comfortable for Europeans. Seen from this perspective, it was the 'resilient regimes', not the western neoliberal market agenda imposed on the region, which was largely responsible for the socio-economic malaise of the area. But there is something that goes even deeper than this. Until the recent past the countries analysed in this special issue were not 'worlded', but instead othered, atomized and delegated to a hinterland as the 'others' of a civilized humanity that is exclusively coded as the liberal West (Dabashi, 2012: 43). Liberal values have been promoted as universal standards by both the US and the EU in the region and this approach has not been called into question, despite the Arab uprisings' call for social justice, social and economic rights, and fair development (Teti, 2012; Pace & Cavatorta, 2012). Todorov (1994: 1) defined this persistent attitude as 'the unwarranted establishing of the specific values of one's own society as universal values'.[2] In light of this persistence, this collected volume joins in the call for a paradigm shift that not only 'decentres the study and practice of Europe's international relations' (Onar & Nicolaïdis, 2013: 283), but also decentres the study of the Arab world as it is currently pursued in the West. In order to reshape the mental schemes and the related terminology through which to analyse the historical processes unfolding in the Middle East and North Africa, 'Arab Spring and peripheries' focused on the local agency of individuals and groups that are located outside of institutionalized power, paying particular attention to the spaces for discursive contestation for those who, because of their constructed otherness, are placed outside mainstream society, politics, media and education.

Notes

1. We thank one of the anonymous reviewers for this point.
2. As noted by Thierry Hentsch (1992: xiv), ethnocentrism is very often the 'precondition of our vision of the Other' (1992: xiv).

Disclosure statement

No potential conflict of interest was reported by the author.

References

Achcar, Gilbert (2013) *The People Want: A Radical Exploration of the Arab Uprisings* (Berkley, California: University of California Press).

Bachelard, Gaston (1951) *L'Activité rationaliste de la physique contemporaine* (Paris: Presses Universitaires de France).

Bergh, Sylvia I. & Daniele Rossi-Doria (2015) Plus ça change? Observing the dynamics of Morocco's 'Arab Spring' in the high atlas, *Mediterranean Politics*, 20(2). doi:10.1080/13629395.2015.1033900.

Collado, , Ángela Suárez (2015) Territorial stress in Morocco: from democratic to autonomist demands in popular protests in the Rif, *Mediterranean Politics*, 20(2). doi:10.1080/13629395.2015.1033908.

CNN (2011) Dozens of Syrians reported killed in Daraa, Available at http://edition.cnn.com/2011/WORLD/meast/03/25/syria.unrest/index.html?hpt=T1

Dabashi, Hamid (2012) *The Arab Spring: The End of Postcolonialism* (London, New York: Zed Books, Distributed in the USA exclusively by Palgrave Macmillan).

Elghamry, Khaled (2015) Periphery discourse: an alternative media eye on the geographical, social and media peripheries in Egypt's spring, *Mediterranean Politics*, 20(2). doi:10.1080/13629395.2015.1033902.

El-Shorbagy, Manar (2013) Egyptian women in revolt: ordinary women, extraordinary roles, in: Dan Tschirgi, Walid Kazziha & Sean F. McMahon (Eds) *Egypt's Tahrir Revolution* (London: Lynne Rienner Publication), pp. 89–109.

Farha, Mark & Salma Mousa (2015) Secular autocracy vs. Sectarian democracy? Weighing reasons for christian support for regime transition in Syria and Egypt, *Mediterranean Politics*, 20(2). doi:10.1080/13629395.2015.1033903.

Fortier, Hedwige (2015) Transition and marginalisation: locating spaces for discursive contestation in post-revolution Tunisia, *Mediterranean Politics*, 20(2). doi:10.1080/13629395.2015.1033904.

Gerges, Fawaz. 2014. Introduction: a rupture. In Gerges, Fawaz (ed): "The New Middle East Protest and Revolution in the Arab World" Cambridge: Cambridge University Press, p. 1–40.

Guazzone, Laura & Daniela Pioppi (2012) *The Arab State and Neo-Liberal Globalization: The Restructuring of State Power in the Middle East* (London: Ithaca Press).

Hentsch, Thierry (1992) *Imagining the Middle East* (Montreal: Black Rose Books).

Khalid, Maryam (2015) The peripheries of gender and sexuality in the "Arab Spring.", *Mediterranean Politics*, 20(2). doi:10.1080/13629395.2015.1033906.

Kühn, Manfred (2015) Peripheralization: theoretical concepts explaining socio-spatial inequalities, *European Planning Studies*, 23(2), pp. 367–378. doi:10.1080/09654313.2013.862518.

Molina, Irene Fernández (2015) Protests under occupation: the spring inside Western Sahara, *Mediterranean Politics*, 20(2). doi:10.1080/13629395.2015.1033907.

Onar, Nora Fisher & Kalypso Nicolaïdis (2013) The decentring agenda: Europe as a post-colonial power, *Cooperation and Conflict*, 48(2), pp. 283–303. doi:10.1177/0010836713485384.

Pace, Michelle & Francesco Cavatorta (2012) The Arab Uprisings in theoretical perspective – an introduction, *Mediterranean Politics*, 17(2), pp. 125–138. doi:10.1080/13629395.2012.694040.

Teti, Andrea (2012) The EU's first response to the "Arab Spring": a critical discourse analysis of the partnership for democracy and shared prosperity, *Mediterranean Politics*, 17(3), pp. 266–284. doi:10.1080/13629395.2012.725297.

Todorov, Tzvetan (1994) *On Human Diversity* (Cambridge (MA): Harvard University Press).

Zurayk, Rami & Anne Gough (2014) Bread and olive oil: the agrarian roots of the Arab Uprising, in: Fawaz Gerges (Ed.) *The New Middle East: Protest and Revolution in the Arab World* (Cambridge: Cambridge University Press), pp. 107–134.

Index

INDEX

RASD *see* Sahrawi Arab Democratic
  Republic
regional activism 98
regional political organization 97–8
regional reconciliation project 96
regionalism 91, 94; after regionalization in
  Rif 101–2; in Rifian politics 92
regionalist groups 101
regionalist mobilization structures 102
regionalist movement in Rif 97
regionalist parties, prohibition of 101
religious–political militancy 74
Rif 149, 151; 'autonomist spring' in
  98–102; centre–periphery relationships
  and constitution of regionalist
  movement in 93–8; local activist groups
  and elites in 92; protests in 102–3;
  regionalism after regionalization in
  101–2; regionalist movement in 97
Rif Declaration Committee (CDR) 96, 97,
  105n19
Rif Independence Movement 102
Rifian civil society 96
Rifian Party for Solidarity 101
Rifian politics: particularisms of 92;
  regionalism in 92
Rif–state reconciliation 96
Royal Consultative Council for Saharan
  Affairs (CORCAS) 114
Royal Institute for Amazigh Culture
  (IRCAM) 86n16
Rural Morocco 75

Sabra, George 60–1
Sahrawi Arab Democratic Republic
  (RASD) 110
Sahrawi 'Arab Spring' 112–17
Sahrawi Association of Victims of Gross
  Human Rights Violations 114
Sahrawi civil protests 9; in Western
  Sahara 109
Sahrawi civil society 117; organizations 111
Sahrawi cultural difference, Moroccan
  recognition of 122
Sahrawi human rights activists 120
Sahrawi 'Intifada' 114
Sahrawi non-violent resistance 110
Sahrawi pro-independence movement 112
Salafists 26
same-sex behaviour 21
SCAF *see* Supreme Council of the Armed
  Forces
secularism, Myth of Mubarak 63–4

self-immolation 43; in Tunisia 39
sexual minorities: boundaries and
  potentialities for 17; concerns of 17; in
  periods of transition, conceptualizing
  strategies of 19–21; researching in
  Arab World 18–19
sexuality: dominant discourses of 47;
  of women 43–4
6th of April Youth Movement, The 134, 139
social media 150–1; alternative media
  structure emergence 133–7; blogs 137;
  Facebook **134,** 134–5; methodology
  131–2; role in Egypt 141; role in
  political debates, in Arab Spring
  129–30; as tool for organizing street
  protests 46–7; Twitter 135–6, **136**;
  YouTube 136–7
social movement theory 111
social networking sites (SNSs), role in
  Egyptian revolution 130
socio-economic factors, manipulation of 6
South Africa, same-sex behaviour in 22
Southern Moroccan periphery, opportunity
  structure of 74–7
SSNP *see* Syrian National Social Party
'state of exceptionalism' 102
strategies, Arab Spring 6, 149–51
Supreme Council of the Armed Forces
  (SCAF) 140
Syria: Arab Spring in 5; Christians
  protested in 54; pre-revolutionary
  state in 52–3; strategies of co-opting
  peripheries 148
Syrian Christians 8, 54, 55, 148–9; absence
  of protestors 56; alternative factors
  driving acquiescence 60–2; assurances
  of post-al-Assad secularism by
  revolutionaries 58–9; fear of Islamists
  57–8; political and socio-economic
  inclusion of 148; refugees 58; secular
  protections 56–7; socio-economic
  grievances lack 59–60; and uprising
  56–60
Syrian National Social Party (SSNP) 55
Syrian revolt, disparate reaction of
  Christians during 53–4

Tamaynaute 81
tansikiyat 118, 124n18
Tansikiyya Arbia Tighedouine 80
theory of orientalism 36
Tindouf refugee camps 114–15
top-down approach 1–2